"In our time the doctrine of the last things ~~problematical~~ for many people, and the idea ~~of a life after death has lost~~ the obvious plausibility it had in previous centuries. In this book Anthony Thiselton provides a comprehensive and illuminating discussion of biblical views on these issues. Thiselton skillfully employs philosophical analysis in the service of expounding biblical texts. This book illuminates these issues in a masterly and perceptive way and provides many new and helpful insights. I warmly recommend it."

— VINCENT BRÜMMER
Utrecht University

"Despite the eschatological turn in much of twentieth-century theology, too little attention has been dedicated to the actual content of the 'last things' in recent literature. As a leading New Testament scholar and theologian acquainted with all of the problems and pitfalls in this area of study, Anthony Thiselton is admirably equipped to tackle this subject. This comprehensive and accessible work will become an important point of reference not only for scholars and teachers but also for those ministering to the dying and the bereaved."

— DAVID FERGUSSON
University of Edinburgh

THE LAST THINGS

A New Approach

Anthony C. Thiselton

Originally published in the United States of America in 2012
as *Life After Death: A New Approach to the Last Things*
by Wm B. Eerdmans Publishing Co., Grand Rapids, Michigan

First published in Great Britain in 2012

Society for Promoting Christian Knowledge
36 Causton Street
London SW1P 4ST
www.spckpublishing.co.uk

British Library Cataloguing-in-Publication Data

A catalogue record for this book is available from the British Library

ISBN 978-0-281-06347-5
eBook ISBN 978-0-281-06832-6

First printed in Great Britain by Ashford Colour Press
Subsequently digitally printed in Great Britain

Produced on paper from sustainable forests

Coopers of Stortford

Traditional service, great value and fantastic ideas...

The Coopers of Stortford £5 voucher is exclusively for our valued customers. Please use it to get £5 off any purchase you make of £25 or over. It can be used with an order from the catalogue, on-line, over the phone or visit us and redeem it in our Bishop's Stortford store.

Terms and Conditions

- Can be redeemed on purchases of £25 or over (not including postage and packing).
- Only one voucher per order.
- Cannot be used for orders already placed with Coopers of Stortford.
- Cannot be used in conjunction with any other offer.
- Cannot be used to pay for Coopers of Stortford gift vouchers.
- Only original vouchers accepted.
- Coupon has a cash value of £0.001.

Coopers of Stortford 11 Bridge Street, Bishop's Stortford CM23 2JU Tel: 0844 482 4400

Coopers OF STORTFORD

Coopers of Stortford
Use in our catalogue, on-line or in-store

*Five Pound
Gift Voucher*

*£5 off any purchase of £25 or over (p&p not included)

Coopers
OF STORTFORD

Welcome to Coopers of Stortford's latest catalogue which is packed full of great value ideas. As one of our most valued customers we would like to say thanks for your custom by offering you a special £5 gift voucher* for you to spend. Simply choose from our latest catalogue, enter the voucher code on-line or quote REU20 if ordering by phone. Go on treat yourself – we look forward to hearing from you very soon.

Valid until 18th April 2012

Code: **REU20**

Contents

Acknowledgments

I owe sincere thanks in many directions for the publication of this book, which reflects my practical concern for this subject. However, two people deserve special thanks. My wife, Rosemary, has once again corrected all the proofs, as well as helping in other ways. My secretary, Mrs. Karen Woodward, has typed the entire manuscript with efficiency, speed, and patience, while also preparing lecture outlines and fulfilling other University duties. In addition to these two, Mr. Milton Essenburg has brilliantly edited the typescript, and I am grateful to him, Mr. Jon Pott, Ms. Linda Bieze, among others at my US publisher Eerdmans, for seeing another book through the press.

ANTHONY C. THISELTON, FBA
Emeritus Professor of Christian Theology
University of Nottingham

Abbreviations

AB	Anchor Bible
ANF	*Ante-Nicene Fathers*
AV	Authorized Version
BDAG	W. Bauer, F. W. Danker, W. F. Arndt, and F. W. Gingrich, *A Greek-English Lexicon of the New Testament and Other Early Christian Literature*, 3rd edn. 2000
ConBNT	Coniectanea Biblica Neotestamentica
EDNT	*Exegetical Dictionary of the New Testament*
FC	Fathers of the Church
FRLANT	Forschungen zur Religion und Literatur, des Alten und Neuen Testaments
HTR	*Harvard Theological Review*
ICC	International Critical Commentary
JETS	*Journal of the Evangelical Theological Society*
JSJSup	Supplements to the *Journal for the Study of Judaism*
JSNTSup	Supplements to the *Journal for the Study of the New Testament*
JTS	*Journal of Theological Studies*
LCC	Library of Christian Classics
LW	*Luther's Works*
NEB	New English Bible
NICNT	New International Commentary on the New Testament
NIDOTTE	*New International Dictionary of Old Testament Theology and Exegesis*
NIGTC	New International Greek Testament Commentary
NIV	New International Version

NJB	New Jewish Bible
NovTSup	Supplement to *Novum Testamentum*
NPNF	*Nicene and Post-Nicene Fathers*
NRSV	New Revised Standard Version
NTS	*New Testament Studies*
REB	Revised English Bible
SJT	*Scottish Journal of Theology*
SNTSMS	Society for New Testament Studies Monograph Series
TDNT	*Theological Dictionary of the New Testament*
TDOT	*Theological Dictionary of the Old Testament*
WBC	Word Biblical Commentary
WTJ	*Westminster Theological Journal*
WUNT	Wissenschaftliche Untersuchungen zum Neuen Testament

A New Approach?

I very much hope that pastors and churchgoers, as well as scholars, teachers, and seminary students, will benefit from this book. I have signposted three or four more technical clusters of two or three pages, which the non-specialist reader may prefer to omit. However, I hope no less that scholars and teachers will read this work, not least because a number of features and arguments are genuinely new and distinctive. About half of the chapters include logical clarifications of biblical problems, which may at first seem "philosophical" but have been included, not to draw on philosophical arguments to impose them onto the Bible but entirely to solve certain supposed contradictions or paradoxes which often perplex many ordinary readers.

These following twelve chapters vary greatly in their degree of novelty. Hence this Introduction offers the opportunity to survey what is new in each chapter, one by one, and to survey the arguments of each in advance of reading this book.

Chapter 1 was not originally part of this book, and was the last chapter to be written. This is because the interest of the New Testament writers concerning "the Last Things" relates not primarily to individual death or to individual survival after death, but to *the great last acts of God*, namely, the Return of Christ in glory, the resurrection of the dead, and the Last Judgment. Yet in the end there seemed insufficient reason to omit what remains a pressing concern for so many, including the writer. Many tell me that clergy are often nervous or ill prepared to speak on this subject. This may perhaps constitute the least original chapter of the twelve. It owes something to Jürgen Moltmann on mourning and death, and to Wolfhart Pannenberg on wholeness of meaning.

Chapter 2 concerns the basis for a reverent but confident belief in the resurrection of the dead, although resurrection is discussed more directly in Chapters 7 and 8. Chapter 2 remains especially relevant to those who hold doubts about any kind of Christian hope in life after death. Such doubt is not limited to those outside the Church. Only exceptional Christians never experience even the faintest doubt about what lies beyond death. Our hope and confidence cannot be based on the capacities of human beings to survive death and to become immortal. Such confidence depends entirely on *God's promise* of resurrection and new creation. Everything depends here on *trust in God,* not on self-reliance. In section 2.3, however, I introduce a new concern about the *language of promise.* The "informal logicians," or philosophers of language, J. L. Austin and John Searle, give special attention to the status of *promise* as "self-involving," "performative," or "illocutionary" language, in which the speaker *commits* himself or herself to *act* and to *do* something. Promises may limit the speaker's options about what courses of action still lie open freely to choose to follow. Such voluntary and self-chosen limitation constitutes a source of wonder at the sheer graciousness and love of God, when God makes such promises to us. But because this is self-chosen, this does not limit God's freedom to do as he wills. The speaker must stand by any promise in a *more-than-verbal* way, if the promise has been made faithfully and with commitment. Again, I include this section on performative language entirely for the sake of clarifying biblical material, and for assuring those who still experience doubts in the face of death. It does not add an alien philosophical distraction. It has still to do with trust and with the faithfulness of God. Finally, we look again at hearing God's voice through the Bible. Before the eighteenth century this was universally affirmed. But modern biblical criticism, as such, does not suggest an *alternative* to this view. We cite many who practice biblical criticism yet hear God through the Bible.

Chapter 3 concerns the Word of God, the sacraments, and God's covenant as confirmations of his promise, lest we persist in doubting God's gracious promises. John Calvin defines a sacrament as an external sign by which the Lord seals in our conscience his promises of goodwill toward us, in order to overcome the weakness of our faith. I not only consider Luther, Calvin, Melanchthon, and other Protestant Reformers, but I also take up the arguments of the Roman Catholic writer Mervyn Duffy about "performative" or "illocutionary" language in liturgy and sacraments. His discussion includes the work of Austin, Habermas, and Chauvet. We then show how Baptism, the Lord's Supper, and the address of the Word of God are all confirmations and assurances of God's pledge and promise to all Christians, especially to all who may be weak in faith. In this context I also consider the Jewish Passover *Sēder* as that which clearly calls for self-involvement and appropriation.

Chapter 4 examines the biblical material on Christians as those who "wait for the revealing of our Lord Jesus Christ" (1 Cor. 1:7). But what does *waiting* or *expecting* amount to? In the history of the Church this has been understood very differently. Some believe they should *expect* the End in a fever pitch of excited anticipation. But there have been two different traditions among Christians. Others think that they should live life entirely normally and calmly. Much of what encourages the former view is to see expectation as being primarily a *psychological state* or "inner" process. But I draw on the thought of the philosopher Ludwig Wittgenstein to show that, while expectation *may involve* psychological elements, nevertheless the *primary* emphasis of expectation lies on a state of *readiness*. It points to *being ready* in an observable, behavioral way, which has little to do with "inner states." Again, this is not to explore philosophy as such, but to draw on Wittgenstein's insights for a logical clarification of biblical and theological language.

Chapter 5 provides one of the easiest and best explanations of this readiness. The biblical material seems at first sight to convey the following two different doctrines or notions about what follows after death: do we depart from this life to be with Christ *immediately?* Or does an *"intermediate state"* intervene while other events take place? Since both traditions seem to be affirmed in the biblical writings, we must engage with this supposed contradiction or "paradox." To shed light on this problem I have drawn on the work of the linguistic philosopher Gilbert Ryle, not to expound his philosophy for its own sake but to explore whether his way of solving paradoxes sheds light on how to understand most clearly these two contrasting biblical traditions. To my knowledge, this has not been explored or discussed elsewhere. In this chapter I have also included a discussion of claims that the book of Revelation teaches a millennium. This raises questions about the interpretation of Revelation, which is undertaken partly here but mainly in Chapter 11.

Chapter 6, on the Return of Christ, often called the *Parousia*, also draws on a lifetime of study of language, including the status of *metaphor*. A further philosophical discussion receives some attention which relates to P. F. Strawson's logical distinction between *assertion* and *presupposition*. This seems to shed some light on Paul's much-discussed words "we who are alive and remain," or "we who are alive who are left" (1 Thess. 4:17). This constitutes, however, a relatively minor issue against the background of the teaching of Jesus, Paul, Hebrews, Revelation, and the witness of the early Church. Hence we also explore other parts of the New Testament, constantly bearing in mind the scope and limits of metaphor. The place of imagery remains a complex issue, as George Caird and others have shown.

Chapter 7, on the resurrection of the dead, again expounds the basic contrast between hope in *natural human capacities* to survive death and the *Creator's sovereign act of resurrection and new creation*. God, "who raised Christ from the dead," will raise us "through his Spirit" (Rom. 8:11). The most distinctive part of this chapter examines what Paul means by the *spiritual body*. "Spiritual" here certainly does not mean "immaterial." Paul has a special meaning of *spiritual*, especially in 1 Corinthians, which is all-too-often forgotten today. The Holy Spirit provides an ongoing, *ever-fresh, dynamic, and forward-looking* postresurrection existence, which is characterized and led by the Holy Spirit himself. We argue that the Holy Spirit does not change his nature and activity in giving ever-fresh newness of life.

Chapter 8 is yet another chapter to draw on some further philosophical analysis. Geoffrey Rowell and others have been persuasive in arguing for the need after death for a gradual process of purification from sin. This is said probably to take place in Purgatory, for all but exceptionally saintly Christians. Paul, however, seems to imply that holiness will become an *immediate gift of the Holy Spirit* in the resurrection itself. Can holiness, seemingly against all common sense, be instant? Here I have drawn on O. R. Jones's neglected book *The Concept of Holiness* to argue that holiness is not primarily a virtue as such, independent of situation, but a *disposition* which always relates to concrete situations. This becomes a key to understanding what is distinctive to the postresurrection life by the Holy Spirit's gift and power. We also add to the traditional discussion of three views of what *eternal* means, a fourth distinctive view. Rather than arguing that it means "timelessness," everlasting duration, or even simultaneity, in common with the scientific and theological work of David Wilkinson, we argue for a *transformed dimension of time*, especially in view of the many meanings of *time* in this earthly life.

Chapter 9, on "hell" and "wrath," addresses issues concerning which students and church members constantly ask me. It was the least attractive of the twelve chapters to write, and Jürgen Moltmann suggests that any serious concept of "hell" undermines the sovereign grace of God and love of God, especially to speak the last word. It was the case, however, that from

Irenaeus to Augustine there were three main views on this subject in the early Church, and it seems right to give each of these a fair hearing. In some places the chapter leaves some particular questions open-ended and unanswered, because there are some questions to which *God does not wish us to know an answer in this life.* On the other hand, the *wrath* of God is not always a negative concept. *The opposite to love is not wrath, but indifference.* Wrath may indicate deep concern about a path that leads to decline and to self-destruction, and may actually be motivated by a loving concern for our welfare and character. Yet wrath is not an *eternal* characteristic or quality of God, like faithfulness, holiness, righteousness, and love.

Chapter 10 provides both traditional material and a further example of some logical clarification drawn from those who are technically philosophers. I discuss the Last Judgment and its necessary relation to justification by grace through faith. But the two extrabiblical contributions derive, first, from work on "onlooks" by Wittgenstein, Donald D. Evans, and others, and, second, from further discussions of "verdictives" and "exercitives" as performative language, again in the writings of Austin, Searle, and others. But both of these extrabiblical contributions, once more, are simply to clarify biblical language. Theologically, I argue that judgment can be awaited with joy, if it is seen as vindicatory as well as definitive and public. It is the time when all doubt and ambiguity disappear, and a definitive evaluation of all things becomes public.

Chapter 11 belongs together with Chapter 12. These chapters gave me the chance to explore so much about most people's chief concern, namely, the destiny and "last state" of the redeemed. In Chapter 11 I chiefly examine the biblical teachings on heaven, while in Chapter 12 I include many speculations of my own, although with the warning that they may indeed be speculations. If "hell" was the least attractive chapter, these chapters were the most attractive and absorbing. The incarnation, cross, and resurrection of Jesus Christ remain utterly central, even after the resurrection of the dead. The all-sufficiency of Christ's work may even enhance the state of the redeemed, as well as making them "blameless," and remain a cause of glory to believers. Further, as Chapter 12 especially emphasizes, the dynamic, ongoing work of the Holy Spirit will not only bring ever-fresh renewal but will also enhance future experience well beyond whatever the five senses, or sense experience, could provide, with its severe earthly limitations. In death we may all part with them reluctantly or even nostalgically, but the new life of the Holy Spirit will eclipse and enhance anything that we experienced in this earthly life.

Chapter 12 confirms that the glory of God remains at the center of the stage, not the state of believers. To enjoy postresurrection existence does not blot out our identities or any recognition of friends. It *transforms,* rather than *abolishes,* all that we have known of life. *But the key factor remains that of "being with God."* We meet him face to face. Resurrection, and the life which follows it, involves Christ, the Holy Spirit, and God, who loves us. It is the work of the whole Holy Trinity. Belief in this future depends on God's promise, and this invites trust. Wonderful as the postresurrection life will be, including our relation with other persons, to be face-to-face with God will eclipse every other wonder. In the present, everything works towards that great Day when "God may be all in all" (1 Cor. 15:28). To be face-to-face with God, we repeat, will be the greatest wonder of all.

CHAPTER 1

Death, Dying, and the Meaning of Life

Geoffrey Rowell represents a widespread view, declaring, "Heaven, hell, death and judgement, are the traditional Four Last Things of Christian theology."[1] If this is correct, we must certainly include chapters on the four themes mentioned under this title, and popularly they probably remain the subjects of most concern. Nevertheless, J. A. T. Robinson declares, "The interest of the modern man [or woman] in Christian eschatology, if he has any interest at all, centres on the fact and moment of death. He wants to know whether he will survive it, and in what form. . . . In the New Testament, on the other hand, the point round which hope and interest revolve is not the moment of death, but the day . . . of the appearance of Christ in . . . glory . . . [and] the doctrine of resurrection."[2] The main focus in the New Testament and in this book, therefore, lies not chiefly in the experience of the individual, but on the last great cosmic acts of God, namely, the Return of Christ (often called after the Greek term the *Parousia*), the Last Judgment, and the resurrection of the dead, as well as what follows these "Last Things."

For this reason, the first draft of this book included Chapters 2 to the end, but not this first chapter. But Rowell is no less right than Robinson. For most people "heaven, hell, death and judgement" are expected subjects among the Last Things. We therefore include death and individual destiny, although Robinson is also right about the doings of God rather than simply the experiences of humankind, and the corporate and cosmic empha-

---

1. Geoffrey Rowell, *Hell and the Victorians* (Oxford: Clarendon, 1974), 1.
2. J. A. T. Robinson, *In the End, God: A Study of the Christian Doctrine of the Last Things* (London: James Clarke, 1950), 10.

sis. This twofold theme is one of several which separate the Christian view of resurrection from the pagan or religious view of immortality. The two conceptions are poles apart: the former is based entirely on the promises and sovereign grace of God; the latter is based on the supposed human capacity to survive death.

1.1. Facing Death: The Inevitability of Dying

There is a practical or existential element to the present book. The author is in his seventies, brought back to life after a near-fatal stroke. It remains a stunning source of perplexity, puzzle, and mystery why so many in their seventies, eighties, and beyond, often seem less to contemplate the inevitability of death, which may come at any time, than many young people or previous generations. Jürgen Moltmann addresses this head-on. Many, he urges, live life as if death did not exist. But this does not help us to live life to the full at all. He writes, "To push away every thought of death, and to live as if we had an infinite amount of time ahead of us, makes us superficial and indifferent. . . . To live as if there were no death is to live an illusion."[3]

We can easily see, Moltmann claims, how readily honesty about death can be liberating and life-enhancing. To be reprieved from serious illness, or to have experienced near death, far from deflecting us from this life, can give our present life a new depth. It is those who repress the thought of death, who turn life into an idol, who perhaps have also deeply repressed anxieties about death.

Part of the reason for this is the age in which we live, especially in Western culture. Geoffrey Rowell shows how in earlier times death was a central concern to virtually all human life. Even in Victorian times the death rate made confrontation with death inevitable. Cholera epidemics were often devastating, he claims. Rowell writes, "In 1840 the annual death rate per 1,000 persons in England and Wales was 22.9; by 1880 it had fallen to 20.5, and in 1900 it was still 18.2; but by 1935 it had decreased to 11.7. . . . In 1840 there were 154 infants under a year old who died out of 1,000 live births, and this figure remained fairly constant until 1900."[4] Today, most of

---

3. Jürgen Moltmann, *The Coming of God: Christian Eschatology* (London: S.C.M., 1996), 50.

4. Rowell, *Hell and the Victorians*, 12; Tim Lambert also has a website, "A Brief History of Life-Expectancy in England."

the Two-Thirds still-developing World experiences what many in America and Europe think they have left behind. In Christian theology, too, death, and life after death, remained an important subject. Henry Venn, an evangelical pietist, encouraged parents to allow their children to witness the deathbeds of Christians, as did the high churchman John Warton. If we were to consider Africa, India, or much of the Two-Thirds World today, we should find how different is the experience of death among children or near families, not to mention times and places of war.

Moltmann compares the horror with which people faced "sudden death" in the medieval and Renaissance periods, with the contrasting modern Western hope for exactly that: a quick and painless death. Earlier generations feared "sudden death" because such death gave no time for preparation for the next life. But in an age which today tries to suppress the thought of death, this attitude "paralyzes our energies for living. . . . It makes us arrogant or depressive; it spreads indifference, coldness of heart, and spiritual numbness. . . . We shut ourselves up in the prejudices that cut us off from new experiences, and wall ourselves up. To live as if there were no death is an illusion which is the enemy of life."[5] This becomes a vicious circle. For the self-love or "narcissism" of modern life not only makes an idol of life, but makes notions of death marginalized, and meaningless, and absurd, as if it were simply "the end" of everything good. Part of the suppression of death leads to fast living: to fast food, to fast cars, to fast relationships, or to fast meetings.

If further evidence is required, whereas in previous generations the elderly lived and died at home, fully respected, amid the circle of family and friends, today the dying are shunted off to hospitals, where they often become anonymous "cases" or "patient-requirements." Moltmann notes that whereas the churchyard used to be situated in the center of the village, today cemeteries are often on the periphery of towns and cities. Death is no longer the public, solemn event it used to be. Moltmann notes, "Dying and death are privatised. . . . There is an unconscious suppressive taboo on dying, death and mourning."[6] No one any longer makes the attempt to stand still, and in the case of men to raise their hats, when a hearse passes. Often people may look the other way.

In the Old Testament, the worst feature of death was possible separation from God, after a life of communion with him. One stream of thought

5. Moltmann, *The Coming of God,* 51.
6. Moltmann, *The Coming of God,* 56.

conceives of death as a descent to She'ōl, which occurs 65 times, and is rendered *hadēs* in the Greek Septuagint. In English it is sometimes netherworld or the grave. Ryder Smith comments, "Here he [the dead] could hardly expect to 'live', but he went on existing in a bloodless, juiceless way, the 'shade' or shadow of his former self."[7] She'ōl or Hades might be called "horrible," and the Hebrew notion of death signified not only the momentary "physical" or observable event, but also the state which followed it.

Richard Bauckham explains, "Ancient Israel shared the conviction of the Mesopotamian peoples that 'he who goes down to Sheōl [the underworld] does not come up' (Job 7:9: 'As the cloud fades and vanishes, so those who go down to Sheōl do not come up'; cf. Job 10:21; 16:22; 2 Sam. 12:23)."[8] In 2 Sam. 12:23 David asserts, "Now he is dead. . . . Can I bring him back again? . . . He will not return to me." A single instance of necromancy (1 Sam. 28:3-25) is narrated, but this was explicitly rejected by the Law (Lev. 19:31; Deut. 18:10-12) and the Prophets (Isa. 8:19; 65:2-4) more than once. If some references speak of God's intervening to "bring them up" (Pss. 9:13; 30:3; Isa. 38:17), this metaphorically applies only to being rescued from near death (cf. Ps. 107:18; Isa. 38:10; 3 Macc. 5:51; *Ps. Sol.* 16:2). Jonah's language is modeled on a psalm in his thanksgiving for deliverance from the fish (Jonah 2:2-9). Ezekiel condemns Pharaoh to She'ōl, or to the pit (Hebrew, *bôr*; Ezek. 31:16).

After the Exile a series of changes emerged. The earliest expectation of deliverance from She'ōl comes in Isa. 26:19: "Your dead shall live, their corpses shall rise. O dwellers in the dust, awake, and sing for joy! . . . The earth will give birth to those long dead." In postbiblical literature a notion of a division into that of the righteous and godless arose, the former entering what Persian thought conceived of as "Paradise." According to Jeremias, "Hades" (Greek, *hadēs*; LXX) then came to be used only as a place of punishment (*Eth. Enoch* 22; Josephus, *Antiquities* 18.14).[9] By the time of the New Testament, the Rich Man (in the Parable of the Rich Man and Lazarus, Luke 16:23) was "in Hades, where he was being tormented." In 1 Pet. 3:19 Christ preached "to the spirits in prison" (some read, "to the spirits [who are now] in prison"). Jesus is depicted as declaring, "Today you will be with me in Paradise" (Luke 23:43; originally from the Persian

7. C. Ryder Smith, *The Bible Doctrine of Salvation* (London: Epworth, 2nd ed. 1946), 92.

8. Richard Bauckham, *The Fate of the Dead: Studies in the Jewish and Christian Apocalypses,* NovTSup 93 (Atlanta: Society of Biblical Literature, 1998), 16.

9. Jeremias Joachim, "*hadēs*," *Theological Dictionary of the New Testament* (henceforward *TDNT*), ed. G. Kittel and G. Friedrich, vol. 1 (Grand Rapids: Eerdmans, 1964), 146-49, esp. 147.

word for *garden*), discussed further in Chapter 4. Lazarus did not experience resurrection, but only restoration to life, since presumably he eventually died again (John 11:11-44).

Nevertheless the canonical writings, especially the New Testament, place all their emphasis on resurrection, in spite of very occasional references to immortality in the Apocrypha, in the light of Hellenistic, not purely Jewish, influence. We still await God's full and final salvation. We have devoted Chapter 4 to "waiting." It is vital to take seriously the fact that "The *last* enemy to be destroyed is death" (1 Cor. 15:26; my italics). Paul does not say in the abstract, "Death has been swallowed up," but "When this perishable body puts on imperishability, . . . *then* the saying that is written will be fulfilled: 'Death has been swallowed up in victory. . . . Where, O death, is your sting? The sting of death is sin . . .'" (1 Cor. 15:54-56). Insofar as on the cross Jesus won for us forgiveness of sin and justification by grace through faith, believers face a "stingless death." Insofar as in life elements and effects of sin still remain, death is not without sorrow, until the yonder side of it. As Moltmann insists, since God is God of the living, life is far more than a preparation for death.[10]

We must consider one further aspect of "facing death." Many of us have long-term projects, ambitions, and hopes. This may range from finishing writing a substantial book to witnessing the marriage of a son or daughter, or the graduation of our children or grandchildren. Reinhold Niebuhr and Jürgen Moltmann both address the problem of life's being "cut off" before a hoped-for completion.[11] Niebuhr regards this as part of the "sting" of death, which may seem surprising since this sting is connected with sin. But God is in control of time. If the kingdom of God or the world really needs the completion of what we are doing, God will give us time to finish it. This is not to devalue or to forget the real pain of disability, or degenerative illnesses. But if it is *purely* an investment of self-centered hopes, for ourselves or others, it may seem to be cut short. Pannenberg rightly reminds us that this is a matter of *trust*. We all aim at some kind of security, but our "relationship [with God] is . . . destroyed when a person tries to replace trust with security."[12]

---

10. Moltmann, *The Coming of God,* 50.

11. Reinhold Niebuhr, *The Nature and Destiny of Man,* vol. 2: *Human Destiny* (London: Nisbet, 1943), 303; Moltmann, *The Coming of God,* 116-18; and Jürgen Moltmann, *In the End — the Beginning: The Life of Hope* (London: S.C.M., 2004), also 116-18.

12. Wolfhart Pannenberg, *What Is Man? Anthropology in Theological Perspective* (Philadelphia: Fortress, 1970), 35.

Nevertheless Moltmann argues that any reasonable human being tries to map out plans for their lives, and sometimes these cannot be completed because death intervenes. In postmortal resurrection it will have become irrelevant to wish to live our life all over again. God's creative act of resurrection means *then* "the chance to become the person God meant us to be."[13] This may be applied to the child who dies at birth or in infancy, the boy run over by a car, and the multitude of those who die because of malnourishment in war, especially in Africa or the Two-Thirds World. Further, Moltmann comments, "The idea that for these people death is the finish would plunge the whole world into absurdity."[14] Their life would have no meaning. Pannenberg extends this approach with reference to the promise by God of postresurrection life. He asserts, "The power and faithfulness of the biblical God stands behind the promises. They create courage for a future that is not yet visible."[15] This overlaps with the main argument in Chapter 2, which we extrapolate in more detail below.

1.2. Mourning for the Deaths of Others

It is not surprising that in both the Old Testament and the New, mourning customs were elaborate and involved family and friends. Mourning and grief flows from the love which the mourner lavished on the deceased. Moltmann observes, "*The greater the love, the deeper the grief;* the more unreserved the surrender, the more inconsolable the loss. Those who give themselves utterly in love with someone else die themselves in the pains of grief, and are born again."[16] He adds, "The person who cannot mourn has never loved."[17]

The Old Testament contains many examples of mourning. The Hebrew *'ābal*, "to mourn," and *'ābēl*, "mourning," occur together about 45 times; and the word *sāphad*, "to mourn, to beat the heart, to lament," occurs also over 40 times. When he heard from Reuben of the supposed death of Joseph, "Jacob tore his garments, and put sackcloth on his loins, and mourned for his son many days. All of his sons and all his daughters sought to comfort him; but he refused to be comforted" (Gen. 37:34-35). We also read in Genesis: "Sarah died [after 127 years] . . . and Abraham

13. Moltmann, *The Coming of God,* 117.
14. Moltmann, *The Coming of God,* 118.
15. Pannenberg, *What Is Man?* 41 and 44.
16. Moltmann, *The Coming of God,* 119 (my italics).
17. Moltmann, *The Coming of God,* 119.

went in to mourn for Sarah and to weep for her" (Gen. 23:2; Hebrew, *sāphad*). In 2 Sam. 13:36-39, "The king and his servants wept very bitterly. . . . David mourned for his son day after day. . . . The heart of the king went out, yearning for Absalom." When his three sons were killed, "their father Ephraim mourned many days, and his brothers came to comfort him" (1 Chron. 7:21-22). Mourning took place not only for a son or wife, but for a public figure, as when "all Judah and Jerusalem mourned for Josiah [and] Jeremiah also uttered a lament for Josiah, and all the singing men and singing women have spoken of Josiah to this day. They made there a custom in Israel" (2 Chron. 35:21-25).

In the New Testament we similarly read of lamentation and mourning for the dead. Probably the most widely known passage concerns the death of Lazarus: "When Jesus saw her [Mary] weeping, and the Jews who came with her also weeping, he was greatly disturbed in spirit and deeply moved. . . . Jesus began to weep. So the Jews said, 'See how he loved him!'" (John 11:33-36). This underlines the point about the direct connection between intense mourning and intense love. Both the Old and New Testaments associate mourning with weeping. The Hebrew word *bākâ* can mean both mourning and weeping, and lament. The Greek in John 11:33-36 uses both *klaiō*, "to weep," and *embrimaomai*, "to be angry or be deeply moved," stressing either indignation at what in principle ought not to happen, or deep emotion, or both. Paul uses *klaiō*, "to weep," in his injunction, "Rejoice with those who rejoice; weep with those who weep" (Rom. 12:15). No Christian should be left to mourn and to weep *alone*.

A frequent New Testament Greek word for "to mourn" is *thrēneō*. The disciples, Jesus says, will mourn his death and absence (John 16:20). Children played games of weddings and funeral lamentations (Matt. 11:17 and par. Luke 7:32), where *thrēneō* refers to ritual mourning or lamentation. The Septuagint uses the word to translate *qînâ*, the regular Hebrew song or meter of lament, in some cases antiphonal lament (Jer. 9:19). Funeral rituals and extended lamentations are found in Greco-Roman culture (e.g., in Homer, *Iliad* 24.721; *Odyssey* 24.60-61; Plutarch, *Solon* 21); in Near Eastern culture, including Persia, the Old Testament, and Judaism; and in the New Testament.[18] The New Testament also uses the word for "grieving" (Greek,

18. G. Stählin, *"thrēneō," TDNT*, vol. 3, 148-55; F. Danker, *A Greek-English Lexicon of the New Testament and Other Early Christian Literature* (Chicago: University of Chicago Press, 3rd ed. 2000) (also called BDAG), 458-59; Saul M. Olyan, *Biblical Mourning: Ritual and Social Dimensions* (Oxford: Oxford University Press, 2004); and Rachel Hachlili, *Jewish Funerary Customs: Practices and Rites in the Second Temple Period*, JSJSup 94 (Leiden: Brill, 2005).

pentheō). James 4:9 brings together "Lament and mourn and weep," and Rev. 18:11 depicts merchants as "weeping and mourning" for Babylon, the city of trade. Any great loss can evoke mourning.

This strong evidence from the biblical and ancient world shows how far modern Western culture has strayed from those customs. Mourning was long, public, and serious, and accepted by all as an important dimension of grief at the loss of a loved one. Moltmann notes how significant this change is for the mourner. He writes, "People who shut themselves off from the mourning process, or who cut it short, will discover in themselves insurmountable depression and increasing apathy. . . . Listening to each other and talking to each other generates a dialogue in the face of death . . . until the loss is accepted . . . through the transformation of the mourner."[19] That is why the biblical era reflects not only the dignity and acceptance of mourning but also particular public rituals, which may extend over long periods.

This is not least because in mourning-counseling there are recognized stages in the long process of mourning. One of the earlier writers to popularize this notion was Elisabeth Kübler-Ross in her book *On Death and Dying* (1969 and 1970). She distinguished the five stages of (1) denial and isolation; (2) anger; (3) "bargaining"; (4) depression; and (5) acceptance and hope.[20] Most writers accept the notion of processes and "stages" in mourning but doubt whether this process is invariable, or can be neatly classified into successive stages universally. Most of these stages, but not all, or even necessarily in that order, occur, and time considerations may vary greatly. Many have suggested other schemes with caution. C. M. Parker suggests the four stages of (1) numbness and shock, in which loss and death seem unreal; (2) a phase of yearning to recover the loss; (3) a period of disorganization and despair; and (4) a gradual and slow return to resolution and reorganization.[21] All these descriptions tend to underline the seriousness and necessary acceptance of mourning. The biblical material suggests that this should *not be an isolated process,* but carried out in the context of the love and support of others, ideally of a family or supportive Church.

Among the most painful kinds of mourning is without doubt grieving

---

19. Moltmann, *The Coming of God,* 119 and 121.

20. Elisabeth Kübler-Ross, *On Death and Dying* (New York: Simon & Schuster, 1969 and London: Tavistock, 1970).

21. Colin M. Parker, *Bereavement* (Harmondsworth: Penguin, 3rd ed. 1998; Hove: Routledge, 4th ed. 2010).

for the death of a child, especially for a son or daughter, which some claim to be more stressful than even the loss of a husband or wife. This may include grieving for the loss of a baby in a stillbirth, or even a fetus. Much that was begun in hope seems unfinished. Hopes for a happy witness of future successes are crushed. The well-known philosopher Nicholas Wolterstorff, for example, wrote *Lament for a Son* as an honest and intense expression of his grief at the loss of his son in a mountaineering accident, as an irreversible loss amid faith.[22] Grief also extends to the loss of the capacities of disabled people who may die prematurely, or to any form of what Moltmann calls a shortened "spoiled life." Yet, as we suggested in the previous section, resurrection means not the resumption and extension of a spoiled life, but "the chance to become the person God meant us to be."[23] Joanna Stephens has argued that the condition of someone with Down syndrome, for example, is so intrinsic to their identity that, on the basis of the wounds of Christ after his resurrection (John 20:27), there may still remain certain marks or effects of this condition without inhibiting resurrection power, capacities, or perfection.[24] We shall argue in Chapter 7, on the resurrection of the dead, that identity, communication, and recognition characterize the resurrection mode of existence, as Ernst Käsemann comments. This must qualify the "never" of Wolterstorff's *Lament*.

We must remind ourselves again that those who mourn see only the preresurrection, this-worldly, side of death. From the perspective of faith, one believes that death has a postresurrection side also. After we experience the great cosmic events of the resurrection of the dead and the Coming of Christ, we shall see death retrospectively, in the light of the resurrection. As Pannenberg reminds us, this perspective is the only one in the light of which even a full understanding of the Person of Christ, or Christology, makes sense.[25]

1.3. Death and the Meaning of Life

If death constitutes *only* the end of life, we face meaninglessness. For Christians this is self-evident. Paul comments, "If Christ has not been

---

22. Nicholas Wolterstorff, *Lament for a Son* (Grand Rapids: Eerdmans, 1987).

23. Moltmann, *The Coming of God,* 117.

24. Joanna Stephens, Unpublished dissertation (Nottingham, 2008), 27-34.

25. Wolfhart Pannenberg, *Systematic Theology* (3 vols.; Grand Rapids: Eerdmans and Edinburgh: T&T Clark, 1991, 1994 and 1998), vol. 2, 277-396.

raised, then our proclamation has been in vain, and your faith has been in vain. . . . If the dead are not raised. . . . If in this life only we have hope in Christ, we are of all people most to be pitied" (1 Cor. 15:14-19). Gone is not only the hope of postmortal resurrection, but also apostolic preaching and Christian faith. Further, in Paul's words, "You are still in your sins" (v. 17). If God's work in us is not yet complete, it is like trying to guess the meaning of a half-finished picture or sculpture. Paul writes, "Now we see in a mirror dimly, but then we shall see face to face. Now I know only in part, but then shall I know fully" (1 Cor. 13:12). The mirror to which he alludes was of polished bronze, not like the mirrors of today.

For unbelievers the situation appears no better. Paul sees a parallel between human death and the creative act of God in resurrection in the "dying" and new life of vegetation (1 Cor. 15:37). "What you sow does not come to life unless it dies" (15:36). Holmes Rolston and Arthur Peacocke speak of a "cruciform naturalism," in which the suffering and dying of all things in the animal and vegetable world leads to a transformative principle which humankind experiences as sowing and reaping: "individual organisms must die. . . . Life must be perpetually redeemed in the midst of perishing. . . . This 'giving birth' requires labour. . . . Biological nature is always giving birth . . . something is always dying, and something is always living on."[26] Jesus said, "Unless a grain of wheat falls into the ground and dies, it remains just a single grain; but if it dies, it bears much fruit" (John 12:24). But if we never witness, or believe in, the time of "much fruit," the mere dying of the grain remains senseless, meaningless, and merely destructive.

If, as Pannenberg and others maintain, meaning emerges only in the light of *the whole*, that whole remains incomplete prior to the complete work of God in the resurrection. Wilhelm Dilthey speaks, in Pannenberg's words, of "the process of history, the *meaning* of the individual elements of life — the characteristic relationship of life's parts, expressing their relation to the whole of life."[27] Pannenberg comments that this is constantly changing. That is why, while Dilthey was content to see meaning determined at the very end of life, Pannenberg looks for meaning in the light of *a greater* whole, which includes the purposes of *God*. Pannen-

26. Holmes Rolston, "Kenosis and Nature," in *The Work of Love: Creation as Kenosis*, ed. John Polkinghorne (Grand Rapids: Eerdmans and London: S.P.C.K., 2001), 57-58 (cf. 43-65); cf. Arthur Peacocke, "The Cost of New Life," in ibid., 21-41.

27. Wolfhart Pannenberg, *Theology and the Philosophy of Science* (Philadelphia: Westminster, 1976), 78.

berg refers to the ongoing march of history in the interpretation, fulfillment, and meaning of prophecy. For example, he writes: "Very few of them [the prophecies] occurred exactly according to the prediction. Time and time again the course of events surpassed the words, giving them a new meaning and a new reference."[28] Hence, he continues, "The eschatological event which binds history into a whole brings about final knowledge of God."[29] He recognizes that *in this life* "revelation . . . is given to us only by way of *anticipation* of the coming End for all men" (his italics).[30] For even if we were to accept Dilthey's insight, a single human life, even at its end, is only a fleeting moment in the history of the whole world or universe.

The provisional meaning of events can be seen retrospectively when other events shed light on them. Things may often look differently in youth and old age. Pannenberg writes, "What formerly seemed insignificant may perhaps appear later as of fundamental importance; and the reverse may be true. The final significance of the events of our life, Dilthey once said, can be measured only at the end of our lives."[31] What seems to be a missed or lost opportunity may be seen later as a providential deliverance from making a mistake. Jesus said to Peter, "You do not know now what I am doing, but later you will understand" (John 13:7). But even old age can have only limited understanding of the events which serve to shape an individual. Only a postresurrection vision of the whole can see a *definitive* meaning where a variety of factors which concern other lives converge, and we arrive at *the* meaning of the whole, as publicly endorsed by God at the Last Judgment.

To many the idea of retrospective assessment of meaning from a postresurrection viewpoint may seem fanciful and speculative. The philosopher of religion John Hick discusses *evidential* criteria in his work on the principle of verification and that of falsification, as first formulated by the positivist (or materialist) philosopher A. J. Ayer, and others. Yet, all the

---

28. Wolfhart Pannenberg, "The Revelation of God in Jesus of Nazareth," in *New Frontiers in Theology*, vol. 3, *Theology as History*, ed. James M. Robinson and John Cobb (New York: Harper & Row, 1967), 120; cf. 101-22.

29. Pannenberg, "The Revelation of God in Jesus," in *Theology as History*, ed. Robinson and Cobb, 122-23.

30. Pannenberg, "The Revelation of God in Jesus," in *Theology as History*, ed. Robinson and Cobb, 131.

31. Wolfhart Pannenberg, "Eschatology and the Experience of Meaning," in *Basic Questions in Theology*, vol. 3 (London: S.C.M., 1973), 201; cf. 192-210.

same, Hick recognizes that there is a place for "eschatological verification" — for events now to become *later* verifiable, when a fuller view becomes possible.[32]

It would be a mistake, however, to lose sight of Pannenberg's contention that even *before* the resurrection we can have an advance or *anticipatory* understanding or meaning. It is simply false to claim that we all have to wait until after the resurrection before we can have *any* access to a provisional, but reasonable meaning. This comes about by faith. By contrast, the postresurrection experience will provide an *unrevisable* and *definitive* meaning. This is a major part of the meaning of the Last Judgment, as we shall see in Chapter 10. In the present, we already possess a *provisional,* working notion of meaning, which it is reasonable to accept. This meaning of language when we speak of God, Christ, or the Holy Spirit, or of the purposes of God, has remained reasonably constant and stable over many generations and various cultures. Christianity does not use a ghetto language which bears no analogical relationship to language about the everyday world. Such language may often lack complete precision, exact equivalence, and even total unanimity, but it is serviceable enough for the Church down the ages to speak of a stable tradition, and to find the Bible intelligible for the decisions of daily life, as Luther and Calvin stressed.

We conclude with perhaps two or three exploratory pages which take us into more technical and philosophical questions. It must be of interest to many, however, that appeal to such widely diverse thinkers as Wittgenstein, Pannenberg, Gadamer, and perhaps also Habermas, each from different academic disciplines, may seem to lend pastoral support to some (not necessarily to all) of the above arguments. All of these four see the intelligibility of language and meaning as resting upon a close relation between language and life. If a Christian claims, for example, that forgiveness of sins is central to his or her faith, but lives a deeply guilt-ridden life, this detracts from the meaning of "I believe in the forgiveness of sins."

(1) There is great force in the attention which Ludwig Wittgenstein gives to the context-in-life or "surroundings" of language. Commenting on the integral relation between language and human life or behavior, he remarks, "One learns the game (life and its meaning) by watching how

---

32. John H. Hick, *Philosophy of Religion* (Englewood Cliffs, NJ: Prentice Hall, 4th ed. 1990), 103-6.

others play."[33] In popular religion, it is sometimes said of the witness of practical conduct, "Christianity is caught, not taught." What we see is often more convincing than what we hear. Wittgenstein, however, does not express the *entire* truth. If the meaning of Christianity depended only on the contemporary conduct of the Church, there would be no way of reforming or of correcting inadequate or wrong behavior, and there have been dark times when the criterion would fail. Yet there is much truth in Wittgenstein's observation. Wittgenstein shows how the meaning of language about pain and language about love reveals its difference *in the light of human behavior which surrounds it.* He writes, "One does *not* say, 'That was not true pain, or it would not have gone off so quickly.'"[34] But a person would hardly say, "I love you dearly — Oh, it's all right; it's gone off now!" The "surroundings" determine meaning. Thus, in this world the Bible and a stable Christian tradition of language and behavior are like the "backing" which gives currency to meaning. We do not have to find it on our own. Once the boundaries or horizons of meaning become infinitely expanded, after the resurrection, that meaning will become definitive.

(2) Wolfhart Pannenberg similarly speaks in the context of biblical revelation of "an intertwining both of . . . words and events."[35] What happens if we seek a *definitive* meaning? Then, Pannenberg comments, "We should have to wait for the end of history, to possess all the evidence needed to determine history's *meaning*" (his italics).[36] One day, after death, we may encounter "the idea of God as the all-determining reality."[37] But in the present "the totality of reality is not available to an experience in a complete state. It is still incomplete: the future is still open. . . . our experience of our own lives and of the world is temporal. . . . The totality of reality itself is not yet given."[38] As a matter of rational faith, which anticipates that death is not the end, God is always present only in "anticipations of the *totality* of reality, in models . . . still subject to confirmation or refutation by subsequent experience."[39] More than a score of philosophers of re-

33. Ludwig Wittgenstein, *Philosophical Investigations* (Oxford: Blackwell, 2nd ed. 1958), sect. 54; cf. sect. 23.

34. Ludwig Wittgenstein, *Zettel* (Oxford: Blackwell, 1967), sect. 504.

35. Pannenberg, "The Revelation of God in Jesus," in *Theology as History,* ed. Robinson and Cobb, 120.

36. Pannenberg, *Theology and Philosophy of Science,* 162.

37. Pannenberg, *Theology and Philosophy of Science,* 309.

38. Pannenberg, *Theology and Philosophy of Science,* 310.

39. Pannenberg, *Theology and Philosophy of Science,* 310 (my italics).

ligion have established careful arguments to support our use of cognitive meaning, not only about life, but also about God.[40]

(3) Hans-Georg Gadamer attacks both the individualism and rationalism of the Enlightenment. He argues that "the anticipation of meaning that governs our understanding" does not spring from the conscious reflection of the individual, "but springs from the commonality that binds us" to the words and deeds of the community, which he calls "the tradition."[41] Individual reflection is only "a distorting mirror" which cannot accurately understand the meaning of life and history.[42] To grasp meaning, he urges, we must "remain open to the other person. . . . But this openness always includes our situating the other meaning *in relation to the whole* of our own meanings."[43] Gadamer, therefore, holds to a communal, and larger, context to grant meaning to what would otherwise seem ambiguous or obscure.

(4) Jürgen Habermas diverges from Gadamer at various points. He is primarily interested in social science and communicative action, whereas Gadamer is primarily concerned with dialogue, hermeneutics, and the philosophy of history. Nevertheless Habermas argues that bare, abstract, individual reflection is not enough, and like Pannenberg and Gadamer he agrees that the individual's place within history (often called his or her historically conditioned "historicality") is bound to make the individual's "interests" play a part in the search for meaning. He shares with many the concept of the "hermeneutical circle," that the "parts" cannot be understood without reference to "the whole." "The full understanding of the individual already presupposes that of the whole."[44] In his later work he discusses how "system" relates to "life world" in the communication of meaning.[45] Recovery of meaning always depends on an "interpretative framework." Indeed, if we were to bring to Habermas's view of communicative action a Christian vision which he presumably does not share, only

40. For example, R. S. Heinbeck, *Theology and Meaning* (London: Allen & Unwin, 1969); Ian T. Ramsey, *Religious Language* (London: S.C.M., 1957).

41. Hans-Georg Gadamer, *Truth and Method* (London: Sheed & Ward, 2nd rev. ed. 1989), 293.

42. Gadamer, *Truth and Method*, 276.

43. Gadamer, *Truth and Method*, 268 (my italics).

44. Jürgen Habermas, *Knowledge and Human Interests* (London: Heinemann, 2nd ed. 1978), 173 (quoting Dilthey); cf. 171-80.

45. Jürgen Habermas, *The Theory of Communicative Action* (2 vols.; Cambridge: Polity Press and Beacon Press, 1987), vol. 2, 119-282; cf. 323-26.

after the resurrection would human self-"interests," with their distorting effects, disappear from view. We discuss this further in a later chapter.

With no belief in life after death, the interpretative framework, or *"whole,"* has become too restricted and narrow to speak of meaning with any confidence. The *possibility* of a postmortal life changes this. For Christian believers this possibility depends not on some supposed human capacity to survive death (as in Plato), but on the divine promise of new creation and resurrection. We explore this in the next chapter, and also in a subsequent one. Only from a retrospective viewpoint acquired *after* resurrection can the "meaning" of our lives become definitive. Disbelief in life after death makes life meaningless; belief in life after death invites a working and provisional meaning, which is grounded in God's promise and human trust; postresurrection experience will bring access to a full and definitive meaning of all things. Chapters 7 and 8 will expound this further.

CHAPTER 2

Things Not Seen

2.1. The Problem for Doubters

The Last Things comprise, after death, especially the Return of Christ, the Last Judgment, the resurrection of the dead, and the transformed postresurrection life, or the final state of the redeemed. But huge skepticism arises in an "evidence-based" culture about trying to describe and predict things which we cannot yet see. It may understandably seem to be the height of folly to describe what many will perceive as no more than speculations about what lies beyond the grave. Much extrapolation from present states of affairs cannot but remain speculative or even products of wish fulfillment. Extrapolating from the love of Jesus Christ cannot yield more than a general and vague hope.

In his earlier thought, the philosopher Ludwig Wittgenstein doubted whether we can speak of the "Beyond." This was not because he was a materialist, like Bertrand Russell and A. J. Ayer. It was because, while remaining relatively open-minded about the "Beyond," he believed that "propositions can express nothing that is higher [than the present world]."[1] Further, within the boundaries of this world, "At death the world does not alter, but comes to an end. Death is not an event in life; we do not live to experience death."[2] We experience not "death," with all that this may entail, but only the event or process of *dying*. We need a wider frame of reference than "this world" to talk about postmortal existence. Wittgenstein be-

---

1. L. Wittgenstein, *Tractatus Logico-Philosophicus* (Eng. and Ger.; London and New York: Routledge and Kegan Paul, 1961), 6.42 (p. 145).

2. Wittgenstein, *Tractatus*, 6.431 and 6.4311 (p. 147).

lieved, in his earlier thought, that "propositions" must concern this world and this life. He acknowledged, "There are, indeed, things that cannot be put into words," but we must remain silent about "what we cannot speak."[3]

Those who may be uneasy about language concerning what lies beyond the world include many Christians. Friedrich Schleiermacher (1768-1834), usually considered to be the first modern theologian, asserts that concerning the Last Things we may at best hope for no more than a general pattern to which we may "approximate."[4] He insists that "an exact construction" of events at the End "is not to be thought of."[5] Christians can only extrapolate on "the consummation of the Church" from what we know of Christ: "All that might go to form a definite picture falls asunder."[6] Schleiermacher might have cited an ancient precedent. Augustine of Hippo (354-430) speaks on the one hand of hoping in God "until the day breaks, and the shadows are removed." He says, "In the morning I shall stand up and . . . will see salvation, and I shall for ever give praise to God."[7] On the other hand, he admits: "During this wandering pilgrimage . . . in this still uncertain state of human knowledge, . . . who can distinguish . . . except you [God]?"[8] It is hard enough to understand our own world and our life, let alone what lies beyond it.

Many try to circumvent the comments of evidence-based philosophers by appealing to analogy, symbol, or myth. Even in the physical sciences, we have become accustomed since the late nineteenth century to rely on "models" *(Bilder* and *Darstellungen)* to conceptualize what lies at the frontiers of knowledge. Heinrich Hertz, who gave his name to the frequency, or cycles-per-second, of pitch or notes in music, drew on Neo-Kantian philosophy to show that the human mind can use "models" for scientific description, where literal propositions seem to run out.[9] But many still disparage metaphor, models, and analogy as suggesting imprecise thinking. Georg Hegel (1770-1831) insisted that philosophers use the

---

3. Wittgenstein, *Tractatus,* 6.5222 and 7 (p. 151).

4. Friedrich Schleiermacher, *The Christian Faith* (Edinburgh: T&T Clark, 1989; Ger. 1st ed. 1821; 2nd ed. 1830), 696.

5. Schleiermacher, *The Christian Faith,* 706.

6. Schleiermacher, *The Christian Faith,* 708.

7. Augustine, *Confessions,* 13:14:15, ed. Henry Chadwick (Oxford: Oxford University Press, 1991), 282.

8. Augustine, *Confessions,* 13:14:15.

9. Cf. A. Janik and S. Toulmin, *Wittgenstein's Vienna* (London: Wiedenfeld and Nicolson, 1973), 132-48.

critically evaluated *concept (Begriff)*, while religious people rely on mere *imagery* or representations *(Vorstellungen)*. His disciple David F. Strauss pressed this further, arguing that Christians use "myth" when the status of his narrative or account cannot be sustained as claiming truth. In his view *myth* denoted *ideas expressed as a narrative of events.*

Some suggest that religious people rely on anthropomorphisms, as when a young child once interpreted the application of air brakes in a train as "the train sneezed." It might be argued that Janet Martin Soskice and others have successfully shown that metaphor can be used to convey cognitive truth; while Paul Ricoeur and Max Black demonstrated that the interaction or intersection between two semantic domains in metaphor constitutes a respectable and even necessary way of conveying truth.[10] Many, however, remain uneasy about metaphors and analogies, even if we use them every day. Later, especially in Chapter 11, we shall argue that symbols, metaphors, and analogies play an important role in the Bible. In the book of Revelation, for example, a cluster of symbols together cancel out unwanted meanings and constitute a primary genre. It was never intended to be a celestial underground or subway map, bearing the legend "You are standing here" and sketching out a possible continuous journey ahead. But for the present we must not be diverted by anticipating issues which we later discuss in full. Our "problem" receives an answer which is even more fundamental than debates about symbol and metaphor.

Before we proceed to look at this core "answer," however, we may consider the application of evidence-based criteria not only to issues in the physical sciences (for which it is correct), but to *all* belief.

(1) John Locke (1632-1704) showed that a "reasonable" belief did not depend on mere intensity of conviction. *Certainty* involves more than psychology or intensity of belief, and it is correct to ask whether we are "entitled" to the beliefs we hold. This is very different from the twentieth- and twenty-first-century popular assumption that anyone is "entitled" to believe anything.[11] Locke did suggest that an "entitled" belief could rest on revelation.

---

10. Janet Martin Soskice, *Metaphor and Religious Language* (Oxford: Clarendon, 1985), 97-161; Paul Ricoeur, *The Rule of Metaphor* (London: Routledge & Kegan Paul, 1978); and Max Black, *Perplexities: Rational Choice, Metaphor, Poetic Ambiguity* (Ithaca: Cornell University Press, 1990).

11. John Locke, *Works* (London: Rivington, 12th ed. 1824), vol. 3, 274-75; cf. Nicholas Wolterstorff, *John Locke and the Ethics of Belief* (Cambridge: Cambridge University Press, 1996), xv-xvi.

(2) William K. Clifford (1845-79) proposed the view that no statement is worthy of belief unless all possible evidence points to the truth of the statement. It is immoral, he argued, to believe without sufficient evidence, and immoral belief cannot be *entitled* belief.[12] He suggests the example of a shipowner who sends people to sea in a ship about whose seaworthiness he has serious, well-founded doubts. He persuades himself that a kindly Providence will ensure the safety of the ship. Clifford insists that it is wrong to believe on insufficient evidence. With Locke, he rightly argues that belief entails responsibility and public effects. But, unlike Locke, he restricts *entitlement* to unambiguous *positivist* or physical evidence. That is to say, this evidence must be seen or verified through one or more of our five *physical* senses: sight, sound, taste, smell, or touch. Clifford's shipowner example rests on evidence taken from the physical world. But if, after death, it is assumed that this-worldly physical evidence lies beyond possibility (*a priori*, or by the nature of the case), how can we argue that the absence of physical evidence remains *relevant*? What *kind* of evidence should we expect to find?

(3) Alfred J. Ayer (1910-89) expounded a version of Clifford's argument that appeared to be confirmed by language and logic. It was known as Logical Positivism. In the first edition of *Language, Truth, and Logic* (1936), he argued that claims to truth depended on *verification by the experience of the senses.* He acknowledged only one exception, namely, if we are dealing with logical, tautological, or mathematical issues which belong to the logical rather than to the physical realm. In the second edition he broadened this criterion of truth to "verification in principle."[13] Propositions about God or ethics become "non-sense"; they have no truth that can be measured by their verifiability. Most of us cannot "see" atoms, let alone subatomic particles, but with the right scientific equipment, their activity could be verified: they are verifiable in principle by extreme magnification or other scientifically observable changes. At the time, the sentence "There are mountains on the other side of the moon" could be verified only in principle until in later years space rocketry made actual verification possible.

Can we say, however, that the criterion of verification or even of verifiability can be *verified by what we can see,* or by what we experience? Or is this formally a logical tautology, which says that we can see only what

---

12. W. K. Clifford, "The Ethics of Belief," in Clifford, *Lectures and Essays* (1879), repr. in Clifford, *The Ethics of Belief and Other Essays* (New York: Prometheus, 1999).

13. Alfred J. Ayer, *Language, Truth and Logic* (London: Gollancz, 1946), 48-49, for example.

we see? The argument *accords a privileged status to the principle of verification,* which contradicts what it asserts because it is itself not based on observable criteria. In the end, it was widely acknowledged during the 1950s that this merely represented old-fashioned positivism or *materialism disguised in linguistic dress* as a linguistic or logical theory. It merely reformulated older materialism in a logical form. Yet in my early days as a university lecturer, I was astonished and appalled by the number of ordinary people who had fallen under its spell. We must turn to a more serious and fundamental issue.

2.2. A First Step: Promise and Trust

It so happens that the phrase "things not seen" occurs in Heb. 11:1: "Faith is the assurance [Greek, *hypostasis,* better, *reality*] of things hoped for, the conviction of things not seen [Greek, *pragmatōn elenchos ou blepomenōn*]." Oscar Cullmann rightly understands that things are "not seen" because *they have not happened yet.* They are, in his words, "things which are future . . . a reference to the time process."[14] Christian thinking in the biblical era started from the temporal distinction between "formerly," "now," and "then," rather than the spatial contrast between here and Beyond. This does not imply that the contrast between visible and invisible did not play a part. The New Testament writers were well aware of this distinction. Nevertheless, the time contrast between past, present, and future remains a more primary one. Terms such as "the Day," "the hour," and "the right time" or "favorable moment" (Greek, *kairos*) perform a fundamental role. In apocalyptic, or "the Last Things" under the broader name of *eschatology,* "the two ages" (Greek, *aiōnes*) play a decisive part.

This provides the backcloth against which we suggest a succinct answer to the "problem" of "Things Not Seen" in an evidence-based culture. We may look beyond the present only on the basis of *promise.* If the future were the product of human imagination or of projection, it would remain sheer speculation. The question which Schleiermacher, Augustine, and an evidence-based culture face may be answered by the extent to which the promises of God are specific about certain matters. As Wolfhart Pannenberg has argued about divine intervention in history and in the

---

14. Oscar Cullmann, *Christ and Time: The Primitive Conception of Time and History* (London: S.C.M., 1951), 37.

world, belief in divine intervention is a matter of "theism" and belief in the God of the Bible.[15] This stands in contrast to Deism, or a merely rationalist or human belief in a Supreme Being, typical of many in the Enlightenment era. Similarly, belief in the validity of divine *promise,* and its significance for truth and as a speech-act, is part and parcel of belief in the biblical God.

Hebrews 11:1 makes it clear that to accept God's promise as effective does entail faith. This does not render belief or faith irrational or contrary to reason. As Pannenberg, again, asserts, credibility does not mean credulity. Martin Luther distinguished faith as *appropriation* of a promise, and what it is to believe *(credere).* "Belief," Luther insists, *can* be "an easy thing [i.e., "over-easy].... Such faith is human, like any other activity of man [or woman].... It is faith about God, not faith in God."[16] In entirely positive terms, he declares, "Faith is a living, daring, confidence in God's grace, so sure and certain that a man [or woman] would stake his life upon it a thousand times."[17] Such faith, Luther says, will make a person "glad and bold and happy" to be good to everyone, and to suffer everything in love to God.

Trust may waver, as many Christians find. Suddenly, when facing imminent death, we may seem to reach the edge of an unknown world, and, in understandable panic, may even contemplate an unwelcome encounter with an unknown God. But stable reflection will suggest that God has made himself known in Christ, and has revealed a Bible and sacraments full of specific promises. One writer writes of the "Christ-likeness" of the biblical God. At such times, we may reflect on the dominical sacraments as pledges and promises. John Calvin repeatedly urged this function of sacraments, both of Baptism and the Eucharist or the Lord's Supper.[18] This is the subject of Chapter 3. It may be that in an attempt to avoid presumption, we are tempted to fall into despair. Yet Jürgen Moltmann asserts that both are equally denials of hope or trust. He writes, "Presumption is a pre-

15. Wolfhart Pannenberg, *Basic Questions in Theology,* vol. 3 (London: S.C.M., 1973), 14; cf. 25-26 and 67-68.

16. *Luther: Early Theological Works: The Epistle to the Hebrews,* ed. James Atkinson, LCC 16 (London: S.C.M., 1962), 210.

17. Luther, "Preface to the Epistle to the Romans" in *LW,* vol. 35 (Philadelphia: Fortress, 1960), 370; also in *Martin Luther,* ed. E. G. Rupp and B. Drewery (London: Arnold, 1970), 95-96.

18. John Calvin, *Institutes of the Christian Religion,* ed. H. Beveridge, 4.14.1-9 and 4.17.5 (2 vols.; London: James Clarke, 1957), vol. 2, 491-97 and 559-60.

mature, self-willed anticipation of fulfilment of what we hope for from God. Despair is the premature, arbitrary anticipation of the non-fulfilment of what we hope for from God. Both forms of hopelessness . . . cancel the wayfaring character of hope. They rebel against the patience in which hope *trusts* in the God of *promise*."[19]

Trust, like faithfulness, implies that the ultimate good cannot have yet arrived. This, again, is the message of Hebrews 11. In v. 1 of Hebrews 11, "being sure" (NIV), even "assurance" (NRSV) of what we hope for, implies the process of trust. Attridge and Lane better suggest "the reality" of things hoped for.[20] The readers are exhorted to exercise bold confidence (10:19). But faith is oriented not only to the past but also to *the future*. This clearly emerges in the comparison of "these all died in faith without having received the promises" (11:13, 39). Noah built the ark on the basis of what he believed would yet happen in the future, for which he had at present no visible evidence (11:7). This was Israel's faith when the people arrived on the banks of "the Red Sea," or Sea of Reeds (11:29), or when they splashed blood on their lintels (11:28); or when Joshua marched around Jericho (11:30).[21] Trust defines what it is to be a Christian.

In the Old Testament trust is required because of the dependability of God. Lack of trust may suggest that the person concerned may not deeply believe that God is dependable.[22] Rather than trust, we may search for supposed ways of finding self-security. Isa. 26:3-4 provides an example: "Those of steadfast mind you keep in peace — in peace because they trust in you. Trust in the LORD forever, for in the LORD GOD you have an everlasting Rock" (NRSV). In a special way trust is called for when some threat to life or to security becomes apparent. In Isa. 30:15b this occurs when Assyria threatens to invade Jerusalem: "In quietness and in trust shall be your strength." In Isa. 7:4-9 Ahaz is urged to trust in a time of crisis. But, as Walter Moberly points out (see n. 22), trust can be misplaced. A notorious illusion is trust in wealth, especially when one is on the brink of personal ca-

---

19. Jürgen Moltmann, *Theology of Hope: On the Ground and the Implications of a Christian Eschatology* (London: S.C.M., 1967), 23 (my italics).

20. H. W. Attridge, *The Epistle to the Hebrews* (Philadelphia: Fortress, 1989), 308; and W. L. Lane, *The Epistle to the Hebrews* (Waco: Word, 1991), 328.

21. Cf. Anthony C. Thiselton, "Hebrews," in *Eerdmans Commentary on the Bible*, ed. J. D. G. Dunn and J. W. Rogerson (Grand Rapids: Eerdmans, 2003), 1472-76.

22. R. W. L. Moberly, "*b-ṭ-ḥ*," *New International Dictionary of Old Testament Theology and Exegesis* (hereafter *NIDOTTE*), ed. Willem A. VanGemeren (Carlisle: Paternoster, 1996), vol. 1, 644-49, esp. 645.

lamity or death (Job 31:24; Prov. 11:28). Jeremiah regularly speaks of those who "trust in falsehood" (Jer. 7:8; 13:25; 29:31).

In the Psalms, oppression and suffering have the function of bringing forth trust in God as vindicator or deliverer. The Psalmist can say, "They trusted, and you delivered them" (Ps. 22:4); "O my God, in you I trust; do not let me be put to shame; do not let my enemies exult over me" (Ps. 25:1-2). The facile always picture "deliverance" as coming in the form for which we already hope. This would undermine the notion of trust as *"putting ourselves in God's hands"* for *his* decision. It is this above overly innocent portrait, which the book of Job, through the "adversary," seeks to undermine as a formula that can be applied to every case. Job and Ecclesiastes counteract any facile application of the general optimism of Deuteronomy or Proverbs to every conceivable case. Faced with the threat of Assyrian invasion, King Hezekiah displayed trust when he took the threatening letter from Assyria into "the house of the LORD and spread it before the LORD" (2 Kings 19:14). The taunting of the Assyrians had the effect of provoking trust. The faithfulness of God to his promises does not exclude a fulfillment which may come as a surprise.

Probably one of the most popular biblical narratives known to children is David's discarding conventional resources of war or defense in the shape of "Saul's armor." When he faced humanly insuperable odds in the form of the "giant," Goliath, "David said to the Philistine, 'You come to me with sword and spear and javelin; but I come to you in the name of the LORD of hosts. . . . that all this assembly may know that the LORD does not save by sword and spear; for the battle is the LORD's, and he will give you into our hand" (1 Sam. 17:45, 47). As when someone is facing death, trust may not necessarily exclude all fear, or every particle of doubt. Trust in a promise does not imply cocksureness or a bland over-confidence. The similarly popular narrative of Shadrach, Meshach, and Abednego facing torture and death in a blazing furnace illustrates this admirably. They courageously trusted that "Our God . . . is able to deliver us from the furnace of blazing fire" (Dan. 3:17). But they realistically added: "But if not, . . . we will not worship the golden statue" (Dan. 3:18). They simply cast themselves on God, and placed themselves in his hands. Moberly calls this addition "crucial," for although God's character suggests deliverance, he comments, "for *reasons known only to himself,* he may not do so."[23]

This remains no less prominent in the New Testament. Paul speaks of

---

23. Moberly, *"b-ṭ-ḥ,"* *NIDOTTE*, vol. 1, 649 (my italics).

Abraham as "hoping against hope" (Rom. 4:18), although the whole passage (Rom. 4:1-25) is about sure trust and faith in God's promises: "No distrust made him waver concerning the promise of God" (Rom. 4:20). Paul further explains: "Hope that is seen is not hope. For who hopes for what is seen? But if we hope for what we do not see, we wait for it with patience" (Rom. 8:24-25). In an "evidence-based" culture, this seems to go beyond the realm of the physical sciences. But to discard Paul would undermine faith and hope. Paul asserts, "We wait for the hope of righteousness" (Gal. 5:5). We "shall all be alive" (1 Cor. 15:22). We experience the Holy Spirit only as the "first fruits" (Greek, *aparchē*) and pledge *(arrabōn)* of much more of the same kind yet to come. We long to see the fruition of God's purposes for the world (Rom. 8:18-25), where "eager expectation" suggests "stand on tiptoe." The Lord's Supper is instituted "until he comes" (1 Cor. 11:26). It is more likely that this refers to the Return of Christ, or the *Parousia*, than to the once-fashionable idea of a "liturgical" coming. Wolfhart Pannenberg rightly states that the nature of this sacrament as a sign "is an expression of the 'not yet' of our Christian life."[24]

The teaching of Jesus also contains this future-looking or "unfulfilled" aspect. Joachim Jeremias well sums up the "reversals" which have yet to take place, especially in the parables.[25] He discusses not only the Parable of the Wheat and the Tares (Matt. 13:24-30) and the Seine Net or Dragnet (Matt. 13:47-48), but also that what is hidden becomes manifest (Matt. 10:26 and par.); the poor will become rich (Luke 6:20); the last will become first (Mark 10:31); the small will become great (Matt. 18:4); the hungry will be filled (Luke 6:21); the weary will find rest (Matt. 11:28); those who mourn will be comforted (Matt. 5:4); those who weep will laugh (Luke 6:21); the sick will be healed, and the blind will receive sight (Matt. 11:5); prisoners will be freed (Luke 4:18); and the lowly will be exalted (Matt. 23:12; Luke 14:11; 18:14).

To the witness of Jesus, Paul, and the Old Testament must be added that of Hebrews. C. K. Barnett rightly compares Hebrews with "the Pilgrim's Progress from the City of Destruction to the Celestial City."[26] Christians have yet to enter into the "rest." In this life they have no abiding city,

24. Wolfhart Pannenberg, *Systematic Theology* (3 vols.; Grand Rapids: Eerdmans and Edinburgh: T&T Clark, 2004), vol. 3, 353.

25. Joachim Jeremias, *The Parables of Jesus* (London: S.C.M., 2nd ed. 1963), 221-22.

26. C. K. Barrett, "The Eschatology of the Epistle to the Hebrews," in *The Background of the New Testament and Its Eschatology: In Honour of C. H. Dodd*, ed. W. D. Davies and D. Daube (Cambridge: Cambridge University Press, 1956), 373-83.

but seek the city which is to come (Heb. 13:14). In their attitude of trust and expectation the readers resemble the Old Testament saints (Heb. 11:10, 14, 16). God has prepared the city to which they journey (11:16). Ernst Käsemann well conveys this promising stance of Hebrews. He wrote the first draft of his study on Hebrews while he was imprisoned by the Nazis in 1937. He declares, "Hebrews intends to show the Christian community the greatness of the promise given it. . . . *It calls it to a way,* to the goal to which it points by way of promise. . . . One possesses the *euangelion* [gospel] on earth only as *epangelia* [promise]. . . . The form of existence . . . *can only be that of wandering (pilgrimage, die Wanderschaft)*" (his italics).[27] Israel "wandering" through the wilderness in trustful response to God's promise appears as an "antitype of Christianity." This is "constitutive for the entire letter."[28] Referring to the whole of the New Testament and Christian theology, Moltmann uses "The Way of Jesus Christ" to underline "the aspect of process . . . leading from his resurrection to his parousia," and that it is "a 'Christology of the way.'"[29]

Hebrews, Paul, the teaching of Jesus, and the Old Testament may appear to embrace the whole biblical witness, with the possible exception of the Johannine writings. But while he does lay very great stress on the present, even in John, as Ulrich Simon argues, "Present fulfilment does not rule out future hope; on the contrary, the work of Christ inspires every hope for the future. Thus John has not abandoned common New Testament eschatology"[30] (John 5:25, 28). C. K. Barrett also underlines the place of future resurrection in John, and G. E. Ladd has long argued that the "now and not yet" of the New Testament constitutes a unifying theme. We have yet to consider in due course the Revelation of John.

All this calls attention to the positive and critical role of *promise.* It places a question mark against an "evidence-based" understanding of *all* reality, not simply "science." Secondarily, promise invites neither cocksureness, nor presumption, nor despair, but *trust.* In Luther's language, faith and trust are the personal *appropriation of promise.*

27. Ernst Käsemann, *The Wandering People of God* (Minneapolis: Augsburg, 1984), 17 and 19.

28. Käsemann, *The Wandering People of God,* 20.

29. Jürgen Moltmann, *The Way of Jesus Christ* (London: SCM, 1990), xiv.

30. Ulrich Simon, *The End Is Not Yet: A Study in Christian Eschatology* (London: Nisbet, 1964), 36.

2.3. Promise and Language

Promise is not a hypothetical assertion about the future. This would reduce its status to the formal logician's analysis of such hypothetical statements as "The King of France is bald," which is an old favorite of logicians.
They use it to demonstrate that some propositions have no truth-value at
all, at least as they stand. They similarly cite statements about a "round
square." John R. Searle brilliantly illustrates the different *direction of fit* between words and the world, in the case of statements and promises. Statements, he points out, *mirror* the world which they *describe*. Thus they
demonstrate a direction of fit in which the *word reflects the world*. But in
the case of promises, and some other modes of language, *words can shape
the world*. The direction of fit begins with the word and points to a *changed
world*. Searle comments, "Some [utterances] . . . get the words (more
strictly their propositional content) to *match the world*, others . . . get the
world to match the words."[31] He draws on the Elizabeth Anscombe analogy
of the shopper and the store detective. The shopper reads the words
"beans, butter, bacon, and bread," and uses the list to *make the world* (in
this case, that of the kitchen at home) *match the words*. But if the store detective writes down the names of what the shopper took from the shelf, in
this case *the words match the world*. They mirror what the shopper has
taken. The detective's list "has a *word-to-world* direction of fit (as do statements . . .); the shopper's list has the *world-to-word* direction of fit (as do
. . . promises)."[32]

Promises make the world match the words because they constitute valid
performative utterances, or are *illocutions*. More than twenty years prior to
Searle, J. L. Austin produced the first and classic study of performatives.
These are utterances, he claimed, "in which to *say* something is to *do*
something."[33] Similarly, he says, an "illocutionary act" is the "performance
of an act *in* saying something."[34] Austin spent a large part of his lectures
discussing "happy" or effective conditions for valid or operative performatives. These entail the speaker's being authorized to perform the act and
the appropriateness of procedure followed, which must rest on accepted

31. John R. Searle, *Expression and Meaning: Studies in the Theory of Speech Acts* (Cambridge: Cambridge University Press, 1979), 3 (my italics).

32. Searle, *Expression and Meaning*, 4 (his italics).

33. John L. Austin, *How to Do Things with Words* (Oxford: Clarendon, 1962), 12 (his italics); from Lectures in 1955.

34. Austin, *How to Do Things with Words*, 99 (his italics).

convention. I cannot simply "name" a rowing boat on the local lake by smashing a ginger-beer bottle against the side and saying, "I name this boat the *QE 3*," but the Queen or shipping magnate's wife can say these words in relation to the appropriate ship, because she is the authorized person to do it, probably with a champagne bottle. For example, "I baptize you, John," might be an effective performative, but "I baptize you infant no. 4267" would not. "My seconds will call on you" would have served as a performative in the days of duels, but now it would seem an empty, irrelevant, and foolish utterance.

Austin's immediate successor in this field, Donald D. Evans, calls this "conventional" or "institutional" force, in contrast to "causal" force.[35] Many of the first attempts of Continental theological scholars, such as Ernst Fuchs, to speak of the speech-event *(Sprachereignis)* simply disregarded what Austin and Evans called conditions for the operative effectiveness of performatives. If we were speaking of illocutions or performatives in a Christian context, we might see the covenant as an institutional mechanism.

Most of my previous discussions of speech-act theory and of performative utterances have followed complex paths.[36] But here I simply make the main point about promising. I will, however, pause to make two comments about precursors of Austin. Perhaps the first in premodern times to identify what were, in effect, *speech-acts* was William Tyndale (c. 1494-1536). He saw that the effectiveness of Scripture lay largely in its *capacity to perform actions* and to *shape the world*. As I have argued more than once, he identified what amount to eighteen different speech-acts which the Bible regularly performs. The Bible *"promises, names, appoints, declares, gives, condemns, curses, binds, kills, drives to despair, delivers, forbids, ministers to life, wounds, blesses, heals, cures, and wakes."*[37] Reflection will confirm that these eighteen linguistic functions are *actions,* performed *in* the saying of the words. Here the institutional framework, we shall argue, includes the covenant.

The second precursor or anticipator in this respect of Austin is Wittgenstein. He was aware of speech-acts, but did not develop or fully ap-

---

35. Donald D. Evans, *The Logic of Self-Involvement* (London: S.C.M., 1963), 68, 70.

36. Anthony C. Thiselton, *Thiselton on Hermeneutics: Collected Works with New Essays,* ed. John R. Hinnells, Ashgate Contemporary Thinking on Religion (Grand Rapids: Eerdmans and Aldershot: Ashgate, 2006), 53-150.

37. William Tyndale, *A Pathway into the Holy Scripture,* in his *Doctrinal Treatises and Introduction to Portions of Scripture* (Cambridge: Cambridge University Press, Parker Society, 1848), 8-9 (my italics).

ply them. He wrote that in a formal oration "We mourn our brother" is an expression (or *act*) of *mourning*; it is "not to tell anything to those who are present"; it is not a description of what we are doing.[38] He also examined the logic of "I believe." He argued that belief represented mostly a "disposition . . . shown me in the case of someone else by his behaviour." Wittgenstein writes: "If there were a verb meaning 'to believe falsely' it would not have any significant first person present indicative." This is because, he observes, "My own relation to my words is wholly different from other people's."[39]

A promise, Austin and Searle urge, "*commits* the speaker to a certain course of action."[40] It is a *commitment*. Theologically this would be startling if we had not become accustomed to the notion of a theology of *covenant*. It is a sign of the majesty, humility, faithfulness, and love of God that he regularly *commits himself* to take given courses of action. This excludes or rules out an array of alternative options. It bears directly on the old question, "If God cannot lie, can he be truly omnipotent and almighty?" One response is to say that this is a *logical* "cannot," not an empirical or contingent one of experience. A fuller explanation is to say that true omnipotence allows God the *voluntary choice to exclude certain actions, if he wills* to do so. In Karl Barth's theology *God's freedom* would seem to imply this.

The *commissive* force of promise can be seen in two ways. First, as H. A. A. Pritchard observes, "Promising seems to *be* binding ourselves" (his italics).[41] Second, promise is an act for which the speaker (or, in some cases, his or her authorized deputy) takes personal *responsibility*. J. L. Austin asks us to imagine the reaction of an anxious parent when perhaps the child sends a cricket ball through a neighbor's window. If the parent exclaims, "He promises [not to do it again], don't you, Willy?" this is hardly a true performative because it is without any personal commitment on the part of the child.[42]

From yet another angle the point is made by a specialist in jurispru-

38. Ludwig Wittgenstein, *Philosophical Investigations* (Oxford: Blackwell, 2nd ed. 1958, Ger. and Eng.), II.ix.189.

39. Wittgenstein, *Philosophical Investigations,* II.x.190, 191, and 192.

40. Searle, *Expression and Meaning,* 8, 22; cf. Austin, *How to Do Things with Words,* 156-57 (my italics).

41. H. A. A. Pritchard, "The Obligation to Keep a Promise," in *Moral Obligation: Essays and Lectures* (Oxford: Clarendon, 1949), 169.

42. Austin, *How to Do Things with Words,* 63.

dence, Charles Fried, in his book *Contract as Promise*. Fried first discusses contracts and contract law, and he makes two points about promise. First, he says, "The device that gives *trust* its sharpest . . . form is *promise*" (my italics).[43] Next, he says, "Promising is *binding,* because we not only see reliance, but invite it."[44] Promise entails both reliance, he argues, and the communication of intention, which *commit* the one who makes the promise. Promise is a purposive action through language, which involves the one to whom the promise is addressed in cooperation, for his or her benefit. Fried argues for the moral integrity of contract, since it rests on self-commitment, self-involvement, and promise.

This corresponds precisely to points which Walther Eichrodt makes about God's willingness to make commitments in the promise of the covenant. He speaks of the constant fear among Gentile nations in the ancient world before Christ of arbitrariness, whim, or caprice among pagan deities. With the God of Israel, he asserts, such arbitrariness is excluded. He writes, "With this God, men [people] *know exactly where they stand; an atmosphere of trust . . .* is created" (first italics mine; second, his).[45] By his own will and purpose, God commits himself to honor what he has promised to do in the covenant. Therefore, his people "know exactly where they stand," and can trust God. *Covenant,* in effect, is an agreed deal or arrangement. We shall return to this subject in this chapter.

In the Old Testament we read of God's promises to Abraham (Gen. 12:1-3; 15:1-8); to Noah (Gen. 9:11); to Abraham, Isaac, Jacob, and Moses (Exod. 6:6; 19:5-6; 32:13); to David (2 Sam. 5:3, 19); and to Israel and the Church to come (Jer. 31:31). God's promise is taken up in the New Testament (Rom. 4:3, 13-25; Gal. 3:14-29; Heb. 6:13; 10:23; 11:11). The Hebrew of the Old Testament simply uses the general words for "to say" (*'āmar, dābār);* the Greek of the New Testament uses a specific word for "to promise," or "promise," namely, *epangellomai, epangelia*. The promise of God, Frederick Danker suggests, occurs in Acts 2:39; Rom. 4:13-14; 9:9; Heb. 7:6; 2 Pet. 3:9; and in numerous other places; the verb occurs in Rom. 4:21; Tit. 1:2; Heb. 10:23; 12:26; and elsewhere.[46] On several occasions God confirms his promise by an oath (Ps. 132:11; Isa. 45:23; Heb. 6:13-14; 7:21). Philo of Al-

---

43. Charles Fried, *Contract as Promise: A Theory of Contractual Obligation* (Cambridge, MA: Harvard University Press, 1981), 8; cf. esp. 7-27 and 40-73.

44. Fried, *Contract as Promise,* 11.

45. W. Eichrodt, *Theology of the Old Testament,* vol. 1 (London: S.C.M., 1961), 38.

46. F. Danker and W. Bauer, *A Greek-English Lexicon of the New Testament* (BDAG), 355-56.

exandria confessed to puzzlement about how this could make logical sense (Philo, *Sacrifices* 91-94; *Special Laws* 3:203-7).[47] To add "It is true that" to a self-evident truth adds nothing to it, as P. F. Strawson has shown, except perhaps the personal endorsement of the one who speaks; so it would be if the true and faithful God adds an oath. But the oath has as its aim not the defense of formal logic but assurance to the addressee, especially if he or she is weak in faith. It allows the believer "a steadfast anchor" (Heb. 6:19). Karl Barth declares that God's "self-witness as the promise, pledge, and assurance" to believers invites reliance on God and a secure relationship with God.[48]

The important factor about commissive language consists both in the *binding or faithfulness* and in the *exclusion* of other options, or *self-limitations,* which together invite trust, and, in the case of promise, bring about the future shaping of the world. All this comes from the *language* of promise. The self-limitation of God is seen partly in creation itself, but especially in Christ, and does not at all undermine his omnipotence or almightiness, but enhances it. Our source of wonder is that God should choose to bind himself, and to limit his options, in this way.

Jürgen Moltmann sees God's self-limitation in creation, although his formulation may perhaps be controversial. God's "freedom" does not consist in his exercising power *over* people, as if they were pawns, playthings, or a piece of property. In creation, Moltmann argues, God not only goes out of himself to create an "other," but also internally withdraws into himself to make room *for* the other. He draws partly on the thought of Isaac Luria. He writes, "We must, after all, assume a *self-limitation* of the infinite, omnipresent God. . . . God must have made room for this" (his italics).[49] The universe, he argues, was made possible through a "shrinkage" process in God. This may become more plausible when we consider evil in the world and human suffering, and what an affront human evil is to God. Creation is God's expression of *love.* Moltmann urges, *"A God who cannot suffer cannot love either."*[50]

---

47. Cf. Anthony C. Thiselton, "Oath," in *New Interpreter's Dictionary of the Bible* (Nashville: Abingdon, 2009), vol. 4, 309-12.

48. Karl Barth, *Church Dogmatics,* II/2 (Edinburgh: T&T Clark, 1957), sect. 34:3, p. 233; cf. 233-59.

49. Jürgen Moltmann, *The Trinity and the Kingdom of God: The Doctrine of God* (London: S.C.M., 1981), 109. Cf. Gershom Scholem, *Major Trends in Jewish Mysticism* (New York: Schocken, 1954 and 1995), 244-86.

50. Moltmann, *The Trinity and the Kingdom of God,* 38 (my italics).

Yet, even if we regard Moltmann's argument as speculative, we cannot deny God's self-limitation in Jesus Christ. In the Person of Christ, he emptied himself or "humbled himself" (Phil. 2:8), for "God was in Christ reconciling the world to himself" (2 Cor. 5:19). Phil. 2:8 reads: "He humbled himself, and became obedient to the point of death, even death on a cross." Martin Hengel shows more clearly than most what "death on a cross" meant. It was offensive and shameful even to mention crucifixion in educated society; the cross signifies shame; it was "a horrific, disgusting business," which was usually "reserved for hardened criminals, rebellious slaves, and rebels against the Roman state. . . . Crucifixion represented . . . uttermost humiliation."[51] The barbaric infliction of pain was vengeful and extreme.

In Christ, Eberhard Jüngel declares, "God *has defined himself*" (his italics).[52] In Christ we encounter "the self-definition of God in human language," and hence in Christ God becomes "thinkable" and "conceivable."[53] This allows for "the speakability of God."[54] Yet language in relation to God not only speaks *about* God. Language, above all, is *from* and *to* him, in the second person. Promise is made in this mode of language (cf. Austin's "He promises, don't you, Willy?"). Jüngel insists, "One of its [language's] essential functions is that of *address*. . . . The word of address affects not only the *consciousness* of the person addressed, but *his whole being*" (first italics, Jüngel's; second and third, mine).[55] Promise comes *from* God; prayer is addressed *to* God.

The examples of God's self-limitation from creation and from the cross are not as far apart as we may think. As we noted in the previous chapter, Arthur Peacock and Holmes Rolston argue convincingly that the principle of dying in order to bring life and regeneration is built into the grain of the universe, which Rolston calls "cruciform nature."[56] Giving birth, Rolston argues, involves labor pains. Something is always dying; and

---

51. Martin Hengel, *The Cross of the Son of God* (London: S.C.M., 1986), 129, 175, and 179; cf. L. L. Welborn, *Paul the Fool of Christ* (London and New York: T&T Clark and Continuum, 2005), 248-53.

52. Eberhard Jüngel, *God as the Mystery of the World* (Grand Rapids: Eerdmans and Edinburgh: T&T Clark, 1983), 350; cf. 220.

53. Jüngel, *God as the Mystery of the World*, 152-69.

54. Jüngel, *God as the Mystery of the World*, 229.

55. Jüngel, *God as the Mystery of the World*, 11.

56. Cf. John Polkinghorne, ed., *The Work of Love: Creation as Kenosis* (Grand Rapids and Cambridge: Eerdmans, 2001), 21-65; Rolston, "Kenosis and Nature," in ibid., 37.

something is always regenerating: "The whole creation has been groaning in travail together until now" (Rom. 8:22). Creation will be set free from its bondage to decay. Hence it waits for the End "with eager longing" (Rom. 8:19).

Wolfhart Pannenberg, at all events, concludes, "The promises [of God] put the human present, with all the pain of its incompleteness and failure, in the light of the future of God that comes to us as our salvation. This does not mean that the promised future is already present. . . . The distinctive tension between Already and Not Yet . . . is typical of the situation of the Christian community. . . . All the promises of God are Yes and Amen (2 Cor. 1:20)."[57] Far from being restricted to the evidential perspective of the physical sciences, Jürgen Moltmann suggests, "on the contrary it stands in *contradiction* to the reality open to *experience now and heretofore.*"[58] Christ's resurrection is not "a mere return to life," but constitutes and promises "a conquest of the deadliness of death . . . a conquest of godforsakenness."[59] The future is not an extrapolation from the present, but an inbreaking of the word of promise that creates the new; it surpasses all expectation. Yet this does not ignore the moment-by-moment experience of waiting for the fulfillment of the promise. Walther Zimmerli writes, "Anyone who speaks of promise and fulfilment knows of veiled purposes and distressed waiting; he knows of walking, and not only of standing still; he knows of a summoning, and not only of a looking on."[60]

In addition to my own examples of the application of "performatives" to parts of the Bible, we suggest that many constitute good textual examples. They include: Donald Evans, Dieter Neufeld, Richard Briggs, Alexandra Brown, J. Eugene Botha, and Karl Donfried, as well as others. I have sought to apply performative utterances to blessing and cursing in the case of Jacob and Esau, and again, in the case of Balaam and Barak (against W. Zimmerli, E. Jacob, L. Dürr, O. Grether, and others); to Christological authority to forgive sins; and to promising. These have been collected together in Part II of *Thiselton on Hermeneutics: Collected Works.*[61] Donald

57. Pannenberg, *Systematic Theology,* vol. 3, 545.

58. Moltmann, *Theology of Hope,* 103 (my italics).

59. Moltmann, *Theology of Hope,* 211.

60. W. Zimmerli, "Promise and Fulfilment," in *Essays in Old Testament Interpretation,* ed. Claus Westermann (London: S.C.M., 1963), 97; cf. 89-122.

61. Thiselton, *Thiselton on Hermeneutics,* 53-67 (also from *JTS* 25 [1974]: 282-99); "Speech Act Theory as One Tool among Many: 'Transforming Texts,'" in *Thiselton on Hermeneutics,* 69-98, and "More on Christology: Christology in Luke . . . ," 99-116, from *New*

Evans applies performative utterances mainly to the divine act of creation and its human response.[62] Dieter Neufeld applies speech-act theory to confessions in 1 John.[63] Eugene Botha uses the approach to John 4:1-42.[64] Richard Briggs discusses a general approach, especially with respect to confessions of faith, the forgiveness of sins, and teaching.[65] Alexandra Brown concentrates on preaching in 1 Corinthians, especially 1 Corinthians 1 and 2.[66] Karl Donfried sees the whole of 1 Thessalonians, especially 1 Thess. 2:1-12, not only as an apologia but also as a speech-act.[67] This does not exhaust the list. Mervyn Duffy applied speech-act theory to the language and ritual of the sacraments in 2005, and Kevin Vanhoozer uses speech-act theory to enhance the authority of Scripture.[68]

All this is simply to add force to the relevance of performative language to the *commissive, active, binding,* and *world-changing* nature of promise. This is not merely a passing fad of philosophers and linguisticians. The promise of God provides the basis for our language about the Last Things, and the basis on which we can proceed. It addresses the problem of any who doubt, and helps us to see the magnanimity, graciousness, and sheer love of the God with whom we shall one day come face-to-face.

Horizons in Hermeneutics (Grand Rapids: Zondervan, 1992), 31-35 and 283-303, and in Joel Green (ed.), *Jesus of Nazareth* (Grand Rapids: Eerdmans, 1994), 453-72; and "More on Promising," 117-29, from *The Promise of Hermeneutics* (Grand Rapids: Eerdmans, 1999), 223-39.

62. Evans, *The Logic of Self-Involvement*, 145-68.

63. Dieter Neufeld, *Re-conceiving Texts as Speech Acts: An Analysis of 1 John* (Leiden: Brill, 1994).

64. J. Eugene Botha, *Jesus and the Samaritan Woman: A Speech-Act Reading of John 4:1-42* (Leiden: Brill, 1991).

65. Richard S. Briggs, *Words in Action: Speech Act Theory and Biblical Interpretation* (Edinburgh and New York: T&T Clark, 2001), 147-298.

66. Alexandra R. Brown, *The Cross and Human Transformation: Paul's Apocalyptic Word in 1 Corinthians* (Minneapolis: Fortress, 1995), 14-104.

67. Karl Donfried, "The Epistolary and Rhetorical Context of 1 Thessalonians 2:1-12," in *The Thessalonians Debate: Methodological Discord as Methodological Synthesis*, ed. K. P. Donfried and J. Beutler (Grand Rapids: Eerdmans, 2000), 31-60.

68. Mervyn Duffy, *How Language, Ritual and Sacraments Work according to John Austin, Jürgen Habermas and Louis-Marie Chauvet* (Rome: Pontifical Gregorian University, 2005).

CHAPTER 3

The Sacraments, the Covenant, and the Bible: Completing the Argument for Doubters

3.1. Promise, the Sacraments, and the Word

Many Christians, on the brink of death, may forget that for fifty or more years they have received and appropriated the sacraments, as signs of God's assurance and promises from God. If we use the 1662 Book of Common Prayer, we will have heard in the second post-Communion prayer, "Thou [God] dost assure us thereby of thy favour and goodness towards us; and that we are very members incorporate in the mystical body of thy Son." Some in the tradition of the Reformation may be fearful of presumption, as if going through a Church ceremony and ritual could of itself secure a safe passage through death. Yet it was above all the Reformers, including Luther, Melanchthon, Calvin, Tyndale, and Cranmer, who most characteristically insisted that the two dominical sacraments, authorized by Christ, constituted *effective signs of divine promise* or *pledges*. Speaking of the sacraments, Philipp Melanchthon wrote: "The gospel is the promise of grace. The locus of signs [sacraments] is very closely related to promises as seals which remind us of the promise, and are certain witnesses to the divine will toward us, testifying that we shall certainly receive what God has promised."[1]

John Calvin defines a sacrament as "an external sign by which the Lord seals in our conscience his *promises* of good will towards us in order to sustain the weakness of our faith."[2] Melanchthon takes up this latter

---

1. Philipp Melanchthon, *Loci Communes Rerum Theologicarum*, in *Melanchthon and Bucer*, ed. Wilhelm Pauck, LCC 19 (London: S.C.M., 1969), 133-40.

2. John Calvin, *Institutes of the Christian Religion*, 4.14.1, ed. H. Beveridge (London: James Clarke, 1957), vol. 2, 491-92.

phrase. He asserts, "Signs are given for the purpose of stirring up faith."[3] Calvin declares, "There never is a sacrament without an antecedent promise."[4] Protestants may indeed not wish to presume on a mechanical process. Luther writes, "The Pope puts trust in the consecrated water. . . . The consecrated water is Satan's goblin bath [*kobelbad*]."[5] But when Word and sacrament cohere in the setting of an authentic worshipping community, the sacraments achieve their status as a promise of God. They become "sacramental signs of the covenants . . . enacted by words, . . . a pledge of grace."[6] Hence in Martin Bucer's view, while "the inward word" comes from the Holy Spirit, "the outward word" includes the "spoken word" of the Bible and preaching, and the "visible word" of the sacraments.

This understanding of the sacraments is not peculiar to the Reformers. Mervyn Duffy sees them as having the same "performative" force as the explicit illocutionary acts or performatives of the preached word.[7] He well describes the respective approaches of J. L. Austin, Jürgen Habermas, and Louis-Marie Chauvet as summing up the impact of performative language. Duffy coins the aphorism, "Words do not merely label, they transform."[8] But Chauvet, he points out, draws on Aquinas as well as on Augustine. With P. Bourdieu, he uses the term *"habitus"* to denote dispositions to act in certain ways. The illocution releases the springs of the *habitus,* in which "Rituals are stagings which unfold the illocutionary-performative dimensions of language."[9] When Christians come together, this is not simply to exchange information, but to become and to be the Church, the people of God and the body of Christ. They celebrate the bond with the founding community and generations that follow.[10] The Church professes belief in the forgiveness of sins: "None discover themselves to be sinners, unless they discover themselves to be *pardoned* sinners."[11] Duffy's declaration, "The ritual [or Lord's Supper] functions to slice away time between the present and

3. Melanchthon, *Loci Communes,* in *Melanchthon and Bucer,* 135.

4. Calvin, *Institutes,* 4.14.3 (vol. 2, 492).

5. Luther, "Sermons in Castle Pleissenburg, 1539," in *LW* 51 (Philadelphia: Muhlenberg, 1959), 303-12.

6. Calvin, *Institutes,* 4.14.6 and 7 (vol. 2, 494-95).

7. Mervyn Duffy, *How Language, Ritual and Sacraments Work according to John Austin, Jürgen Habermas and Louis-Marie Chauvet,* Tesi Gregoriana Serie Teologia 123 (Rome: Pontifical Gregorian University, 2005), 19-202.

8. Duffy, *How Language and Sacraments Work,* 152.

9. Duffy, *How Language and Sacraments Work,* 168.

10. Duffy, *How Language and Sacraments Work,* 178.

11. L.-M. Chauvet, *Symbol and Sacrament* (Minneapolis: Collegeville, 1955), 433.

'*illo tempore*' of the origins," coheres with the Protestant research on "remembrance" *(anamnēsis).*[12] The Eucharist dissolves the time gap between Calvary and the present, as in the words of the Black Spiritual: "Were you *there* when they crucified my Lord?" A worshipper at the Lord's Supper is no further from the cross than the penitent thief to whom Jesus said, "Today you will be with me in Paradise" (Luke 23:43).

Promise, as both Catholics and Protestants agree, is part of *proclamation,* which involves the self. Duffy and Aquinas are no less emphatic than Luther and Calvin about this.[13] Aquinas may indeed be less explicit than Calvin about understanding the sacraments as proclamation, but it is implicit in his contrast between the angels seeing Christ face-to-face, and human beings seeing him by faith, and through word and sacrament.[14] Calvin is explicit. He writes, "The right consideration of signs . . . depends chiefly on promise."[15] Incidentally, like Oscar Cullmann, he sees this as a vital part of the argument for infant baptism. The Lord's Supper is "proclamation," not least because Paul specifically said, "You proclaim the Lord's death" when you participate in the Lord's Supper (1 Cor. 11:26; Greek, *katangellete*). We must keep in mind that this is a proclamation, not just information. To quote Duffy one last time, "Sacraments clearly *do* things; they are actions of Christ and his Church."[16] Calvin asserts, "The Lord not only reminds us of this great gift of his goodness . . . but passes it, as it were, from hand to hand, and urges us to recognise it . . . not to be ungrateful . . . but rather proclaim it . . . and celebrate it with thanksgiving . . . (1 Cor. 11:26)."[17] On the brink of death, we may be tempted to forget the faithful participation in the sacraments. Yet to recall them is not presumption, but faith. As Calvin stresses so many times, "The office of the sacrament is to aid the infirmity of the human mind, assisting it in rising upwards, so as to perceive the height of spiritual mysteries."[18]

For the Reformers this never stands in contrast to the hearing of the Word of God, but as a different mode of the same action. Admittedly

---

12. Duffy, *How Language and Sacraments Work,* 233.

13. Duffy, *How Language and Sacraments Work,* 241-42.

14. Thomas Aquinas, *Summa Theologiae* (London: Eyre & Spottiswoode, 1963), 3, Q. 80, art. 2, reply to obj. 1-2.

15. Calvin, *Institutes,* 4.14.2 (vol. 2, 529).

16. Duffy, *How Language and Sacraments Work,* 248 (his italics); also *Code of Canon Law,* 840.

17. Calvin, *Institutes,* 4.17.37 (vol. 2, 595).

18. Calvin, *Institutes,* 4.17.35 (vol. 2, 593).

Bucer's phrase "visible words" seems to privilege sight over other senses, whereas often in hearing the Word, the ear has become privileged. But in participation in the sacraments God permits sight, hearing, touch, taste, and even perhaps smell to become avenues of communication. To some this may penetrate to the subconscious. The Word of God operates on many levels. Yet the Word of God has many methods of communication. Each supplements the other. Some Protestant clergy seek to maintain the Reformers' equal balance by wearing the same robes for both Word and sacrament. Our discussion of performative language underlines this co-equal effect. Scripture and its expositors, Calvin asserts, function like glasses, "so Scripture dissipates the darkness, and shows us the true God clearly."[19] This applies not only to the Eucharist or the Lord's Supper, but also to Baptism. Schnackenburg, a Roman Catholic writer on Baptism in Paul, whose book on the subject has been translated into English by a prominent Baptist, asserts that pledge and promise lie at the heart of Baptism.[20]

Baptism and the Lord's Supper focus on the death and resurrection of Christ. Readings of Scripture, especially from a Lectionary, and preaching extend our horizons almost without limit. Karl Barth comes near to, but perhaps not quite reaches, the "performative" dimension of Scripture in the technical sense, when he speaks of "The Speech of God as the Act of God."[21] He insists that the speech of God is not "only talk": "The Word of God is itself the act of God. . . . The Word of God makes history: 'He spoke, and it was done; he commanded, and it stood fast' (Ps. 33:9)."[22] God's Word denotes "a *promise,* a *judgement,* a claim."[23] It is not an empty pledge, but revelation is a contemporary act and actualization of the Word of God by the Holy Spirit.

We do not have to restrict ourselves to the Reformation era to find this perspective. Athanasius, for example, writes: "The Scriptures . . . were spoken and written by God through man who spoke of God," although the Scriptures must be read with pure motives. If we truly understand them and hear them, we "may escape the peril of the sinners and thus fire at the Day of Judgement, and receive what is laid up for the Saints in the King-

19. Calvin, *Institutes,* 1.6.1 (vol. 1, 64).

20. Rudolf Schnackenburg, *Baptism in the Thought of St. Paul* (Oxford: Blackwell, 1964), 87.

21. Karl Barth, *Church Dogmatics* (Edinburgh: T&T Clark, 1957-75), II/1, sect. 5, 3, 143-62.

22. Barth, *Church Dogmatics,* II/1, sect. 5, 3, 143-44.

23. Barth, *Church Dogmatics,* II/1, sect. 5, 3, 150.

dom of Heaven, which 'eye hath not seen, nor ear heard' (1 Cor. 2:9)."[24] Supremely, however, the sacraments, and especially Christ himself, represent "the embodied word." On the brink of death, are all these many assurances, and modes of assurance, to be cast aside? Some writers could even condemn such doubt as a lack of trust. The writer of the Epistle to the Hebrews protests, "How can we escape if we neglect so great a salvation? It was declared at first through the Lord, and it was attested to us by those who heard him, while God added his testimony by signs . . . and the Holy Spirit" (Heb. 2:3-4).

3.2. Promise and Covenant

The relationship sealed by the covenant stands at the heart of Christian Baptism and the Lord's Supper, as signs of the covenant. But in chronological terms our earliest example of God's entering into a covenant relationship is the covenant with Noah, which included his descendants and all future humanity (Gen. 6:18; 9:8-17). God committed himself never to flood the earth and thus to bring about its destruction. A relationship of trust has been established. The rainbow becomes a sign of this covenant (Gen. 9:13-17). The sentence, "I have set my bow in the clouds, and it shall be a sign of the covenant between me and the earth" (v. 13), does not mean that God created the rainbow only after his promise to Noah, but that the already created rainbow now counts as a sign of grace. It serves to remind humanity of God's pledge as a commissive promise, and thus acts as *reassurance* of this promise. God commits himself in order that humanity may *know where they stand,* and enjoy a *secure relationship* with God. This covenant is established "forever" (v. 11; cf. Isa. 24:5).

The covenant with Abraham first takes the form of a promise and commitment to give the land of Canaan to him and to his descendants (Gen. 15:18-20). The covenant is made in answer to Abraham's question, "How do I know that I shall possess it [the land]?" (Gen. 15:8). Abraham is commanded to collect animals for sacrifice, and while a deep sleep and "terrifying darkness" fall upon Abraham, a flaming torch (representing God) passes between pieces of the dismembered animals to show the solemnity and gravity of the commissive act and its irrevocable nature. The

24. Athanasius, *On the Incarnation,* 56 and 57, in *Christology of the Later Fathers,* ed. E. R. Hardy, LCC 3 (London: S.C.M. and Philadelphia: Westminster, 1954), 109-10.

covenant is then "made" (Hebrew, *kārath*, "to cut"), as the flame divides the animals. Like the covenant with Noah, it appears to be an unconditional promise. Abraham will not live to see its fulfillment to his descendants, but God has performed an extraordinary act to demonstrate in a momentous way an assurance of the divine commitment and promise. Paul stresses that the promise is without conditions in Gal. 3:17.

A second covenant with Abraham follows in Gen. 17:1-10. In this case the emphasis falls on the promise of numerous offspring: "I will make you exceedingly faithful; and I will make nations of you . . . an everlasting covenant to be God to you and your offspring after you" (Gen. 17:6-7). To "establish" the covenant underlines, again, God's commitment to perform the promise. It will be an "everlasting" covenant (Gen. 17:7, 13, 19). There is, however, at least a hint of conditions: "This is my covenant, which you shall keep" (17:10). Whereas the rainbow was a sign of the covenant with Noah, and the fire and sacrifice was a sign of the first covenant with Abraham, now circumcision clearly becomes a sign of this third covenant (Gen. 17:10-14): "Every male among you shall be circumcised . . . throughout your generations . . . including the slave born in your house" (Gen. 17:10-12). Any who does not participate in the covenantal sign "shall be cut off from his people; he has broken my covenant" (17:14). People may despise the promise of God by deliberate failure to participate in the sign. We shall compare, in due course, failing to participate appropriately in the sign of the new covenant, the Lord's Supper (1 Cor. 11:27-32). It becomes clear a little later that the covenant passes through Sarah to Isaac (Gen. 17:21).

Abraham's faith, or his appropriation of the covenant promise, is tested to the limit. First, he faces the problem that Sarah has become normally too old to conceive a son. How can God's promise now be fulfilled? We learn in Gen. 18:11 that "Sarah and Abraham were old, advanced in age," yet the messengers from God asked, "Is anything too wonderful to the Lord? . . . Sarah shall have a son" (Gen. 18:14). His second challenge to trust occurred after the miracle of the birth of Isaac, when God said, "Take your son, your only son Isaac, . . . go to the land of Moriah, and offer him there as a burnt offering" (Gen. 22:2). In Kierkegaard's famous words, Abraham is commanded "to slay the son of promise." In the end, on the point of "not withholding his son" (v. 12), Abraham took the "ram caught in a thicket" and offered it up instead of his son (22:13).

A fourth covenant is made with Israel under Moses. God says, "I will take you as my people, and I will be your God" (Exod. 6:7). All the events surrounding the Exodus, the deliverance from slavery in Egypt, and especially the Passover and even the Ten Commandments, belong within this frame of God's covenant with his people. We examine again the Passover covenant in the Liturgy or Jewish *Haggadah* and *Sēder* shortly below, in this chapter and section.

The New Testament alludes to the various promises to Abraham. Hebrews refers to "the land he had been promised" (Heb. 11:9); to "the power of procreation" (Heb. 11:11); and to the provision of "one person, and this one as good as dead." Abraham "died in faith, without having received the promise" (Heb. 11:13). Paul refers to the covenant promise to the ancestor of many descendants (Gal. 3:6-9, 17-18; Rom. 4:3-13), and to Abraham's belief that God gives life "to the dead" (Rom. 4:17). Abraham believed, "hoping against hope" (4:18), "when he was already as good as dead. . . . No distrust made him waver concerning the promise of God" (Rom. 4:19, 20). Søren Kierkegaard (1813-55) discusses Abraham's appropriation of promise in his *Point of View for My Work as an Author* and in his *Fear and Trembling*.[25] Even Isaac could not fully "understand" what was happening. Abraham abandoned "worldly understanding."[26] His agony lay in "disappointed expectation." All the horrors were concentrated in one moment (Gen. 22:2). Abraham acted "on the strength of the absurd. . . . The paradox cannot be mediated . . . a paradox capable of transforming a murder into a holy act, [which] well pleased God."[27] Conventional ethics ran out; Abraham was invited to trust in God, whatever "logic" dictated. "Testing" faith, or a "trial of faith," Kierkegaard insisted, has nothing to do with God's testing hypothetical cognitive knowledge, but with the changing or transforming of the person who is "tested." We may not agree with all of Kierkegaard's remarks, but at least they show the special demands of human trust in God's promise.

God's "taking Israel as his people" reaches a climax in the renewed covenant at Sinai.[28] Exod. 19:8 takes up Exod. 6:6-8, and the Ten Commandments (Exod. 20:2-17) serve as the people's part of the covenant. The term "book of the covenant" is traditionally applied to Exod. 20:22–23:33. At the end of God's declarations, God "gave him [Moses] the two tablets of

25. Søren Kierkegaard, *Fear and Trembling*, ed. Walter Lowrie (New York: Doubleday, 1941 and 1954), 27-37 and 42-64; also in A. Hannary, ed. (London: Penguin, 1985), 44-55.

26. Kierkegaard, *Fear and Trembling*, 27.

27. Kierkegaard, *Fear and Trembling*, 64; cf. 88; and Anthony C. Thiselton, *New Horizons in Hermeneutics* (London: Harper-Collins and Grand Rapids: Zondervan, 1992), 564-66.

28. Cf. Rolf Rendtorff, *The Covenant Formula: An Exegetical and Theological Investigation* (Edinburgh: T&T Clark, 1998), 13-17 and 45-47.

the covenant, tablets of stone, written with the finger of God" (Exod. 31:18; cf. Exod. 32:15). In Exod. 34:10 God declares, "I hereby make a covenant." What emerges is that God makes a commitment at Sinai, and promises to do wonders on the people's behalf. It is clear from the Exodus account, however, that the Sinai covenant involves a mutual commitment.

Later books of the Pentateuch reaffirm earlier covenants: "I will remember my covenant with Jacob; I will remember my covenant with Isaac . . . and Abraham" (Lev. 26:42). Deuteronomy, especially chapters 4–11 and 29–31, takes up many details about the covenant.[29] God keeps his covenant with every generation.

Jeremiah looks forward to the new covenant, in place of "a covenant that they broke," namely, when "I will write it [my law] on their hearts, and I will be their God, and they shall be my people" (Jer. 31:33). "I will forgive their iniquity, and remember their sin no more" (Jer. 31:34). Ezekiel renews the promise: "I will bring you within the bond of the covenant" (Ezek. 20:37). It is "a covenant of peace" (*shālôm*, peace or well-being) that makes God's people "secure" (Ezek. 34:25). Isaiah speaks of an everlasting covenant and of God's "steadfast love" in the same chapter as that in which he speaks of the effects and effectiveness of God's Word (Isa. 55:3; cf. vv. 10-11).

In the New Testament the covenant finds a special focus in the words of institution of the Lord's Supper or Eucharist. The Lord's Supper is an effective sign of God's pledge or promise, "This is my blood of the covenant . . . poured out for many" (Mark 14:24; Matt. 26:28; Luke 22:20). Paul, in an even earlier pre-Pauline apostolic tradition, attributes to Jesus the words, "This sign is the new covenant in my blood" (1 Cor. 11:25).[30] Other contexts may be added. Paul and the apostles are "ministers of a new covenant" (2 Cor. 3:6). Hebrews applies the covenant of Exodus to Christians (Heb. 9:19-20). Sacrifice is made in the context of covenant (Heb. 9:21-22).[31] But the central focus concerns the Lord's Supper or Eucharist as an effective sign of the covenant. Oscar Cullmann comments, "The new covenant, established by the death of Christ, — that is the first idea involved in the Last Supper."[32]

29. Rendtorff, *The Covenant Formula*, 62-69.

30. Anders Eriksson, *Traditions as Rhetorical Proof: Pauline Argumentations in 1 Corinthians*, ConBNT 29 (Stockholm: Almquist & Wiksell, 1998), 74-86 and 100-106, and throughout.

31. For a study of Intertestamental understandings of covenant, cf. Stanley E. Porter and Jacqueline C. R. de Roo (eds.), *The Concept of the Old Covenant in the Second Temple Period*, JSJSup (Leiden: Brill, 2003).

32. Oscar Cullmann and F. J. Leenhardt, *Essays on the Lord's Supper* (London: Lutterworth, 1958), 19.

Admittedly the Greek term for "covenant," *diathēkē,* occurs relatively rarely: four times in the Synoptic Gospels, twice in Acts, nine times in Paul, and seventeen times in Hebrews. But most of these references are to the Lord's Supper. Gal. 3:15 and Heb. 9:16-17 are notable exceptions. H. Hegermann favors the translation "covenant promise," and argues that for the most part it denotes "irrevocable commitment."[33] In Heb. 6:13 it is additionally irrevocable by a divine oath (discussed above). He sees the institution of the Lord's Supper (Mark 14:24) as an application of Exod. 24:8: "Moses took the blood and dashed it on the people, and said, 'See the blood of the covenant that the LORD has made with you.'"

This becomes more cogent when we examine the actual words of institution, and how they might represent a special variant on the words said at the Passover meal. The *Mishnah* sets out an "order" or liturgical tradition, known as the Passover *Sēder.* This follows the dramatic action of Exod. 12:1-51, in order that participants may "re-live" the Passover and appropriate its promises, as if the worshipper were "there." Exod. 12:25-27 declares, "You shall keep this observance. And when your children say, 'What do you mean by this observance?' you shall say, 'It is the Passover sacrifice to the LORD.'" The *Mishnah* adds the comment, "A man must so regard himself as if he came forth himself out of Egypt" (*m. Pesaḥim* 10:5). The *Sēder* states, " . . . because of that which the Lord did unto *me* when *I* came forth out of Egypt."[34] In the Synoptic tradition reflected in Matthew, Mark, and Luke, Jesus commands the disciples to prepare a Passover meal for him to eat with them. (From the standpoint of John's chronology, this must have been "their" Passover, even if it was technically a day earlier, just as today some families enjoy "their" Christmas not exactly on December 25; cf. Mark 14:14; Matt. 26:17-19; Luke 22:7-13.) F. J. Leenhardt shows how the Passover *Sēder* fits the words of the institution of the Eucharist or Last Supper.[35]

The Jewish *Haggadah* begins with the *Sēder:* "Blessed art Thou, O Lord. . . ." The Jewish "grace" is the counterpart of "after blessing [it]" (Mark 14:22, NRSV; Matt. 26:26, NRSV; Luke 22:19) or "after giving thanks" (Mark 14:23; Matt. 26:27). The NRSV intrusion of "it" is a most unfortunate mistake. The Greek simply has, "Taking the bread, he blessed [God]

---

33. H. Hegermann, *"diathēkē," Exegetical Dictionary of the New Testament (EDNT),* ed. H. Balz and G. Schneider (Grand Rapids: Eerdmans, 1993), vol. 1, 299.

34. Cecil Roth (ed.), *The Haggadah* (London: Soncino, new ed. Heb. and Eng., 1934), 36.

35. F. J. Leenhardt, in Cullmann and Leenhardt, *Essays on the Lord's Supper,* 39-43.

and broke it" (Mark 14:22; cf. Matt. 26:26). The NIV rightly has: "Jesus took bread, gave thanks, and broke it" (Mark 14:22; Matt. 26:26; Luke 22:19). Best of all are the REB and NJB. "He took bread, and having said the blessing, he broke it" (Mark 14:22 and pars.). The grace, directed toward God, is not a "consecration" of the bread and wine. Then in place of "This is my body," the Jewish *Haggadah* reads, "This is the bread of affliction that our forefathers ate in the land of Egypt" (Hebrew, *hā' lachmā' 'anya' diyakālû 'abānta' be'ārāts demitsrāyîm*).[36] Joachim Jeremias also explains the words of institution in the setting of a Passover meal.[37] Admittedly Otfried Hofius prefers to state that 1 Cor. 11:23b-25 does not point to "the particularities of a Passover meal."[38] But it is difficult to ignore the arguments of many others to the contrary. What remains without controversy is Cullmann's comment that "Jesus' words about the new covenant" have a unique value "as far as the Lord's Supper is concerned."[39] Leenhardt rightly sees how "This is my body" comes as a bolt from the blue and a surprise when Jesus is expounding "what the Paschal meal meant to the pious Israelite."[40]

The deliverance from Egypt was a manifestation of God's covenant mercies to the "old" Israel; the Lord's Supper is a covenant sign of God's mercies in Christ under the new covenant. Many see a parallel between Baptism as an unrepeatable sign of the new covenant, and circumcision as an unrepeatable sign of the old covenant. Admittedly this claim, too, is controversial. We may digress briefly to note that Ellen Juhl Christiansen argues that Baptism cannot replace circumcision on the basis that "covenant" in the Intertestamental writings serves as an "identity marker."[41] But there are strong arguments to the contrary, not least in a detailed but often neglected study by Pierre C. Marcel, *The Biblical Doctrine of Infant Baptism: Sacrament of the Covenant of Grace.*[42] Marcel discusses the for-

---

36. Roth (ed.), *The Haggadah,* 9.

37. Joachim Jeremias, *The Eucharistic Words of Jesus* (London: S.C.M., 1966), 41-54.

38. Otfried Hofius, "The Lord's Supper and the Lord's Supper Tradition," in *One Loaf, One Cup: Ecumenical Studies on 1 Corinthians 11 and Other Texts,* ed. Ben F. Meyer (Macon, GA: Mercer University Press, 1993), 86.

39. Cullmann and Leenhardt, *Essays on the Lord's Supper,* 20.

40. Cullmann and Leenhardt, *Essays on the Lord's Supper,* 39.

41. Ellen J. Christiansen, *The Covenant in Judaism and Paul: A Study of Ritual Boundaries as Identity Markers* (Leiden: Brill, 1997).

42. Pierre C. Marcel, *The Biblical Doctrine of Infant Baptism* (London: James Clarke, 1953).

mation of the covenant; covenant promises; and the status of the sacraments as following the word of promise. Circumcision is an effective sign
of "entry *into* the covenant" (Marcel's italics), which is God's sovereign
gift.[43] He declares, *"God makes the promise that he will render man capable
of receiving the promise"* (his italics).[44] God's promise extends to children
of believers. "If they refuse the grace of the covenant, it is because they
have *chosen* the way of perdition" (his italics).[45] He then proceeds with
more ecclesiological arguments, such as the argument from silence in relation to the admission of women to Holy Communion.

To resume our main argument, whether or not we wish to argue from
the status of Baptism as a sign of covenantal promise, it remains true that,
in Calvin's words, "Free *promise* we make the *foundation of faith,* because
in it [i.e., in free promise] faith properly consists."[46] Often in the mass media we hear it said that "faith" has sustained someone through trials and
pain. Yet some fear to make it plain in the media that "faith" depends on
what lies behind, or causes, faith. Faith alone is a human psychological
state, unless, like Luther, we define it as the appropriation of the divine
promises or of the divine word. Only in this latter sense could we found
anything on "faith." Calvin also argues that valid faith rests not on human
experience, but on the Word of God.[47] God's "own testimony," Calvin
urges, is a firmer foundation than faith in the popular sense. He writes that
"a full definition of faith . . . is a firm and sure knowledge of the divine favour towards us, founded in the truth of a free promise in Christ . . . sealed
in our hearts by the Holy Spirit."[48] This *does not imply credulity,* for "we
have good ground for comprehending all the promises in Christ. . . . The
promises of God are in him, yea and Amen (2 Cor. 1:20; cf. Rom. 1:3; 1 Cor.
2:2)."[49] Calvin concludes, "Wherever this living faith exists, it must have
the hope of eternal life as its inseparable companion."[50] Once again, at the
risk of repetition, hope beyond the grave depends on *God's promise,* and
trust in this divine promise, and the *covenant, and sacraments as effective
signs of the covenant, confirm* God's promise, and address this assurance es-

---

43. Marcel, *Biblical Doctrine,* 99.
44. Marcel, *Biblical Doctrine,* 103.
45. Marcel, *Biblical Doctrine,* 110.
46. Calvin, *Institutes,* 3.2.29 (Beveridge ed., vol. 1, 494, my italics).
47. Calvin, *Institutes,* 3.2.6-7 (vol. 1, 473-75).
48. Calvin, *Institutes,* 3.2.7 (vol. 1, 475).
49. Calvin, *Institutes,* 3.2.32 (vol. 1, 497).
50. Calvin, *Institutes,* 3.2.42 (vol. 1, 506).

pecially to any Christian who is weak in faith, or becomes tempted to doubt. For any who doubt, sacraments, as effective signs of the covenant, confirm God's promise through all the senses, not only through hearing.

3.3. Completing the Argument: Does God Speak through the Bible?

We have argued that the "evidential" viewpoint is not appropriate for considering human existence and life after death. Even though it is appropriate for the domain of the physical sciences, a view of future or postmortal events does not depend on extrapolating on the basis of the present, or the speculative use of our imagination. It depends on appropriating the promises of God, and trusting him. These promises take the form of commissive illocutionary or performative speech-acts, even though these are embedded in states of affairs. If these speech-acts depend upon an accepted procedure, this procedure can be found especially in the covenant, as well as in Word and sacrament. The sacraments are tangible and visible pledges of assurance concerning God's promissory acts.

Yet one last gap in the argument needs to be filled if the chain of reasoning is to be complete. Can we be certain that the promises of God expressed in the Bible have the status of *divine* promises rather than human words of hope projected into the mouth of God? For some this may not be a genuine question; but for many it is perceived as the most vulnerable point in the argument. We saw in the previous chapter that William Tyndale anticipated modern notions of performative language by, for example, distinguishing between the Bible's *informing* us *about* liberation, joy, and forgiveness, and *liberating us, making us joyful,* and *forgiving us, as effective acts,* with real consequences in life. As we saw, he spoke of naming, blessing, cursing, and waking as acts. But, as I have argued elsewhere, only *God* can perform these acts.[51] Unless God speaks them through the human words of the Bible, these words would remain no more than words; they are not effective performatives. Yet thousands, or more probably millions, have proved these to be *effective acts* in their lives.

We cannot enter here into a full discussion of biblical authority, or of whether, or in what sense, the Bible constitutes the Word of God. A number of theologians, to be sure, comment positively on this. Karl Barth (1886-1968) asserts in his early works, "It is not right human thoughts

---

51. Thiselton, *New Horizons in Hermeneutics,* 283-306.

about God which form the content of the Bible, but right divine thoughts about men."[52] But although Barth preferred later to speak of the Bible as a *witness* to the revelation of God, he never doubted that God spoke through historical human voices. He wrote that in the Bible we encounter "Divine words in human speech."[53]

Among books written on "the theological interpretations of Scripture," we may cite almost at random several very recent works, all after 2001. We may have certain reservations about them, but all stress that the purpose of reading the Bible relates to *communion with God, the presence of God, or hearing the voice of God.* Telford Work speaks of "the Bible's character as the Word of God," and particularly cites Athanasius (c. 296-373) among the Church Fathers who stress communion with God, and the Bible as *God's* "self-revelation."[54] Daniel Treier (2008) insists that reading and interpreting the Bible "need not involve denigrating the faithful labours and valuable contributions of biblical scholars," even if we also hear *God* speaking in Scripture.[55] Jens Zimmermann (2004), with whose work I have both sympathy and reservations, writes, "The main goal of interpretation before the Enlightenment was communion with God."[56] Mark Bowald, whose work also suggests several reservations, nevertheless rightly compares the illusory path on which "we reason our way *to* God" with hearing an authentic address "*from* God" (his italics).[57]

When he speaks of not denigrating the work of biblical scholars, Daniel Treier rightly regards it as mistaken to regard all "biblical criticism" as advocating disengagement of the voice of God. Biblical criticism is of many kinds. Again, while four of the books cited above come from America, in England there is a long tradition of fine biblical scholars who do not separate questions about God from questions about the biblical text. More

52. Karl Barth, *The Word of God and the Word of Man* (London: Hodder & Stoughton, 1928), 43.

53. Karl Barth, *Church Dogmatics* (14 vols.; Edinburgh: T&T Clark, 1957-75), I/2, sect. 19.1, 463.

54. Telford Work, *Living and Active: Scripture in the Economy of Salvation* (Grand Rapids: Eerdmans, 2002), 10, 36-39.

55. Daniel Treier, *Introducing Theological Interpretations of Scripture: Recovering a Christian Practice* (Grand Rapids: Baker Academic, 2008), 199.

56. Jens Zimmermann, *Recovering Theological Hermeneutics: An Incarnational-Trinitarian Theory of Interpretation* (Grand Rapids: Baker Academic, 2004), 18.

57. Mark A. Bowald, *Rendering the Word in Theological Hermeneutics: Mapping Divine and Human Agency* (Aldershot and Burlington, VT: Ashgate, 2007), 17.

than this, they avoid regarding biblical criticism as an *alternative* to the view that God genuinely speaks through the human words of the Bible.

The classic trio at the end of the nineteenth century who anticipated this unity of approach were B. F. Westcott (1825-1901), J. B. Lightfoot (1828-89), and F. J. A. Hort (1828-92). Lightfoot and Westcott were Cambridge professors who became Bishops of Durham. William Baird comments, "Hort, Lightfoot, and Westcott understood the intimate relation between historical theology and biblical research." Compared with the greatest of the Germans, he continues, "They were not like grasshoppers, but as giants in their own right — equal in stature to the tallest of the Germans."[58] But this is by no means confined to the nineteenth century in Britain. Simply to select another recent trio from England, we suggest that today Walter Moberly (2000 and 2006), Francis Watson (1994 and 1997), and N. T. Wright (2003, 2005, and other dates) deserve to be regarded as their successors.[59] They are not alone; others might also be named, including Charles Cranfield, Graham Stanton, Richard Bauckham, Markus Bockmuehl, and many others. N. T. Wright, also former Bishop of Durham, writes that Scripture will come into its own by "prayerful listening" to God as we read it.[60] We would do better to speak of "God's work through Scripture," or "God's authority exercised through Scripture," than simply "the authority of Scripture."[61] For we need to "integrate" notions of biblical authority with God's work as a whole.

Bowald, Treier, Zimmermann, Work, and Henning Graf Reventlow (see below) explicitly agree that the problem which they address arose out of the Enlightenment.[62] Unlike Westcott, Lightfoot, and Hort, or Moberly, Watson, and Wright, many others seemed to imply that to stress the hu-

---

58. William Baird, *History of New Testament Research,* vol. 2 (Minneapolis: Fortress, 2003), 83.

59. R. W. L. Moberly, *The Bible, Theology and Faith* (Cambridge: Cambridge University Press, 2000), and *Prophecy and Discernment* (Cambridge: Cambridge University Press, 2006); Francis Watson, *Text, Church and World: Biblical Interpretation in Theological Perspective* (Edinburgh: T&T Clark, 1994), esp. 1-14, and *Text and Truth: Redefining Biblical Theology* (Edinburgh: T&T Clark, 1997); and N. T. Wright, *The Resurrection of the Son of God* (London: S.P.C.K., 2003) throughout; and other writings.

60. N. T. Wright, *The Last Word: Scripture and the Authority of God* (London: S.P.C.K. and HarperOne, 2005), 114; N. T. Wright, *Scripture and the Authority of God* (London: S.P.C.K., 2005), is similar in approach.

61. Wright, *The Last Word,* 116 and 117.

62. Bowald, *Rendering the Word,* 16-19 and 23; Work, *Living and Active,* 3-11; Treier, *Theological Interpretations,* 27 and 34.

manness of the biblical writers was an *alternative* to hearing the voice of God in the Bible. One example of this trend today can be seen in Heikki Räisänen, *Challenges to Biblical Interpretation,* and especially his essay, "The New Testament in Theology." He writes, "If biblical studies are taken really seriously, traditional ways of using the Bible . . . become unviable."[63] This argument depends largely on the old assumption about "contradictions" in the New Testament, where the concern may often be not with chronology or geography, but with theology. Räisänen agrees with other writers that "in the Enlightenment . . . it all began."[64] He claims that exegesis cannot be reconciled with "theological synthesis." He complains, "Exegetes have acted . . . as systematic theologians."[65] There is even a political polemic to the effect that theological exegetes are unprofessional. To see the Bible as Scripture, he says, has "detrimental effects."[66]

Bowald and Zimmermann see the villain of the piece as Immanuel Kant (1724-1804).[67] But the classic specialist study of this issue, and probably the best, is Henning Graf Reventlow, *The Authority of the Bible and the Rise of the Modern World* (Eng. 1984; Ger. 1980). In an earlier part of his book, he considers the Puritans, Thomas Hobbes, and the Latitudinarians. But the culprit, he rightly argues, is not primarily Kant, but English Deism. He examines examples of Deism in John Toland's *Christianity Not Mysterious* and Matthew Tindal's *Christianity as Old as Creation* (1730). Tindal betrayed consistent hostility to the tradition of the Church.[68] "Natural" religion is sufficient, with no need for revelation. Anthony Collins (1676-1729) spoke of a revelation "whose literal meaning is false, but whose real meaning is consistent with . . . Reason."[69] "Free thinking" must be independent of all authority (which matches Kant's definition of the "Enlightenment" later). He bases much of his argument on the diversity of Scripture. He rejects allegory and typology. His writings betray a definition of "faith" far removed from Luther's, amounting to assent to the truth of propositions,

63. Heikki Räisänen, *Challenges to Biblical Interpretation: Collected Essays* (Leiden, Boston, Cologne: Brill, 2001), 227.

64. Räisänen, *Challenges,* 229.

65. Räisänen, *Challenges,* 229.

66. Räisänen, *Challenges,* 247.

67. Bowald, *Rendering the Word,* 3-13, 16-25; Zimmermann, *Recovering Theological Hermeneutics,* 138-50.

68. Henning Graf Reventlow, *The Authority of the Bible and the Rise of the Modern World* (London: S.C.M., 1984), 329.

69. Reventlow, *The Authority of the Bible,* 355.

not appropriation of God's promises. Reventlow concludes that although the Deists sought to find parallels between revelation and reason, their work "in fact demonstrated precisely the opposite."[70]

Reventlow succeeds in showing that theology and revelation were thrust away from biblical and textual study *as irreconcilable opposites*. But the tradition of serious biblical exegetical study combined with the faithful attempt to hear God's voice through Scripture has an honorable history from the Church Fathers, through the medieval and Reformation Church, to modern times, even *after* the Enlightenment. We need to see the supposed problem for what it is. Are we to approach the Bible in confident, reasonable faith and communion with God, or with an attitude which some, like Räisänen, would mistakenly call *value-neutral* assumptions?

Francis Watson has performed an invaluable service in arguing that what many suppose to be honest, value-neutral inquiry is nothing of the kind. Watson writes, "The primary function of holy scripture is to be read publicly in the context of communal worship. . . . If theology is to be Christian, . . . the ecclesial community must be seen as its primary point of reference. . . . A commitment to academic *secularity* will make one unwilling to accept that 'theology is peculiar here.' The church is represented as a threat to the quest for truth."[71] Hence the Bible is silenced and muzzled, and does not issue in proclamation. But to expect a Christian biblical specialist to ignore his or her "social base" is not value-neutral; it is a deliberate choice of secular values. Watson concludes, "The assumption that faith is incompatible with proper academic standards as openness . . . is ultimately a mere prejudice."[72] To eliminate the relevance of anything that lies beyond the physical world in the case of the Bible is like visiting a doctor who imagines that all that is relevant to the patient is a set of physiological and electronic mechanisms that control both the brain and the body. It is an amazingly reductionist and mechanistic view, which even artists and musicians would find inadequate, let alone people of faith, and should have been associated only with a mechanistic worldview.

So there we have it. To appropriate the promise of God in Scripture is as much a venture of faith as *theism* or *Christianity*. It is not some special "addition" to Christian faith, but part and parcel of what it is to be a Christian. We may support this statement with some examples from the Church

---

70. Reventlow, *The Authority of the Bible*, 383.
71. Watson, *Text, Church and World*, 4, 6, and 7 (my italics).
72. Watson, *Text, Church and World*, 9.

Fathers. In the second century Irenaeus (c. 130-200) speaks of the heretics who "disregard the order and the connection of the Scriptures and . . . dismember and destroy the truth."[73] They distort and rearrange passages, like someone who "rearranges gems," making them form a picture of their own devising, or turning something beautiful "into a dog or a fox" (*Against Heresies* 1.8.1).[74] Irenaeus insists that "the entire Scriptures . . . can clearly, unambiguously, and harmoniously be understood."[75] Irenaeus was deeply grounded in Scripture and tradition, and appealed to apostolic tradition as biblical and Catholic truth.

Clement of Alexandria (c. 150-215) had such wide sympathies with the Greek world and with Christian *gnōsis* that we might imagine that he would not pay special attention to the Old and New Testaments. On the contrary, he cites the classic passage of 2 Tim. 3:15-17 about the Scriptures being "God-breathed" or inspired by God (Greek, *theopneustos*). He quotes Paul's words to the effect that the Scriptures "are inspired by God, being profitable for doctrine, for reproof, for correction, for instruction in righteousness."[76] Heretics and those who deviate from the truth "will not make use of all the Scriptures, and will not quote them entire, . . . but select ambiguous expressions to force them to their own opinions . . . making use of mere words."[77] Scripture is the criterion of truth (*Stromata* 7.16).

Tertullian (c. 160–c. 235) writes, "Where diversity of doctrine is found, *there*, then, must be corruption both of the Scripture and the expositions thereof be regarded as existing."[78] This runs counter to some of Räisänen's claims. He asserts harmony between the ancient Church and the Scriptures. The Scriptures, Tertullian urges, are truly apostolic, embodying the teaching of Christ.[79] Like Clement, Tertullian quotes the verse in 2 Tim. 3:16 to the effect that all Scripture is "God-breathed" or "inspired."[80] His own writings are saturated in the Bible.

Origen (c. 185-253) is also outspoken about their inspiration and authority. He declares, "The Scriptures themselves are divine, i.e. were in-

---

73. Irenaeus, *Against Heresies* 1.8.1; *ANF*, vol. 1, 326.

74. Irenaeus, *Against Heresies* 1.19.1; *ANF*, vol. 1, 344; cf. *Against Heresies* 1.18.1-4 and 2.10.1, 2; *ANF*, vol. 1, 243-44 and 369-70.

75. Irenaeus, *Against Heresies* 2.27.2; *ANF*, vol. 1, 398.

76. Clement, *Exhortation to the Heathen* 9; *ANF*, vol. 2, 196.

77. Clement, *The Stromata* 7.16; *ANF*, vol. 2, 351.

78. Tertullian, *On Prescription against Heretics* 38; *ANF*, vol. 3, 261.

79. Tertullian, *Scorpiace* 12; *ANF*, vol. 3, 645.

80. Tertullian, *On the Apparel of Women* 5; *ANF*, vol. 4, 16.

spired by the Spirit of God."[81] They contain "promises" on the part of God.[82] This certainly includes the Old Testament as well as the New. If we find difficulties and stumbling blocks, this is due to our own limitations and blindness, not to the Bible.[83] All of Scripture is one perfect and attuned instrument of God, producing a variety of notes from one source. Again he states: "The books [of Scripture] were written by the Spirit of God."[84] In numerous places Origen states that the Bible is "clear" and "powerful."[85]

After Nicea, many later Church Fathers endorse this mainstream view. Cyril of Jerusalem (315-68) speaks of "the inspired Scriptures of the Old and New Testament."[86] Basil the Great (330-79) regularly refers to Scripture as "inspired," and warns us that not to study it "grieves the Holy Spirit."[87] Augustine (354-430) speaks of the Bible as "the writings of the Holy Spirit."[88] Christians heard the *voice of God* speaking *through* Scripture. They were *not* unaware of the *human* agency of *the human* writers of the Bible. But the unanimous testimony of the Church Fathers was that God spoke through Scripture.

Often it is suggested that the "secular" view is a "progressive" view, acting on the insights of "biblical criticism." But it is nothing of the kind. We have seen that such biblical critics as Westcott, Lightfoot and Hort, or today such successors as Moberly, Watson, Wright, and others, have no problem in *hearing God speak through Scripture,* which they have studied with utmost rigor and self-criticism. The Fathers were not unaware of different human voices *within* Scripture. But more important than this for them was the divine voice. They could appropriate the promises of God in its pages. John Goldingay gives special attention to such active words which bring about a world-changing or performative effect. He writes, "It is as promise that the word of God is infallible."[89] A statement from a

81. Origen, *De Principiis* 4.1.1; repr. in *ANF,* vol. 4, 349.

82. Origen, *Against Celsus* 6.1; *ANF,* vol. 4, 375.

83. Origen, *Philocalia* 10; cf. R. B. Tollinton (ed.), *Selections from the Commentaries and Homilies of Origen* (London: S.P.C.K., 1929), 27-51.

84. Origen, *Against Celsus* 5.60; *ANF,* vol. 4, 569.

85. Origen, *Against Celsus* 7.59; *ANF,* vol. 4, 635.

86. Cyril, *The Catechetical Lectures* 33.

87. Basil, *Letters, Letter* 22; *NPNF,* ser. 2, vol. 8, 127-28.

88. Augustine, *Confessions* 7.21.27.

89. John Goldingay, *Models for Scripture* (Grand Rapids: Eerdmans and Carlisle: Paternoster, 1994), 212.

writer who is known for his attacks on "fundamentalism" might be useful to show that one may respect the special status of the Bible or hearing God's voice through it, without in the least neglecting its "human" side. James Barr, for example, asserts, "Involvement with the Bible is analytic in being a Christian."[90] To hear the Bible is what it is to be a Christian.

The promises of God mediated through the Bible provide a valid starting point for writing about life after death, the future resurrection, and the Last Judgment. To face death with a mistaken view of the Bible is to ask us to lose all legitimate grounds for hope about postmortal existence, which God himself has promised. We may now consider more explicitly "eschatological" issues, or the content of "the Last Things."

90. James Barr, "Has the Bible Any Authority?" in James Barr, *Explorations in Theology,* vol. 7 (London: S.C.M., 1980), 52.

CHAPTER 4

Waiting and Expecting

4.1. Waiting and Expecting in the Biblical Writings

Waiting or expectation characterizes Christians in a variety of contexts and situations. In the earliest writing of the New Testament Paul describes Christians as "waiting for his Son from heaven" (1 Thess. 1:10; Greek, *anamenō*, simply a general term for waiting). In 1 Cor. 1:7, Christians are described as those who are "waiting for the coming of our Lord Jesus Christ"; while in Gal. 5:5, "we wait for the hope of righteousness." In Romans Paul writes that believers "wait for the revealing of the sons of God" (Rom. 8:19); "wait for adoption" (Rom. 8:23); and "wait with patience" (Rom. 8:25). In all five cases in 1 Corinthians, Galatians, and Romans, the Greek word is *apekdechomai,* which the KJV or AV translates "expect earnestly." Frederick Danker translates the word "await eagerly," with all the intensity of a double compound verb, although in 8:25 it may mean simply "wait patiently."[1]

Paul teaches his first converts at Thessalonica also that Christians are people-in-waiting. He explained to the Corinthians that they had not already "arrived" but still waited for Christ's triumphant victory. This was partly to correct their triumphalism (1 Cor. 1:7-8; 1 Cor. 4:8-13, with deep irony). The church at Rome was both calmly to wait for hope to be fulfilled and to wait with eager expectancy for the sons of God to be revealed in

---

1. Frederick W. Danker, *A Greek-English Lexicon of the New Testament and Other Early Christian Literature,* based on W. Bauer's Lexicon (BDAG), 100; also Joseph H. Thayer (ed.), *Greek-English Lexicon of the New Testament* (Edinburgh: T&T Clark, 4th ed. 1901, repr. 1953), 56, suggests "assiduously and patiently to wait for"; cf. Phil. 3:20; Heb. 9:28; Rom. 8:19, 23, 25.

their true splendor, and for the whole creation to be liberated from decay and bondage. Rom. 8:19 speaks of the creation itself as standing on *tenterhooks*, standing *on tiptoe*, or *craning its neck* (Greek, *apokaradokia*) to see the sons and daughters of God revealed in their true status, and creation delivered from frustration or self-contradictory emptiness (Greek, *mataiotēti . . . hypetagē*). Commenting on the first Greek word *apokaradokia*, Charles Cranfield observes, "The basic idea is that of stretching the neck, craning forward *(kara* is a poetical synonym for *kephalē, head)*. The *apo-* is intensive, as is also *apekdechesthai* later in the verse and in v. 23."[2] The whole of creation cranes its neck to see what God has prepared.

We shall turn to other parts of the Bible shortly. But we pause to note a fact which is perhaps surprising. If we look up "expectancy" or "waiting" in books on the Last Things, we seldom find anything at all in the index under this heading. Yet Christians over the generations have been interpreting what it means "to wait" or "to expect" very differently. Some, like Augustine and Luther, advocate calmness and simply going about one's everyday duties. Others try to predict the date of the event of Christ's coming, in spite of prohibitions from both Jesus and Paul, and even encourage a fever pitch of excitement. Yet what does "waiting" or "expecting" actually mean?

"Waiting" can conjure up the most tedious experience. We think of waiting for trains or buses. A waiting room is a static, colorless place, where waiting seems to go on forever and ever. 2 Peter speaks of "scoffers" who impatiently cry in frustration: "Where is the promise of his coming? For ever since our ancestors died, all things continue as they were from the beginning of creation!" (2 Pet. 3:4). To wait "expectantly" may at first appear to be positive and to lack tedium, but can a person remain "expectant" for a very long period? "To wait" or "to expect" seems to be what philosophers often call a polymorphous or multi-meaning verb. Like the verb "to try," its content and substance *vary* according to *what* we are "trying" to do. "Try to sleep" cannot involve the same attitude and actions as "try to lift this heavy weight" or "try to play the piano better." Is it like this in the case of "waiting"? There seems to be no systematic, rigorous study of the diverse meanings and contexts of what "to wait" amounts to. In the next

2. Charles E. B. Cranfield, *The Epistle to the Romans* (Edinburgh: T&T Clark, 1975), vol. 1, 410. J. H. Moulton and George Milligan, *The Vocabulary of the Greek Testament* (London: Hodder & Stoughton, repr. 1952), 56, argue that the verb is very rare in the papyri.

section we shall argue that Ludwig Wittgenstein offered an account of "expecting" in everyday life which sheds a flood of light on "expecting" in the biblical writings and in Christian thought.

Our next task is to explore biblical terminology for waiting and expecting in their various biblical contexts, especially in relation to waiting for the events of the End. But some readers may prefer to skip ahead to the meat of the chapter, which begins after the Hebrew and Greek word studies. There is no need, for example, for the less specialist reader to puzzle over the Hebrew terms Qal or Piel, which are technical grammatical forms. In effect this means skipping over only the next *four* paragraphs, and resuming when we discuss "readiness."

In the Old Testament we find at least three types of waiting with expectancy. Often the Hebrew word *qāwâ* can mean to wait for God's timing and action in one's lifetime. Psalm 37 provides an example: "Those who wait for the Lord shall inherit the land" (Ps. 37:9). "Wait for the Lord, and keep to his way" (37:34). Yet C. Barth points out that in many passages the Hebrew *chākhâ* is used of waiting for God, perhaps in parallelism with "hoping in him" (Isa. 8:17). Here the form *chikkâ* and *qiwwâ* (from *qāwâ*) are parallel, but it remains to be seen, the lexicographers argue, "whether *chikkâ* and *qiwwâ* are fully synonymous here."[3] Barth rejects the suggestion that the words "signify a condition of acute tension."[4] More probably, he argues, the verbs suggest the prophetic call for rest, quietness, and trust. Brown, Driver, and Briggs see the Hebrew Qal of the root *q-w-h* to mean (as a participle) "those waiting for" (Ps. 37:9; Isa. 40:31; Lam. 3:25), and the verb generally to mean first "to wait," then "to look eagerly" (Isa. 5:7; 59:9, 11; Jer. 8:15; 13:16; 14:19; Job 7:2; 30:26; Ps. 39:8). Only as a derivative use may it mean "to lie in wait for" (Ps. 119:95).[5] They also examine *ch-k-h*, understanding the Qal to mean "to wait for" (often with *le* [Ps. 33:20; Isa. 8:17; 64:3; Zeph. 3:8]). The subject may be God, as in "God waits to be gracious to you" (Isa. 30:18).[6]

Daniel Schibler believes that *ch-k-h* in the Piel of the Hebrew verb can mean "to wait," "endure," "expect," "hope," occurring at least 14 times in this form. It characteristically occurs in the latter Prophets (Isa. 8:17; 30:18; 64:4; Hos. 6:9; Zeph. 3:8) and in the Writings (Job 3:21; 32:4; Pss. 33:20;

---

3. C. Barth, "*Chākhâ,*" *Theological Dictionary of the Old Testament (TDOT)*, ed. G. J. Botterweck and Helmer Ringgren, vol. 4 (Grand Rapids: Eerdmans, 1980), 361; cf. 359-63.

4. Barth, "*Chākhâ,*" *TDOT*, vol. 4, 361.

5. Francis Brown, with S. R. Driver and C. A. Briggs (eds.), *The New Hebrew and English Lexicon* (Lafayette, IN: Associated Publishers and Authors, 1980), 875.

6. Brown, Driver, and Briggs, *New Hebrew Lexicon*, 314.

106:13; and Dan. 12:12). Often it lies behind the Greek *hypomenein* in the Septuagint, where the Vulgate translates it mostly with *expectare*. It can overlap, he argues, with the meaning of "hope."[7] He rightly comments, "Much depends on that upon which one waits, for example impatient waiting (for the morning light . . . , 2 Kings 7:9); unduly prolonged waiting (Jehu . . . delays fleeing from imminent danger . . . , 2 Kings 9:3); waiting to do evil (lying in ambush . . . , Hos. 6:9); persevering waiting, even until the time of the end . . . (Dan. 12:12); finally, strenuous waiting, even to the point of longing for death (Job 3:21)."[8] The Old Testament thus provides such a *varied range of meanings* for "to wait," that for Christians "waiting for the revealing of Christ" has no sharply bounded signification.

We have seen that in the New Testament the Greek words *ekdechomai* and *apekdechomai* usually mean "to expect eagerly" or "to await eagerly," as Danker and Cranfield urge. J. P. Louw and E. A. Nida argue that the verbs mean "to continue to remain in a state until an expected event," and hence "to remain until, to wait until."[9] The value of this comment is to extricate the verb from seeming to imply primarily a particular *psychological* or *mental* state, which "eagerly" might be thought to imply. It is also less polymorphous, or varied, than the Old Testament lexicons suggest. We shall see shortly why this is helpful. Louw and Nida also distinguish the verbs from *prosdokaō*, "to await with apprehension." This is clearly more mental and psychological, but does not refer to eschatological waiting (Acts 27:33).[10] The same applies to *mellō*, "to wait, to delay." Finally, the Greek word *menō* or *anamenō* generally means "to remain in a place and/or state," and, again, is often used in an everyday sense of "waited for us at Troas" (Acts 20:5), but also "to wait for his Son from heaven" (1 Thess. 1:10).[11] The very different Greek word *apokaradokia*, "what one eagerly expects," has less to do with "waiting" than the longing which accompanies it in certain special circumstances (Rom. 8:19; cf. Phil. 1:20). The use of the word *apekdechomai* in Heb. 9:28 also involves desire and longing in the same circumstances as in Rom. 8:19.[12]

---

7. Daniel Schibler, *"ch-k-h," NIDOTTE*, vol. 2, 129-30.

8. Schibler, *"ch-k-h," NIDOTTE*, 130.

9. Johannes P. Louw and Eugene A. Nida (eds.), *A Greek-English Lexicon of the New Testament Based on Semantic Domains* (2 vols.; New York: United Bible Societies, 2nd ed. 1989), vol. 1, 152 (Entry 13.28).

10. Louw and Nida, *Greek-English Lexicon*, vol. 1, 313-14 (Entry 25.228).

11. Louw and Nida, *Greek-English Lexicon*, vol. 1, 729-30.

12. Louw and Nida, *Greek-English Lexicon*, vol. 1, 296 (Entries 25.63 and 25.64).

Finally, Louw and Nida address passages in which *ekdechomai* ("to expect"), *elpizō* ("to hope" or "to expect"), and *prosdokaō* ("to expect" or "to anticipate") all relate to "thinking concerning future contingencies."[13] These are at first sight helpful because they comment on "expectation." But these linguisticians face what many philosophers would regard as a serious flaw, by categorizing "expect" under "think" (349). A test case is 1 Cor. 16:11: Is "I am expecting him" primarily about Paul's act of thinking, or about what he is doing about the pastoral situation and his stance? In Heb. 10:27, which Louw and Nida also cite, is "a fearful expectation of judgment" really about "thoughts"? The NRSV translates it "*prospect* of judgment," as if it entirely determined what we "wilfully persist in doing" (v. 26). "Hoping" is perhaps a borderline case, but the Greek word *prosdokaō* is simply used of "expecting a servant to come" (Matt. 24:50) and well fits into the example which we are about to discuss. Simeon "expected" the consolation of Israel (Luke 2:25).

We may conclude this initial section by noting that the New Testament often *implies* a state of waiting or expecting without *using* a word that we can then find in a Hebrew or Greek concordance or dictionary. The concern may be with *readiness*. Matthew 25 offers a good example: "Ten bridesmaids took their lamps, and went to meet the bridegroom. . . . The bridegroom was delayed. . . . There was a shout, 'Look! Here is the bridegroom! Come out to meet him.' . . . The bridegroom came and those who were *ready* [Greek, *hetoimoi*] went with him into the wedding banquet. And the door was shut" (Matt. 25:1-10).

The key to the notion of "expecting" in the New Testament has much to do with the term "ready." From the evidence of 2 Thessalonians (which I argue elsewhere is Pauline), Paul resists the notion of a frenzied or mindless "enthusiasm" or over-excitement, coupled with sober reflection that certain events must take place before the final coming of Christ (2 Thess. 2:1-12). The Thessalonians needed to return to calmer reasonable reflection (Greek, *nouthetein*; 1 Thess. 5:4; 2 Thess. 3:15), just as the Galatians needed to wake up from their "bewitchment" (Gal. 3:1). Robert Jewett comments, "The congregation has been similarly torn away from their reasonable state of mind by an alien power that bewitched them."[14] Some seemed surprised that persecution should befall them while they "waited" for the Return of Christ, or his *Parousia* (1 Thess. 3:4); others sat loose to

---

13. Louw and Nida, *Greek-English Lexicon*, vol. 1, 357 (Entries 30.53-30.55).
14. Robert Jewett, *Paul's Anthropological Terms* (Leiden: Brill, 1971), 367 and 373.

faithfulness in marriage (1 Thess. 4:5-7); some were "shaken in mind" (2 Thess. 2:2, 3); and many apparently abandoned everyday work and employment, in spite of Paul's clear example to the contrary (2 Thess. 3:6-13). Paul therefore exhorts them: "Stand firm, and hold fast to the traditions that you were taught by us" (2 Thess. 3:13). The congregation must be calmly content, if necessary to share Christ's sufferings. "Expecting" the end does not seem to mean a psychological state of obsessive excitement.

4.2. What Is It to "Expect"?: Wittgenstein's Answer

We are not falling into the trap of imposing a meaning onto the New Testament in the light of a modern nontheological writer. Here we face a problem of *language as such*. What does "to expect" *amount to*, in any case? We have already seen that the term is polymorphous or varied in the Old Testament, and that in the New Testament it does not primarily imply a heightened psychological state. Wittgenstein shows that in many contexts in most "surroundings" the primary meaning of the term does not concern a mental or psychological state, but is more akin to "being *ready*."

Wittgenstein elaborates his most homely illustration of the logical grammar or meaning of "to expect" when in *The Blue Book* he expounds "A" expecting "B" to come to his room for tea. He writes: "What happens if from 4 till 4.30 A expects B to come to his room? In one sense . . . 'to expect' . . . certainly does not refer to one process or state of mind going on throughout the interval. . . . At four o'clock I look in my diary and see the name 'B.' . . . I prepare the tea for two; I think for a moment 'does B smoke?' and put out cigarettes; towards 4.30 I begin to feel impatient. . . . All this is called 'expecting B from 4 to 4.30.' And there are endless variations to this process. . . . There is no feature in common to all of them."[15] *The crucial factor in "expecting a visitor for tea" is not primarily what is going on inside someone's head, but the set of observable actions or behavior to which the expectation gives rise.*

Wittgenstein observes that *expectation* does not primarily denote "the sensation of expectation," or even "a state of expectation," even if it means "expecting that so-and-so will happen."[16] Experiencing a sense of tension

---

15. Ludwig Wittgenstein, *The Blue Book and Brown Books: Preliminary Studies for the "Philosophical Investigations"* (Oxford: Blackwell, 2nd ed. 1969), 20.
16. Wittgenstein, *The Blue Book,* 20.

which is relieved by someone's coming is not "the only way or even the most common way of using the word 'expect.'"[17] One common-sense problem finds expression in Wittgenstein's question: "How can we expect something that is not the case . . . a fact which does not exist?"[18] Popular opinion might suggest that we perceive "a shadow of the fact," but reflection shows otherwise. The shadow "is some sort of picture."[19] But the problem is that of having "some sort of picture" before us. Fundamental to expecting is not "having an image" or "a mental event," but "knowing how to go on."[20] The idea of a mental act here is a "curious superstition," as if the mental act could cross the bridge before we reached it: the trouble crops up when we try to imagine "the ideas of thinking, wishing, expecting, believing, knowing. . . ."[21]

In his *Philosophical Investigations* Wittgenstein goes further. He writes: "I want to say: 'If someone could see the mental process of expectation, he would necessarily be seeing *what* was being expected."[22] But, he adds, "to say that someone perceives an expectation *makes no sense*."[23] He asks, "What's it like for me to expect him to come? — I walk up and down the room, look at the clock now and then, and so on."[24] But this event is not a parallel to his arriving and walking through the door. The two are totally dissimilar. "We fail to get away from the idea that using a sentence involves imagining something for every word."[25]

H. H. Price rightly argues that *believing* is often a disposition to respond to a situation in appropriate ways, not primarily a mental state. For example, I do not stop believing when I fall asleep or am knocked unconscious, for it is not a mental event of consciousness.[26] Belief consists of a disposition to respond to situations in particular ways. For example, if this belief is denied, I am likely to defend it. In the same vein Wittgenstein asserts, "We say 'I am expecting him', when we believe that he will come,

---

17. Wittgenstein, *The Blue Book*, 21.

18. Wittgenstein, *The Blue Book*, 36.

19. Wittgenstein, *The Blue Book*, 36.

20. Wittgenstein, *The Blue Book*, 40.

21. Wittgenstein, *The Brown Book*, 143.

22. Ludwig Wittgenstein, *Philosophical Investigations* (Oxford: Blackwell, 2nd ed. 1858), sect. 452 (his italics).

23. Wittgenstein, *Philosophical Investigations*, sect. 453 (his italics).

24. Wittgenstein, *Philosophical Investigations*, sect. 444.

25. Wittgenstein, *Philosophical Investigations*, sect. 449.

26. H. H. Price, *Belief* (London: Allen & Unwin and New York: Humanities, 1969), 20-21, 29-37, 38-41 and more generally 19-91 and 243-314.

though his coming does not *occupy our thoughts* [his italics]. (Here 'I am expecting him' would mean, 'I should be surprised if he didn't come', and that would *not* be called the description of a state of mind)."[27] Similarly, Wittgenstein anticipates Price by observing that what it *means* to believe consists less in some mental or conscious state, such as a feeling of certainty ("That would not interest us"), than: "Let us look and see what are the consequences of this belief, where it takes us."[28]

The conclusion which Wittgenstein reaches is that "An expectation is *embedded in a situation, from which it arises*."[29] "The expectation of an explosion, for example, may arise from a situation in which it is to be expected, but if someone whispers, 'It'll go off now', instead of saying, 'I expect the explosion any moment', still his words *do not describe a feeling*" (although the tone of the words may suggest a feeling).[30] Expecting and believing are not the only words that do not primarily denote a feeling. Wittgenstein writes, "Could someone have a feeling of ardent love or hope for the space of one second, *no matter what* preceded or followed this second? . . . The surroundings give it its importance . . . (A smiling mouth *smiles* only in a human face)"[31] (his italics). Similarly, if I say that I *expect* an event to occur, "the point is: what led up to these words?"[32]

Wittgenstein is dogged by this problem. He first wrestles with "the fulfilment of an expectation" and "expecting" in 1930 in *Philosophical Remarks*.[33] Then, as we have seen, he pursues this in the *Blue Book* and the *Investigations* between 1933 and 1951. He re-appraises the issue in the *Zettel*, mainly from 1945 to 1948.[34] In the *Zettel* Wittgenstein observes that often "I am expecting . . ." may be replaced by "Be prepared for this to happen."[35] We are arguing that this equivalence is very important for New Testament expectations of the *Parousia*. Almost every New Testament scholar asks whether this or that belief passed through Paul's mind as a mental state

---

27. Wittgenstein, *Philosophical Investigations*, sect. 577.

28. Wittgenstein, *Philosophical Investigations*, sect. 578.

29. Wittgenstein, *Philosophical Investigations*, sect. 579 (my italics).

30. Wittgenstein, *Philosophical Investigations*, sect. 582 (my italics).

31. Wittgenstein, *Philosophical Investigations*, sect. 583.

32. Wittgenstein, *Philosophical Investigations*, sect. 586.

33. Ludwig Wittgenstein, *Philosophical Remarks* (Oxford: Blackwell, 1975) and *Philosophische Bemerkungen* (Oxford: Blackwell, 1967), sects. 25-34.

34. Ludwig Wittgenstein, *Zettel* (Ger. and Eng.; Oxford: Blackwell, 1967), sects. 53-68 and 71-72.

35. Wittgenstein, *Zettel*, sect. 65.

when he wrote, "We who are alive, who are left" (1 Thess. 4:17), when all that he probably meant was "We are ready." The *Zettel* repeats sect. 581 of the *Investigations* word for word: "An expectation is embedded in a *situation* from which it takes its rise."[36]

If this applies to Christian expectation of the final coming of Christ, as we believe it does, it explains the varied or polymorphous meaning of *ch-k-h* and *q-w-h* in the Old Testament, the tendency in both Testaments to speak of *waiting* or of *expecting* as calm, measured, and compatible with everyday work. In the New Testament it denotes not a subjective, heightened, psychological state or mental belief about chronology, but an objective state of *readiness* for the Lord's coming. We shall now seek to understand some of the consequences of what Wittgenstein calls "paying attention to the wrong thing" for Christian thought. To concentrate on the question "What is going on in his mind?" he argues, is comparable to concentrating on the constituency of butter when price rises in butter concern not butter as such, but the economic situation. Finally, it is important to note that Wittgenstein is no materialist or behaviourist. He explicitly denies such a stance.[37] The question he asks is not about the nature of reality, but about being committed "to a particular way of looking at the matter."[38]

4.3. Attitudes to "Expectation" in Christian Thought

Christian attitudes to expectation of Christ's coming have varied considerably. Perhaps the most widely known exponents of a calm, steady attitude, which had nothing to do with heightened excitement, were Augustine of Hippo (354-430) (except in *City of God*, bk. 20) and especially Martin Luther (1483-1546). Luther disapproved of fanatical excitement, fueled by eschatological expectation. This is evident, for example, from Luther's letter to his friend, Michael Stiefel. Stiefel predicted the time of Christ's advent by extrapolating from chronology in the book of Daniel, as 8 a.m. on October 19, 1533. Luther wrote to him, "I did not suspect that you would become so excited about this." He writes to Stiefel with calm and balance, pointing out that predictions are of no great significance because Christ did not reveal the timing to human beings. His pastoral concern was "to set hearts at

36. Wittgenstein, *Zettel*, sect. 67 (my italics).
37. Wittgenstein, *Philosophical Investigations*, sects. 307-8.
38. Wittgenstein, *Philosophical Investigations*, sect. 308.

rest."[39] Luther also identified the papacy with the Antichrist, supposedly implied by the "Man of Sin" and the "Lawless One," who "exalts himself above every so-called god or object of worship, so that he takes his seat in the temple of God, declaring himself to be God" (2 Thess. 2:3-4).[40]

If the pope is the Antichrist, the Antichrist is no longer awaited in the future, but is a figure of world history. There is a legend that well sums up Luther's attitude toward "expecting the End." He is credited with saying, "If I knew that tomorrow was the end of the world, I would plant an apple tree today." That is to say, life is to continue normally. Among the Church Fathers, Tyconius the Donatist (d. c. 400), Jerome (c. 345-420), and Augustine of Hippo (354-430) were three of those with most reservations about eschatological excitement. Tyconius's chief work was his *Liber Regularum*, or *Book of Rules* (c. 380).[41] In the North African church Tyconius faced fierce struggles about the nature of the Church, and saw dangers in an exegesis of biblical texts which unduly restricted their meaning. He offered a "spiritual interpretation," which sought to draw from future eschatology and apocalyptic permanently valid principles, rather than a map of future events.

Tyconius's *Book of Rules* provides seven short treatises on the interpretation of Scripture. He seeks to offer "keys and lamps" to the meaning of the Bible, to find paths through "vast forests of prophecy." He combs through Isaiah, Ezekiel, and the Pauline Epistles, expounding Paul's doctrine of the Church as the body of Christ. He seeks to move the historical and authorial sense of texts to see the Bible, as Luther does, as a book which witnesses above all to Christ. Tyconius's sixth *rule* addresses eschatological texts. Verses such as these, he argues, which depict "that hour," or "on that day," refer not to a time in the remote future, but to the whole era of the Church. The Church in its sinfulness may perhaps even *be* the Antichrist (2 Thess. 2:4); the lessons of that verse are for the present. While many interpret "what restrains" (2 Thess. 2:7) as the Roman Empire, for Tyconius it is the Church in the present. Although the *Book of Rules* bears in ecclesiological terms on the Donatist and "Catholic" church, and the

---

39. Martin Luther, "Letter to Michael Stiefel," in *Luther: Letters of Spiritual Counsel*, ed. Theodore G. Tappert, LCC 18 (London: S.C.M., 1955), 101-3.

40. Luther, *Works: Commentaries on 1 Corinthians 7 and 15 and Lectures on 1 Timothy* (St. Louis: Concordia, 1973), vol. 28, 310.

41. Cf. F. C. Burkitt (ed.), *The Book of Rules of Tyconius*, Texts and Studies 3 (Cambridge: Cambridge University Press, 1894); also Kevin L. Hughes, *Constructing Antichrist* (Washington: Catholic University of America Press, 2005), 84-94.

presence of evil in the Church, its primary importance for subsequent generations lay in its enormous influence on Augustine. Except for the special circumstances of *City of God*, especially book 20, Augustine followed Tyconius on eschatology. The main view concerning "expecting" the End was that the Church must be vigilant against moral evil.

Jerome possessed a biblical scholarship unrivaled among the Church Fathers, including knowledge of Hebrew. He translated most of the Bible from the original languages into Latin, in the standard version known as the Vulgate. He anticipated the Reformers in working with the Hebrew canon of the Old Testament in contrast to the Greek canon of the Old Testament and Apocrypha. Jerome had little interest in theological or eschatological speculation, and often, following Origen, opted for a "spiritual" interpretation of biblical texts. He rejected, for example, an interpretation of Daniel in terms of specific future events.[42] He rejected a "millenarian" account of otherworldly future events, regarding these as too materialistic. But with caution he was more willing than Tyconius to consider some speculations about the End-time.[43] Jerome understands Rev. 20:1-3, which includes the binding of the devil and Satan for "a thousand years," as a picture of a time of peace and growth for the Church. The devil may be "bound" by Christians' renouncing moral laxity. Matthew 24 probably refers to the destruction of Jerusalem in A.D. 70, yet it has present relevance in portraying the victory of God.[44]

Augustine reflects the more thoroughgoing influence of Tyconius, where apocalyptic passages are understood to refer to the contemporary Church. The Antichrist is already active in the persecutions of the Church. Tyconius is agnostic about the details of the last days or of the End-time.[45] He understands the millennium as one of rest and peace for believers, or alternatively their reign with Christ. He writes, "While the Devil is bound, the saints reign with Christ during the same thousand years . . . in this present time. . . . It is then of this kingdom militant . . . that the Apocalypse speaks."[46]

42. Jerome, "Preface to Daniel," in P. Schaff and H. Wach, *NPNF*, ser. 2, vol. 6 (Edinburgh: T&T Clark and Grand Rapids: Eerdmans, 1989), 500.

43. Jerome, *In Sophoniam* 1.14.

44. Cf. Brian E. Daley, *The Hope of the Early Church: A Handbook of Patristic Eschatology* (Cambridge: Cambridge University Press, 1991), and Jerome, *Commentary on Matthew*, ed. Thomas P. Scheck, FC 117 (Washington: Catholic University of America Press, 2008).

45. Daley, *The Hope of the Early Church*, 131-50.

46. Augustine, *City of God* 20.9; *NPNF*, ser. 1, vol. 2, 429-31.

The *City of God* followed the Goths' sack of Rome in 410, and offered a theology of history to defend the Christian faith from blame for bringing about this disaster. Augustine argues that Christians belong not primarily to the City of Rome, but to the City of God, or City of Heaven, in the present. This "City" remains in process of traveling toward the End. On earth the two cities are *intermingled.* The visible Church contains both true Christians and those who nominally confess the faith. He does speak of the last judgment in book 20.[47] Unusually, compared with the rest of his writings, the *City of God* speaks of the millennium and of the first and second resurrection.[48] Augustine firmly believed in the end events or the last things, but not in awaiting them in frenzy.

In contrast to Tyconius, Jerome, and Augustine, Victorinus (c. 304) emphasized an apocalyptic perspective and millenarian tendencies, not least because of his experience of oppression, persecution, and martyrdom under Diocletian. Similarly, Lactantius (c. 250-325) writes shortly after these Diocletian persecutions and explicitly cites apocalyptic themes. He writes, "Cities shall be overthrown . . . by continual earthquakes . . . frequent diseases and repeated famines. . . . Waters shall be changed into blood. . . . Prodigies shall confound the minds of men. . . . the darkness of the sun, the colour of the moon . . . and falling stars."[49] Ambrosiaster (d. c. 380), commenting on 2 Thessalonians 2, stresses the activity of the Antichrist, "false signs, deceptive wonders," and Satan being "cast down from the heavens."[50] This suggests a very different mood from that of Augustine and Luther.

These two contrasting mind-sets show how important and far-reaching can be Wittgenstein's analysis of "expect" for the Church. The question is not whether a given psychological state should be encouraged, but whether we are *ready* for the *Parousia.* As the Luther legend implies, a pure and devoted Christian may be *ready* while planting the next apple tree, or continuing daily work. In Pauline theology, the important thing is that believers should possess, as they wait, "the firstfruits" (Greek, *aparchē;* Rom. 8:23) of the Spirit, that quality of life which reflects the gift of the Holy Spirit of Christ, which in the *future* will be revealed in all its fullness. The gift of the Holy Spirit is also a guarantee of the life of the Spirit yet to

47. Augustine, *City of God* 20.1-2, 4-5; *NPNF,* ser. 1, vol. 2, 421-22 and 423-25.

48. Augustine, *City of God* 20.6, 7; *NPNF,* ser. 1, vol. 2, 425-28.

49. Lactantius, *Divine Institutes,* in *ANF,* vol. 7, 16.

50. Ambrosiaster, *Commentarius in Epistolas Paulinas,* ed. H. J. Vogels (Vienna: Hoelder-Pichler-Tempsky, 1969), 241-42.

come (Greek, *arrabōn;* 2 Cor. 5:5; cf. Eph. 1:14). The terms "firstfruits" and "guarantee" may suggest that the future has become already present, but nevertheless in a *partial* way with more to come. This has nothing to do with intense psychological processes, but, rather, with ensuring that one's life bears the fruit of the Holy Spirit. The running argument of Romans 8 is that if anything prompts readiness for the future, this is the Holy Spirit, who is "the Beyond that is Within." Paul speaks of Christians as those who "inherit" (Greek, *klēronomein*) what lies ahead when the right time comes (1 Cor. 6:9-10; 15:50; Gal. 5:21).

If there is tension in the present, it is a *theological* rather than a *psychological* one. N. Q. Hamilton speaks of the "Eschatological Tension of the Christian Life," but as a theological tension.[51] This is because, although the forces of the "new age" in Christ are decisive, the old age and its forces still exercise their limited power in the real world. The key category, again, is that of *promise.* Christians still *wait for* adoption in the fullest sense, for they are still "heirs" (Rom. 8:17). They "*wait for* the hope of righteousness" (Gal. 5:5). In neither case do these examples of waiting refer to a psychological state, but to an objective state of affairs. They are "in Christ"; but the whole corporate reality of "being in Christ" moves toward the future, not yet having experienced the cosmic transformation which will abolish the powers of the former age.

Christians *will* be glorified with Christ, Paul declares, "if in fact we suffer with him" (Rom. 8:17). Even prayer does not have to be an intense psychological experience. Rom. 8:26 shows that the Holy Spirit prompts the prayers of Christians as they struggle in a condition of weakness and frailty. They even use "inexpressible groans" *(stenagmoi alalētoi).* Some scholars relate this impossible-to-understand prayer with the gift of speaking in tongues.[52] Weakness and suffering, however, do not mean that there is no joy: "We rejoice in the hope of the glory of God" (Rom. 5:2). The believer is transformed in a steady but gradual process "into the same image [of Christ] from one degree of glory to another" (2 Cor. 3:18).

Ernst Käsemann rightly insists that the more we appreciate what early Christianity owes to apocalyptic notions of the End, the more we come to appreciate the role of struggle, even with temptation and suffering, as "the

---

51. N. Q. Hamilton, *The Holy Spirit and Eschatology in Paul* (Edinburgh: Oliver and Boyd, 1957), 26-40.

52. Anthony C. Thiselton, *The First Epistle to the Corinthians,* NIGTC (Grand Rapids: Eerdmans, 2000), 957-89 and 1094-1130.

locus of faith" in the Christian life.[53] On one side stands "eschatological enthusiasm" with its intense psychological processes of "expectation."[54] On the other side stands a common-sense recognition of life and the body as "that piece of the world that we ourselves are. . . . man in his ability to communicate. . . . In the bodily [everyday] obedience of the Christian, carried out in the world of everyday, the lordship of Christ finds visible expression . . . and the whole thing becomes credible as Gospel message."[55]

Käsemann rightly stresses the *lordship of Christ* and the *righteousness of God* as central themes of the New Testament, both of which derive especially from apocalyptic. Lordship is expressed not only by God's declaration that Christ is Lord at the *resurrection,* but also by quietly living as one who "belongs to" Christ as Lord as his servant or slave *(doulos)* (Rom. 14:7-9; 1 Cor. 6:19-20; 2 Cor. 4:5; Phil. 2:9-11; 3:8). The cardinal themes of apocalyptic, apart from revelation from God itself, are resurrection, new creation, and universal judgment. The resurrection declares Christ to be Lord. But the practical or existential currency of these two future events during the present period of "waiting" is not psychological intensity, but *living as those counted righteous* in advance of the final public confirmation of this, at the Last Judgment, and *living as those who belong to Christ as slaves to their Lord.* Apocalyptic does not imply an obsession with End events, but with the consequences of judgment (righteousness) and resurrection (living as those who belong to Christ as Lord). Meanwhile, Rudolf Bultmann comments on Rom. 14:7-8, "None of us lives to himself. . . ." "[The Christian] no longer bears the care for himself . . . but lets this care go, yielding himself entirely to the grace of God; he recognizes himself to be the property of God (or of the Lord)."[56] This and 1 Cor. 3:21-23 are mighty expressions of freedom.

Klaus Koch shows how this apocalyptic theme is worked out in the teaching of Jesus also.[57] The parables, he argues, often refer to the kingdom of God as still awaited; yet some verses, for example, Luke 11:20, "the kingdom of God has come upon you," point to its present arrival. He rightly observes that the formula "now already–not yet" has become a truism for

---

53. Ernst Käsemann, "Primitive Christian Apocalyptic," in *New Testament Questions of Today* (London: S.C.M., 1967), 117; cf. 108-37.

54. Käsemann, *New Testament Questions,* 125.

55. Käsemann, *New Testament Questions,* 135.

56. Rudolf Bultmann, *Theology of the New Testament,* vol. 1 (London: S.C.M., 1952), 331.

57. Klaus Koch, *The Rediscovery of Apocalyptic: A Polemic Work on a Neglected Area of Biblical Studies* . . . (London: S.C.M., 1972), 70-78 and throughout.

writers on the Gospels, which allows various interpretations. But in the end the arrival of the kingdom of God allows not only for some degree of decisive liberation and new creation now, but also for a period of waiting and expectation. At the End, resurrection, new creation, and judgment will become fully public. Koch quotes Peter Stuhlmacher as declaring that the righteousness of God does not mean "simply the pardon of the individual," but rather "God's effective salvation-creating justice, which forms the world according to the divine standard."[58]

It is worth noting that both the prophetic stream and the apocalyptic stream of hope are important for Christology. The prophetic stream looks forward to a *man*, perhaps a being like David, who will bring in the kingdom of God in the power of the Holy Spirit and his anointing. The apocalyptic stream sees sin as so deep and widespread that only *God himself* can bring in the kingdom by divine intervention. Jesus Christ fulfills *both* streams of expectation. But our task is to focus on what this perspective implies for waiting and expecting.

Meanwhile Käsemann rightly sees that Christian discipleship in the present is a matter of living out the lordship of Christ in the *everyday world*, even if this requires living with oppression or temptation. Calvin and many Christian thinkers, in effect, endorse this.[59] Calvin writes, "The trials by which the Lord proves and exercises us are severe. . . . But their hopes may stand . . . in the meantime."[60] The Luther legend strikes the right note. If he thought that the world would end tomorrow, Luther would go on planting trees. Wittgenstein is relevant in helping us to understand what it is, and should be, to wait and to expect a future event.

---

58. Koch, *The Rediscovery of Apocalyptic*, 85; and Peter Stuhlmacher, *Gerechtigkeit Gottes bei Paulus*, FRLANT 87 (Göttingen: Vandenhoeck & Ruprecht, 1965), 238. Cf. Anthony C. Thiselton, *The Two Horizons* (Grand Rapids: Eerdmans and Exeter: Paternoster, 1980), 324-26.

59. John Calvin, *Institutes of the Christian Religion*, ed. H. Beveridge, 2 vols. (London: James Clarke, 1957), 3.20-25.

60. Calvin, *Institutes*, 3.20.52 (Beveridge ed., vol. 2, 200-201).

CHAPTER 5

Two Apparent Problems:
The Intermediate State or Immediately with Christ?
Will There Be a "Millennium"?

We have already examined "a new approach" to the concept of *expecting*. This was achieved with the help of the philosopher Wittgenstein's clarification of the term "to expect." It cohered fully with the biblical witness. A similar new approach becomes possible when we seek to answer the question: do the dead enter Christ's presence *immediately*, or are they to await the general resurrection after an interval that is usually called *the intermediate state?* In this case we shall argue that the researches of the secular philosopher Gilbert Ryle suggest an approach which not only allows, but necessitates, a *positive answer to both alternatives without contradiction*.

5.1. An Immediate Departure to Be with Christ
or an Intermediate State before the Resurrection?

Both ways of approaching human destiny are thoroughly biblical. As most Christians know, in Phil. 1:23 Paul declares, "I am hard pressed between the two: my desire is to depart (Greek, *eis to analysai*) and be with Christ, for that is far better. . . ." The Greek *analyō* means "to depart" or "to be loosed," and is a euphemism for death. Similarly, "We would rather be away from the body, and at home with the Lord" (2 Cor. 5:6). On the other hand, the general resurrection appears to denote an event which occurs for the whole people of God at *one moment*, *after* some have died. Paul writes, "The trumpet will sound, and the dead will be raised imperishable, and we shall all be changed" (1 Cor. 15:52). He writes in his earliest epistle, "The Lord himself . . . will descend from heaven, and the dead in Christ will rise first. Then we who are alive, who are left . . ." (1 Thess. 4:16-17). Oscar

Cullmann writes, "The transformation of the body does not take place until the End, when the whole creation will be made new by the Holy Spirit, when there will be no death and no corruption."[1]

Martin Luther imagined the state of the dead as a sleep, in which a person remains so deeply asleep that this state is dreamless, unconscious, without any feeling, and even "removed from space and time."[2] Luther points out that, according to Paul, Christ is "the firstfruits of those who have fallen asleep" (1 Cor. 15:20-21), which for Christians means that "this remnant of death is to be regarded as no more than a deep sleep, and that the future resurrection of our body will not differ from suddenly awaking from such a sleep."[3] Luther adds, "Scripture applies the term 'sleep' to those who are placed into the coffin and grave. These people, however, . . . will simply be transformed, or changed."[4] Paul inherits the Greek word for "to sleep," *koimaō*, from the Greek Old Testament or LXX (the Septuagint), for example, in Gen. 47:30, Deut. 31:16, and 2 Macc. 12:45, where the NRSV translates it "lie down," but it means "to die." Then it becomes a standard euphemism for death in the New Testament (John 11:11, Acts 7:60; 1 Cor. 7:39; 11:30; 15:6, 51; 1 Thess. 4:14-15; 2 Pet. 3:4). The word is also used of natural sleep. The use of the word alone, however, could be due to borrowing from a Jewish euphemism. But we cannot so easily dismiss the idea of waiting in some kind of condition until the future event of the resurrection.

One way of reconciling "the immediate departure" approach and "the intermediate state" approach might be to say that a state of waiting is still "in Christ." Christ indeed said to the dying thief, "Today you will be with me in paradise" (Luke 23:43). Jürgen Moltmann insists, "It [an intermediate period] is not empty, like a waiting room. It is filled with the Lordship of Christ over the dead and the living, and by the experience of the Spirit, who is the life-giver."[5] Moltmann continues, "Christians know that they are safely hidden in Christ (Col. 3:3), . . . but they are not yet in the new

1. Oscar Cullmann, *Immortality of the Soul or Resurrection of the Dead? The Witness of the New Testament* (London: Epworth, 1958), 37.

2. Jürgen Moltmann, *Is There Life after Death?* (Milwaukee: Marquette University Press, 1998), 47.

3. Martin Luther, *Luther's Works*, vol. 28, *Commentary on 1 Corinthians 7 and 15 and 1 Timothy*, ed. Hilton Oswald (St. Louis: Concordia, 1973), 110 (cf. Weimar Edition, vol. 36, 547).

4. Luther, *LW*, vol. 28, 200, on 1 Cor. 15:53 (Weimar Edition, vol. 36, 675).

5. Jürgen Moltmann, *The Coming of God: Christian Eschatology* (London: S.C.M., 1996), 104.

world of the future. . . . The dead are dead, and are not yet risen, but they are already 'in Christ' and are with him in the way to the future. . . . 'Neither death nor life . . . will be able to separate us from the love of God that is in Christ Jesus' (Rom. 8:38-39)."[6]

This almost solves the problem of how the Christian dead can be immediately "with Christ" and yet also enter an intermediate state until the future Coming of Christ and the general resurrection. They are safely "with Christ," and yet they cannot be conscious of being with Christ. Is this, however, the very best and most meaningful explanation? It goes much of the way toward explaining the tension, but not quite the whole way.

Certainly the notion of being "with Christ" at once, even if unconsciously so, would appear to exclude a notion of "Purgatory." We shall consider Purgatory more fully in Chapter 8 when we ask: Is the Holy Spirit's gift of holiness at the resurrection immediate or gradual? Jürgen Moltmann argues that the above consideration effectively makes *Purgatory* invalid.[7] Pope Benedict XII declared in the fourteenth century, "There is a *Purgatory,* that is a state of punishment and purification, in which the souls which are still burdened by venial sins and the temporal punishment for sins, are purified."[8] Thomas Aquinas writes, "The punishment of purgatory is intended to supplement the satisfaction which was not fully completed in the body. Consequently since . . . the works of one person can avail for another's satisfaction, whether the latter be living or dead, the suffrages of the living, without any doubts, profit those who are in purgatory."[9] Most Protestants will at once see this as compromising the once-for-all all-sufficiency of Christ to cover all sin without exception. Geoffrey Rowell, however, attempts to defend Purgatory in a Tractarian or Anglo-Catholic tradition. He disengages it from any notion of punishment or merit, and sees it as a gradual process of purification after death for most, but perhaps not all, Christians. We discuss his view in detail in Chapter 8 when we consider whether the Holy Spirit's gift of holiness, like Christ's gift of righteousness, can *be instant at the resurrection.*

Some modern Catholic theologians have perhaps modified the tradi-

---

6. Moltmann, *The Coming of God,* 105.

7. Moltmann, *The Coming of God,* 97; cf. 96-101 on Purgatory.

8. Pope Benedict XII, *Benedictus Deus* (1336, *On the Beatific Vision of God;* in *Papal Encyclicals Online,* January 2008.

9. Thomas Aquinas, *Summa Theologiae,* Blackfriars ed. (London: Eyre & Spottiswoode, 60 vols., 1963 and *New Advent* online), Part II:2, Q. 71, art. 6.

tional doctrine of Purgatory.[10] Karl Rahner stresses the grace of God, resurrection, and a qualified universalism, but insists that Purgatory remains an official Catholic doctrine, allowing for postmortal growth and development or "ripening."[11] His view seems not hugely different from that of the Anglican, Geoffrey Rowell. Vatican II certainly has formal rules for "Masses for the Dead," so that "the dead may be helped by prayers."[12] We discuss Purgatory in greater detail in Chapter 8.

The upshot of all this is that we are left with two apparently different biblical traditions. The more popular is summed up in the words of Jesus, "Truly, I tell you, *today* you will be with me in Paradise" (Luke 23:43). Paul's language seems to confirm this: "My desire is to depart and be with Christ, for that is far better" (Phil. 1:23). The other tradition, which seems more sophisticated, comes from the earliest writings of the New Testament, 1 Thessalonians: "The Lord . . . will descend from heaven, and the dead in Christ will rise first. Then we who are alive, who are left . . . will meet the Lord in the air" (1 Thess. 4:16-17). Paul also writes, "As all die in Adam, so all will be made alive in Christ. But each in his own order: Christ the first fruits, then *at his coming* those who belong to Christ" (1 Cor. 15:22-23; my italics). We propose to show that a radical difference of logic reveals good reasons for *both* views, that *both* can be entirely reconciled, and that *both* are true in important ways.

5.2. Gilbert Ryle's "Paradox" of the Participant and the Logician

Just as Ludwig Wittgenstein indirectly suggested a new perspective on the logical grammar of "to expect," so the linguistic philosopher Gilbert Ryle (1900-1976) provided indirectly an entirely new perspective on how we can hold together the two biblical traditions which I have outlined. Ryle was a leading "Oxford philosopher" and exponent of what was earlier called "linguistic analysis." His chosen task was to disentangle conceptual confusions and paradoxes. From this point of view, as an exponent of *logic* and *language*, it is hardly relevant that he remained an extrovert, secular philosopher.

10. Karl Rahner, "Purgatory," in his *Theological Investigations,* vol. 19 (London: Darton, Longman & Todd, 1984), 181-93.

11. Cf. Gerald A. McCool (ed.), *A Rahner Reader* (London: Darton, Longman & Todd, 1975), 356-58; and Rahner, *Theological Investigations,* vol. 7 (1971), 287-91.

12. Austin P. Flannery (ed.), *Documents of Vatican II* (Grand Rapids: Eerdmans, 1975), 205.

In *The Concept of Mind* (1949) Ryle sought to dispel conceptual confusions about the relationship between body and mind, although his attack on "the dogma of the Ghost in the Machine," inherited from Descartes, was more than an exposure of a category mistake.[13] To bracket mind and body as two examples from the same category is as bad as uttering a zeugma: "She came home in a flood of tears and a sedan chair."[14] Similarly, we cannot think of "rising hopes" in the realm of mind in the same way as "a rising tide" in the physical or empirical world.[15] Mental "occurrences" and physical occurrences do not constitute two collateral histories. "Mental events" are best thought of, Ryle claims, in an adverbial way, or as a disposition. This is not quite behaviorism or materialism in the fullest sense of these words, although Ryle moves too far in this direction. His rejection of a sharp dualism is biblical, but we should not want to follow him all the way.

Our concern, however, is not with *The Concept of Mind,* but with his book *Dilemmas* (1966; from Lectures given in 1953), and especially with one of its essays, "Achilles and the Tortoise."[16] The book seizes our attention because it addresses "conflicts between theories."[17] The theories appear to be rivals, but this is because each is incomplete, and their formulation often carries with it some confusion. Often we find "quarrels between theories," but this is often because they are "would-be solutions of different problems," not of a single problem.[18] This applies to many theories or "problems" in theology, including the modern Christologies of the 1960s and 1970s, and to interpretations of postmortal existence.[19] Ryle sets himself to examine a series of classic "paradoxes," or logical dilemmas. Many go back to Aristotle, who formulated such material "categories." Often theorists who seem to be at loggerheads prove to be "talking at cross-purposes

13. Gilbert Ryle, *The Concept of Mind* (London: Hutchinson, 1949), 17.

14. Ryle, *The Concept of Mind,* 23.

15. Ryle, *The Concept of Mind,* 24.

16. Gilbert Ryle, *Dilemmas* (Cambridge: Cambridge University Press, 1966), 36-53.

17. Ryle, *Dilemmas,* 1.

18. Ryle, *Dilemmas,* 1.

19. The classic example of this kind of conceptual confusion comes in several essays in *Christ, Faith and History: Cambridge Studies in Christology,* ed. S. W. Sykes and J. P. Clayton (Cambridge: Cambridge University Press, 1972), especially in J. A. T. Robinson's language about a "bat-man" or "Centaur." Part of the German debate about "the Christ of Faith and Jesus of History" since Lessing probably reflects the same problem; cf. Alistair McGrath, *The Making of Modern German Christology* (Oxford: Blackwell, 1986), and Karl-Joseph Kuschel, *Born before All Time: The Dispute over Christ's Origin* (London: S.C.M., 1992), 21-175.

with one another. . . . The two sides are, at certain points, hanging their arguments upon concepts of different categories," though they suppose that they belong to the same category.[20] Thus Ryle examines issues about predestination and freedom, a dilemma about pleasure, and our special concern, the paradox of Achilles and the Tortoise.

This is justly a famous paradox of Zeno of Elea (c. A.D. 490-420). Zeno believed that this paradox illustrated the illusory nature of change. In this respect he sided with Parmenides against Heraclitus. His argument against motion used the analogy of the race course and the arrow. In normal commonsense terms a fast runner (Achilles) will overtake a slow runner (the Tortoise) to reach the destination first. Ryle comments, "Yet there is a very different answer which also seems to follow with equal cogency from the same data."[21] A mathematician might calculate the distance that Achilles has to run, in the first instance, to catch up with the Tortoise, and to allow for the fact, additionally, that *by the time Achilles reaches the starting point of the Tortoise, the Tortoise has moved ahead, however slowly.* As a second stage, we can envisage Achilles catching up with the Tortoise's point of advance, but *by the time he has done this, the Tortoise will have moved yet further on.* Ryle comments, "Ahead of each level that Achilles makes up, there always remains a further, though diminished, lead for him still to make up. . . . *So Achilles never catches the Tortoise.* He whittles down the distance, but never whittles it down to nothing. . . . This is one of the justly famous paradoxes of Zeno. . . . It deserves to rank as the paradigm of a philosophical puzzle."[22] If the reader finds this material too mind-stretching, we have tried to offer a homely analogy in the next paragraph.

How, then, does a series of diminishing leads seem to take the form of an endless sequence of postponements of victory? Ryle himself offers three analogies. But before we look at them, I suggest one very homely analogy of my own, which nonphilosophers may find helpful. My homely analogy compares what we might say to children as they try to sleep on the night of Christmas Eve. We might say, "The sooner you fall asleep, the sooner Christmas morning will be here." As *participants* who are deeply involved, they will find this true. But as *"observers"* parents or other adults will find *plenty to do while the children sleep*: there may be presents to wrap and label; for some, midnight Communion to attend; and so on. They will meet

20. Ryle, *Dilemmas*, 11.
21. Ryle, *Dilemmas*, 36.
22. Ryle, *Dilemmas*, 36-37 (my italics).

early on Christmas morning; but for the children the experience will be immediate. However, "sleeping" is only part of a randomly chosen analogy. It is simply a convenient example which shows how different the "participant" and "observer" perspective may be.

We now return to Ryle's analogies. The first takes the form of measuring time, and also speed in terms of miles per hour. A second takes the form of dividing a cake into diminishing fractions. A third suggests we plant flags on the race course, to mark where Achilles reaches the starting point of the Tortoise; where he has made up the distance to where the Tortoise has next reached; and so on. All of these use a "special partition-procedure."[23] Ryle's pivotal statement is as follows: "Zeno, in his mention of successive leads to be made up by Achilles, is, though surreptitiously and only by implication, referring to the *total* two-mile course run by Achilles in overtaking the tortoise. . . . The reason why at first sight this [i.e., Achilles overtaking the Tortoise] does not seem to be the case is that we are *induced to look at the race through Achilles' own eyes*" (my italics).[24] If we return to the analogy of fractions of the cake, the central point turns on the difference between the question: "How many portions have you cut *off* the object?" (Ryle's italics); and the question: "How many portions have you cut it *into?*" (Ryle's italics).[25] "A certain special way of sub-dividing two miles" yields, or appears to yield, a "nonfinality" only because this perspective is how it appears to Achilles, the *participant, not* to the *spectator* as *observer.*[26]

It is precisely because two different procedures, which he calls *measurement* and *calculation*, intertwine, Ryle argues, that a *paradox* seems to emerge. If they are kept apart as separate, we should *not* have a paradox. "Truisms about the world and human beings" might be called "nursemaids' truisms"; truisms which "give us no news about what happens" might be called "a logician's platitude."[27] *One way* of looking at the supposed problem is to see it *through the eyes of the participant, or existentially;* the other is to see *through the eyes of the spectator, or "ontologically."* If we split a "whole" into infinite parts, we could never succeed in conveying an "infinite" course in finite, limited time.[28] Similarly, in his previous essay on

23. Ryle, *Dilemmas*, 43.
24. Ryle, *Dilemmas*, 44.
25. Ryle, *Dilemmas*, 46.
26. Ryle, *Dilemmas*, 49.
27. Ryle, *Dilemmas*, 52.
28. Cf. Anthony C. Thiselton, *A Concise Encyclopaedia of the Philosophy of Religion* (Oxford: Oneworld, 2002), 271-72.

predestination or "it has to be" Ryle shows that we tie ourselves into knots when we seek to apply the logic of "what is" to that which has not yet occurred. Again, there is a distinction between the "nursemaid," or practical, perspective and the "logician's" perspective, or calculation.

Ryle might well have reacted with horror at the prospect of someone's applying his logical analysis to theology, but theology has been led into several blind spots by category-confusion of the kind that Ryle discusses. Quite simply we propose that (1) "to depart and to be with Christ," i.e., *immediately,* is a *participant or existential perspective;* (2) "to wait until the Coming of Christ" and the general resurrection constitutes a *spectator or ontological perspective. Both* are *valid and true within the context* that gives them meaning and currency.

I have used this kind of solution to "paradoxes" found in the Bible in at least two or three ways, and more. I shall very briefly outline them, in order to amplify the far-reaching importance for theology of distinguishing between the "participant" and "observer" perspective. But some readers, whose interest may be only in the Last Things, may prefer to skip ahead to section 5.3, on the millennium. Our first and most important example concerns justification by grace through faith.[29] The main paradox is that of how Christian believers can be *"simul justus et peccator"* (at the same time righteous and sinner). This relates, as we shall see, to the logical difference between a *historical viewpoint* or frame of reference and an *eschatological viewpoint* or frame of reference. Closely associated with this is another subsidiary "paradox"; how can justification be both present, as when Paul declares, "We are justified by faith" (Rom. 5:1), and future, as when he says, "We eagerly wait for the hope of righteousness" (Gal. 5:5). Johannes Weiss calls it the "pre-dating of what is really an eschatological act."[30] A third alleged "paradox" is whether the advance verdict of God is "real" or merely "counted as," as if it were a legal fiction. An older Catholic writer asks, "How can the false be true, or how can God declare true what he knows to be false?"[31] All three relate to the differences between a historical and an eschatological frame.

All three "paradoxes," especially the main first one, can be reconciled positively by tools and conceptual devices suggested indirectly by Ryle and

29. Anthony C. Thiselton, *The Two Horizons* (Grand Rapids: Eerdmans and Exeter: Paternoster, 1980), 415-23.

30. Johannes Weiss, *Earliest Christianity* (New York: Harper, 1959), vol. 2, 502.

31. Ferdinand Prat, *The Theology of St. Paul* (London: Burns, Oates & Washbourne, 1945), vol. 2, 247.

Wittgenstein. In his book *The Meaning of Righteousness in Paul*, John Ziesler attempted to offer a partial reconciliation by arguing that the noun and the verb introduced a different perspective.[32] But the difference between the noun and the verb does no more than scratch at the surface of the problem. Wittgenstein speaks of the phenomenon of "seeing . . . as. . . ."[33] In the *Zettel* he cites the example of "a kind of puzzle picture." At first glance it looks like "a jumble of meaningless lines." Then we see it as a landscape. He comments, "It all depends on *the system* to which the sign belongs" (his italics).[34] There is nothing "false" about seeing a puzzle picture first as *this*, and then as *that*: both are genuine perceptions. Wittgenstein's most famous example is that of Jastrow's "duck-rabbit." This can be "seen as" a duck facing to the left, or as a rabbit facing upward and a little to the right. Echoing Søren Kierkegaard, we might suggest that *what* is seen remains the same; but *how* it is seen depends on its frame of reference.

Donald D. Evans coins the term "onlooks" for this phenomenon.[35] This relates closely to how God "looks on" Christian believers. Evans comments that this involves "placing *x* within a structure, organization, or scheme. This often involves the description of a status . . . to *x*."[36] Two propositions might be contradictory; but hardly two evaluations. What is "good" in one context may be "fair" or "bad" in another.

I have argued that humankind, whether Christian or not, remains central in the context of *history*, but that Christians, or those counted "put right," are in a right relationship with God (or "rightwised") in the context of *eschatology*. This is why Weiss rightly calls it "a pre-dating of an eschatological act," which belongs "strictly speaking" to the future. In Luther's sense of faith as appropriation, we may appropriate this future in the present. That is why James 2:14-26 uses "faith" in an entirely different way.[37] The confusion and "paradox" come about when we intermingle language

32. John Ziesler, *The Meaning of Righteousness in Paul*, SNTSMS (Cambridge: Cambridge University Press, 1972), 128-210.

33. Ludwig Wittgenstein, *Philosophical Investigations*, sect. 74 and II.xi.193-214; also in *The Blue and Brown Books: Preliminary Studies for the "Philosophical Investigations"* (Oxford: Blackwell, 2nd ed. 1969), 163-74.

34. Ludwig Wittgenstein, *Zettel* (Oxford: Blackwell, 1967), sects. 195, 201, and 228.

35. Donald D. Evans, *The Logic of Self-Involvement: A Philosophical Study of Everyday Language with Special Reference to the Christian Use of Language about God as Creator* (London: S.C.M., 1963), 124-41.

36. Evans, *The Logic of Self-Involvement*, 127.

37. Thiselton, *The Two Horizons*, 422-27.

about history with language about eschatology. We repeat some of these comments in Chapter 10, in a different context.

A second example of dissolving biblical paradoxes relates to a tragically misunderstood passage, namely, Titus 1:12-13. I will risk spending a page and a half on this to show how persistent are the confusions and misunderstandings that can arise about biblical passages, owing to a failure to note logical paradoxes of various kinds. Wittgenstein and J. L. Austin had seen the logical distinctiveness of first-person utterances (a participant's) as against third-person utterances (an observer's). Most biblical commentators and exegetes failed to notice this, and this failure led to nearly two thousand years of misinterpretation of this passage in Titus. Paul (or the writer) commissions Titus to set in order the practical life of the churches in Crete. Yet he puts into the mouth of a *Cretan,* "Cretans are always liars, vicious brutes . . . ," and explicitly adds, "That testimony is true" (Tit. 1:12-13). In 1994 I wrote "The Logical Role of the Liar Paradox . . . A Dissent from the Commentaries . . ." to clarify the true meaning of the passage.[38]

It has always been obvious that to say, "I always tell only lies," and then to add, "This is true," constitutes a contradiction in terms. If the second statement is true, the first is false; only if the second statement is false can the main statement be true. In logic, "*P* implies or entails not-*p*." Most of the commentators spend much ink trying to excuse Paul both of logical stupidity and of racial abuse and prejudice against Cretans. Virtually every commentary had either failed to spot the paradox, or tried to excuse the writer for making a racial stereotypification of monstrous proportions. But this is not an *empirical* statement about Cretans at all. It is a *logical* statement to show the fruitlessness of what the writer attacks as useless arguments and myths. The paradox of the speaking liar is also found in Zeno, but is more closely associated with Eubulides, whose Megarian school, like Zeno, opposed Heraclitus's view of reality as change, movement, or flux. The liar paradox remained familiar in Greece until perhaps a century after Cicero. Apart from a brief revival in the Middle Ages, it regained life in the modern era, when Georg Cantor formulated his paradox in mathematics in 1899, and the Burali-Forti paradox of the "set of all sets" emerged at about the same time. Wittgenstein included as one cause of paradoxes the principle that "My own relation to my words is wholly dif-

---

38. Anthony C. Thiselton, "The Logical Role of the Liar Paradox in Titus 1:12, 13: A Dissent from the Commentaries in the Light of Philosophical and Logical Analysis," *Biblical Interpretation* 2 (1994): 207-23; repr. in *Thiselton on Hermeneutics,* 217-29.

ferent from other people's."[39] We can say, "*He* believes it, but it is false"; but hardly, "*I* believe it, but it is false."[40]

What, then, is Paul, or the writer of Titus, saying, and why did so many generations of commentators seem to miss his point? The writer is attacking arrogant self-assertion (1:7), empty talk (1:10), and "profession of knowledge of God denied by deeds" (1:16). He urges holiness and self-control (1:8), and being a "model of good deeds" (2:7). But the historic reason for thinking that all Cretans were liars arose from the Cretan claim to possess the tomb of Zeus in their island when Zeus was popularly believed to be immortal. The originator of the charge of lying was said to be Epimenides. In the patristic era, claims and counterclaims about the fate of Zeus become prevalent. Origen compares the fate of Zeus with belief in the resurrection of Christ.[41] The slogan "Cretans always tell lies" became an *empirical* or *contingent* statement about Cretans in the context of arguing for the resurrection of Christ.

Meanwhile the tradition of a *philosopher Epimenides,* who formulated paradoxes and logical puzzles, became confused with a tradition of a supposed *prophet Epimenides,* who denounced false claims about Zeus. What the writer to Titus denounces is *empty talk, unrelated to practical life and behavior,* which merely goes round and round in a circle of contradiction. His comment, "*This is true,*" is intended both to show how *ridiculous and profitless* this is, and that he is propounding a *logical* formulation, not an *empirical* one about people who live in Crete. Everything else in this short epistle is about practical *behavior,* which will provide convincing *currency* for talk. The author knows all about first-person utterances and even paradoxes.

We have finished what some may see as a digression, but it functions to illustrate the far-reaching consequences of logical confusion in many directions. Our argument further shows that the difference between "participant" (first-person) utterances and "observer" (third-person utterances), as elucidated by Wittgenstein and Ryle, opens fresh questions and new ways of exploring what look like "rival" theories in more than one area of thought.

This applies to the question of whether the Christian dead pass *immediately* into the presence of Christ, or whether they "wait" in an *intermediate state,* for the Coming of Christ and the general resurrection. The per-

---

39. Wittgenstein, *Philosophical Investigations,* II.x.192.
40. Wittgenstein, *Philosophical Investigations,* II.x.190 (my italics).
41. Origen, *Contra Celsum* 3.43.

son who dies will know nothing of the intermediate state. Admittedly the believer is "in Christ," and his or her "sleep" cannot be interrupted. But it conveys an idea that is not very helpful. The best way is to talk about "the next thing we know," which is to be conscious of Christ. The exegete or theologian, however, may wish to contemplate the continuing acts of God, such as continuing history, waiting and expectation, the "last trumpet," and the resurrection of the dead. In the role of *observer*, he is right. But that is not the practical concern of the dying Christian, whose role is that of *active participant*.

5.3. Will There Be a Millennium? A Further Controversial Issue

This further area of conceptual confusion or controversy is also capable of explanation. It also looks like conflict between different traditions within the New Testament. At first sight Rev. 20:1-10 seems to affirm it, while the Synoptic Gospels, John, Paul, and Hebrews seem either to ignore it or to reject it. The idea is almost entirely based on Rev. 20:1-10, although some attempt to support the notion by a forced exegesis of 1 Cor. 15:22-28 and 1 Thess. 4:15-17.

Revelation 20:1-10 depicts the descent of an angel who holds the key to the abyss and a great chain, and his seizure of "the dragon, that ancient serpent, who is the devil and Satan" to bind him for a thousand years (v. 2). He will throw him into the abyss, and lock and seal it, to prevent his deceiving the nations "until the thousand years be ended" (v. 3). Then the martyrs beheaded for their testimony to Christ are raised to life, and "reign with Christ a thousand years" (v. 4). This is called "the first resurrection" (v. 5); to share in it is to be accounted blessed (v. 6). "When the thousand years are ended, Satan will be released from his prison and will come out to deceive the nations" (v. 7). Gog and Magog march to battle to attack the holy city (v. 8). The devil is thrown into the lake of fire forever (v. 10). The NRSV places in brackets "The rest of the dead did not come to life until the thousand years were ended" (v. 5). Not all MSS contain the phrase which the NRSV puts in brackets.[42]

Does this passage imply a literal or chronological thousand-year reign with Christ, especially one *before* the final Coming or *Parousia* of Christ and the Last Judgment? This claim (in its latter form) is the

---

42. David Aune, *Revelation 17–22*, WBC (Nashville: Nelson, 1998), 1073.

"premillennialist" view defended by J. F. Walvoord and others.[43] "Premillennialism" arose largely from the "Dispensationalist" approach of John Nelson Darby (1800-1882), associated with the *Scofield Reference Bible* of 1909. Like most Apocalyptists, Dispensationalists see history in terms of a sequence of ages or "Dispensations," to which such biblical books as Ezekiel, Daniel, and Revelation were said to point. The popular writer Hal Lindsey went as far as to claim that the founding of the Jewish state in 1948 is one of the most important prophetic fulfillments of the Gospels, and that Daniel and Revelation foresaw associated historical-political events.[44] His influence on many modern American conservatives can be seen in American politics which involve attitudes to Israel. Meanwhile, William Miller (1782-1849) and the Millerites (1840 onward) who were forerunners of the Seventh-Day Adventists, also promoted the idea of a literal millennium. The belief in a literal, earthly, thousand-year reign with Christ was also known as chiliasm. "Premillennialism" is only one version of it, but probably the most influential, namely, that Christ will *first* return from heaven to initiate the thousand-year reign, and at the end of the millennium will return, finally, to inaugurate the final battle against evil forces and Satan, and the Last Judgment. Those who hold these beliefs see "the first resurrection" of Rev. 20:5-6 as one of saints at the beginning of the millennium; those who reject that view usually see it as an allusion to sharing in Christ's resurrection.

Before we look at details of the argument on both sides, we may summarize the chief arguments which each side puts forward. (1) Millennialists cite the fact that some of the theologians of the early Church, and some in the Middle Ages, held this view. Against this, many point out that Origen, Tyconius, and Augustine in the early Church held a "spiritual" interpretation of the thousand years. Luther, Calvin, and many others rejected a chronological interpretation. (2) Millennialists argue that it cohered with the Old Testament and Judaism. Others argue that if Revelation taught a millennium, this emphasis would have been clearer, more explicit, and less ambiguous, and that in any case references to such entities as "Jerusalem" and to Gog and Magog (Rev. 20:8-9) were intentionally symbolic, not referring to historical or geographical entities. (3) "Plenary inspira-

43. John F. Walvoord, *The Revelation of Jesus Christ* (Chicago: Moody, 1966), 291 and throughout; and John F. Walvoord, *Armageddon: Oil and the Middle East* (Grand Rapids: Zondervan, 2nd ed. 1990), esp. 218.

44. Hal Lindsey, *The Late Great Planet Earth* (Grand Rapids: Zondervan, 1970), 53.

tion" of the Bible means that whether or not the millennium is implied elsewhere in the Bible, we must take Revelation 20 seriously. Against this, many others assert that Revelation 20 does not teach a millennium, and that its effective neglect in the rest of Scripture is decisive.

(1) We turn to the first argument in detail. The chief sources cited in the early Church are Justin, Irenaeus, Tertullian, perhaps Hippolytus, and Lactantius. We shall quote their words. Justin (c. 100–c. 165) has no doubt about the applications of Old Testament prophecy to Jesus Christ (*Dialogue with Trypho* 77–79; *ANF*, vol. 1, 237-38). On the last things he asserts: "There will be a resurrection of the dead and a thousand years in Jerusalem [or the saints will live a thousand years in Jerusalem], which will then be built, adorned, and enlarged, as Ezekiel and Isaiah and others declare" (*Dialogue with Trypho* 80; *ANF*, vol. 1, 239). Irenaeus (c. 130–c. 200) may be less specific. He quotes copiously from Revelation. But his allusions to the millennium, if such they are, concern primarily the fall of Satan. God through Christ will "bind 'the dragon, that old serpent' and subject him to the power of man, who had been conquered. . . . The last enemy, death, is destroyed" (Rev. 20:2; 1 Cor. 15:54-55; *Against Heresies* 3.23.7; *ANF*, vol. 1, 457). Elsewhere he quotes "he who has part in the first resurrection" (Rev. 20:6; *Against Heresies* 5.34.2; *ANF*, vol. 1, 564). He also refers to the Antichrist, allegedly from 2 Thess. 2:10-12 and Rev. 19:20, and to Satan's destruction in the lake of fire (Rev. 19:20; *Against Heresies* 5.28.2; *ANF*, vol. 1, 557). But these are not explicit and uncontroversial references to the millennium.

Tertullian (c. 160–c. 235) is more explicit. He writes, "It will be after the resurrection for a thousand years in this divinely built city of Jerusalem 'let down from heaven'" (Rev. 21:2; *Against Marcion* 3.25; *ANF*, vol. 3, 342). "After its thousand years are over, within which period is completed the resurrection of the saints, . . . there will ensue the destruction of the world and the conflagration of all things at the judgment: we shall then be changed . . ." (*Against Marcion* 3.25; *ANF*, vol. 3, 343).

By far the most explicit and convincing, however, is Lactantius (c. 250–c. 325). He writes, "Christ shall descend with great power and . . . a countless host of angels. . . . The wicked shall be destroyed. . . . But the prince of demons himself, . . . being bound with fiery chains, shall be imprisoned, that the world may receive peace, and the earth . . . may rest" (Lactantius, *The Epitome of the Divine Institutes* 72; *ANF*, vol. 7, 254). God will then raise "the righteous dead to eternal life, and will Himself reign with them on the earth, and will build the holy city. . . . Stars will become more brilliant. . . . Beasts become mild. . . . But when the thousand years shall be fulfilled, and the prince of demons loosed, the nations [will] rebel against the righteous, and an innumerable multitude will come to storm the city of the saints" (*The Epitome of the Divine Institutes* 72; *ANF,* vol. 7, 254). The judgment of God will then shake the earth from its foundations.

Many of the thinkers of the early Church, however, notably Origen, Tyconius, and Augustine, come down on the opposite side. Origen (c. 185–c. 254) opted for a more "spiritual" interpretation of biblical prophecies, although his *Hexapla* revealed his concern for the details of the Bible. In *De Principiis* 4.2 he claims that many misunderstand the Scriptures because they look for a "bodily" or historical meaning rather than a "spiritual" one. He refers to Rev. 20:4, of the witness of the martyrs (*An Exhortation to Martyrdom* 30), but insists that many have "a false understanding . . . because they understand scripture not according to the spiritual meaning but according to the sound of the letter" (*De Principiis* 4.2.2). He adds, "The prophetic style is always strewn with types and enigmas" (*De Principiis* 4.2.3). Tyconius compares his *Liber Regularum* in the early 380s, as well as writing a commentary on Revelation, which became lost.[45] He argues that the goal of biblical interpretation is to move beyond the "human sense" to the "mystical." Hence "in that hour" is not a reference to a moment in time, but a symbolic meaning, as understood in the apocalyptic genre (*Book of Rules* 6.108-11). In 2 Thessalonians 2 "the man of sin" is not a particular figure of the last times, but a principle, perhaps representing evil in the Church (Tyconius, *Book of Rules* 3.55).

Tyconius greatly influences Augustine's biblical exegesis. In *On Christian Doctrine,* book 3, Augustine discusses the difference between clear historical signs and enigmatic, ambiguous, or figurative signs. We must not interpret figurative or symbolic signs literally. "Bondage," for example, does not signify being human slaves, but the spiritual bondage of the will (*On Christian Doctrine* 3.6-9). He asserts, "We must guard against taking a metaphorical form of speech as if it were literal" (*On Christian Doctrine* 3.10.14). In *City of God* 20 (c. 427) he specifically addresses Rev. 20:1-10. He says, "While the devil is bound, the saints reign with Christ during the same thousand years [but] understood in the same way, that is, of the time of His [Christ's] first coming. . . . For the Church could not now be called His Kingdom . . . unless the saints were even now rejoicing with Him. . . . It is then of this kingdom militant, in which conflict with

---

45. Kevin L. Hughes, *Constructing Antichrist* (Washington, DC: Catholic University of America Press, 2005), 84-94.

the enemy is still maintained, . . . that the Apocalypse speaks in the words just quoted" (*City of God* 20.9; *NPNF,* ser. 1, vol. 2, 429-30). There are, to be sure, apocalyptic perspectives in *City of God* 20, but this is because of its philosophy of history in the light of the sacking of Rome by Alaric the Goth. Augustine rejects a literal reading of "the thousand years." Rather, it witnesses to the present life of the Church. He remains "agnostic" about the timing and exact sequence of events of the end. Gregory of Rome and Thomas Aquinas broadly follow him. Clearly there is no early unanimous testimony about the millennium. If we can argue from silence, the majority of Church Fathers would probably stand with Tyconius and Augustine on this subject.

If we look at later interpreters, Martin Luther was definitely not millenarian. He certainly rebuked his close follower Michael Stiefel for speculating about the time of the End.[46] He is reputed to have said that if he knew that the final Coming of Christ was about to happen, he would go on planting trees. Arguably, Obbe Philips (c. 1560) and the radical "left-wing" Reformers held the minority view that the millennium was a chronological period.[47]

(2) We turn more briefly to the argument about the millennium in Judaism. This argument may cut both ways and cannot be decisive. If Judaism did reflect this belief strongly, we can argue either that John inherited it, or that it forms part of a symbolic stage setting for something more important. George B. Caird argues in his commentary that it is "demonstrably false" to suggest that the millennium "was so dominant in the first century as to leave him [John] no alternative but to borrow it."[48] R. H. Charles considers it "a late and attenuated form of the old Jewish expectation of an eternal Messianic Kingdom on the present earth."[49]

A larger and much more important related question is the historical or symbolic nature of the language of Revelation, and especially Revelation 20. I address this more fully in Chapter 11. In conservative circles, some sort of breakthrough was achieved by William Hendriksen in his

46. Martin Luther, "Letter to Michael Stiefel and Table Talk Recorded by Anthony Leuterbach" (1533), in *Luther: Letters of Spiritual Counsel,* ed. T. G. Tappert, LCC 18 (London: S.C.M., 1955), 301-4.

47. George H. Williams (ed.), *Spiritual and Anabaptist Writers,* LCC 25 (London: S.C.M., 1957), 213, n. 31.

48. George B. Caird, *The Revelation of St. John the Divine* (London: Black, 1966), 250.

49. R. H. Charles, *A Critical and Exegetical Commentary on the Revelation of St. John,* ICC (2 vols.; Edinburgh: T&T Clark, 1920), vol. 2, 142.

commentary. He did not see Revelation as a map of world history, like an Underground or Subway Map, which usually carries the explanatory words, "You are standing here." Specifically, he pointed out that the themes of Revelation 20 closely reflected those of Revelation 11–14. He argued that Rev. 12:5-11 is parallel with 20:1-3; 11:2-6 and 12:14ff. parallel with 20:2; 11:7 matches 20:7ff.; and 11:17-18 and 14:14ff. match 20:11ff.[50] Because both cycles of events are symbolic, he concludes, "The theory of the premillennialists is at variance with the facts here."[51]

W. Hendriksen pictures the scene when John wrote, "Heathenism is everywhere triumphant. . . . All the nations — with the exception of the Jews — are under the thraldom of Satan. . . . With a sigh of horror we exclaim, 'Is this condition never going to change? . . . Will the light of the glorious gospel never penetrate into the palaces and hovels of Asia and Europe?' . . . The answer is 'Rejoice. . . . He [Christ] shall have domain also from sea to sea. . . . They that dwell in the wilderness shall bow down to him."[52] Satan shall deceive the nations no more. Indeed, in the ministry of Jesus, Jesus cried: "I beheld Satan falling as lightning from heaven" (Luke 10:17-18). Here the "falling from heaven" is caused by the mission of the Seventy.

The binding of Satan, Hendriksen concludes, begins with the first coming of Jesus Christ. Admittedly Satan still exercises a limited power: But the "thousand years indicates that throughout this present gospel age the devil's influence on earth is curtailed. He is unable to prevent the extension of the Church."[53] He is not bound in every sense. In John Bunyan's A Pilgrim's Progress Christian must pass between two lions. He finds that they are bound or chained. Within the lengths of their chains they can threaten and move. But there is a limit to their freedom; in the end Christian passes safely between them. There still remain persecution and oppression. The seer sees the martyrs who have been beheaded (Rev. 1:2, 9; 6:8; 20:4) even while Satan is bound.

The "reign" of the saints or martyrs is sharing in Christ's resurrection. Christ is the "stronger man" who "binds" the strong man who had held the household in thrall (Mark 3:27). Certainly Jude 6 and *Jub.* 5:6 (cf. *1 Enoch* 88) speak of evil spirits or Satan being imprisoned and cast into the abyss.

---

50. W. Hendriksen, *More than Conquerors: An Interpretation of the Book of Revelation* (Grand Rapids: Baker and London: Tyndale Press, 1962; originally 1940), 182.

51. Hendriksen, *More than Conquerors,* 185.

52. Hendriksen, *More than Conquerors,* 186-87.

53. Hendriksen, *More than Conquerors,* 188.

But Robert Mounce and others point out that in Rev. 20:1-10 the focus is upon martyrs rather than all saints, and "There is no specific indication that their reign with Christ takes place on earth, or that it necessarily follows the second advent."[54] The binding of Satan, he argues, is consistent with a reference to the present age: the passage does not represent him as "completely inactive."[55] The judgment is "the vindication of the martyrs."[56] He clinches the argument about the relevance of the passage to its historical and social situation by concluding: "The essential truth of the passage is that the martyr's steadfastness will win for him the highest life in union with God and Christ. It is a commentary on the Lord's saying in Matt. 10:39, 'He that loses his life for my sake will find it.'"[57]

If Mounce and Hendriksen are correct, the third argument about plenary inspiration falls to the ground as irrelevant. To question a millennium before the final Coming of Christ is not to marginalize Revelation 20, for it may be doubted whether it demands such an interpretation. Yet George Caird is among those who still believe that Revelation in part addresses world history, as well as avoid the notion of a millennium which is at odds with the rest of the New Testament. He observes, "It would seem that John expected the millennial reign of Christ and the martyrs to be different in degree, but not in kind, from the reign which Christ had exercised ever since his resurrection. . . . The first resurrection is not a postponement of heavenly bliss. . . . Already they are before the throne of God and serve him day and night in his Temple."[58] But to catalogue a chronological chart of future events "is to unweave the rainbow. . . . John uses his allusions not as code . . . but for their evocative and emotive power."[59] "'If only we knew,' the martyrs have cried, 'where it is all going to end.'"[60] John makes current events and persecutions intelligible and credible. Christ is already the Victor, and the New Jerusalem shall come, when God will wipe away all tears and will make all things new (Rev. 21:4-5).

This becomes confirmed by Robert Gundry's convincing argument that "the description of the new Jerusalem in Rev. 21:1–22:5 deals in sym-

---

54. Robert H. Mounce, *The Book of Revelation* (Grand Rapids: Eerdmans and London: Marshall, Morgan & Scott, 1977), 351.
55. Mounce, *The Book of Revelation*, 352.
56. Mounce, *The Book of Revelation*, 354.
57. Mounce, *The Book of Revelation*, 359.
58. Caird, *The Revelation of St. John*, 255.
59. Caird, *The Revelation of St. John*, 25.
60. Caird, *The Revelation of St. John*, 261.

bolism."[61] It has "unheard of dimensions, having gates that consist of a single pearl, being paved with gold that can be seen through, and so on."[62] The new Jerusalem is holy and descends from heaven (Rev. 21:2). Gundry concludes: "John wanted his Christian audience . . . to see in the new Jerusalem not their future dwelling place, but . . . their future selves."[63] There is no reason to interpret "the beloved city" in Rev. 20:9 differently. Yet we cannot pretend that our discussion leaves no loose ends.

The controversy is likely to continue. David Aune's bibliography shows how many have written on this issue.[64] In America, debates go on, especially in conservative circles, for example, in the *Westminster Theological Journal* and the *Journal of the Evangelical Theological Society.*[65]

It may be difficult to convince a literal millennialist about the symbolic parallels between Revelation 11–14 and Revelation 20. For some of the book of Revelation, as Caird argues, does concern world history, although much or most of it addresses us through symbol. This is where the previous part of this chapter, which we called "a new approach," perhaps comes into its own for the present question also. Is Rev. 20:1-10 first and foremost *written for the observer,* who looks for a map of events after a "first" final coming of Christ, or even between the foundation of the Jewish state and the final Coming of Christ? Or does John address the *"participant" or existential situation* of the first and subsequent readers? We saw in our discussion of the "intermediate state" how drastically an observer and participant perspective appeared differently to each kind of audience.

We should not confuse this with Rudolf Bultmann's demythologizing program, which attempted to reduce *all* observer perspectives to existential ones. Even some conservative charismatic groups show sympathy (even if not consciously or deliberately) with an existential account of Christ's lordship. They often sing, "We build him a throne." They mean to say, rightly, that the participant cash value of calling Christ "Lord" can be seen in the extent to which we are genuinely his obedient slaves or servants. But if this were the whole truth, it would also say, wrongly, that

61. Robert H. Gundry, *The Old Is Better: New Testament Essays in Support of Traditional Interpretation,* WUNT 178 (Tübingen: Mohr Siebeck, 2005), 399; cf. 399-411.

62. Gundry, *The Old Is Better,* 399.

63. Gundry, *The Old Is Better,* 408.

64. Aune, *Revelation 17–27,* 1069-71.

65. For example, J. A. Hughes, "Revelation 20:4-6 and the Question of the Millennium," *WTJ* 35 (1973): 281-302; M. G. Kline, "The First Resurrection," *WTJ* 37 (1975): 360-75; and S. H. T. Page, "Revelation 20 and Pauline Eschatology," *JETS* 23 (1980): 31-45.

Christ's lordship depends on human recognition of it, or even on the worship and obedience of the Church. We cannot exhaustingly and without reminder reduce the whole "observer" perspective to the existential. That is why Paul is at pains to assert that "God declared Christ Lord at the resurrection" (Rom. 1:4). But the book of Revelation is addressed to persecuted Christians and to those soon to be martyred as an assurance of God's victory in Christ. He addresses them in their existential situation as "participants" in the death and resurrection of Christ, even if parts of Revelation 21 and 22 carry also an "observer" or propositional perspective of Christ's ultimate victory and the blessing of the righteous.

The fundamental point is that "prophecy" is a practical, participatory address of the gospel, as most of the Church Fathers, Aquinas, Luther, Calvin, and Wesley defined prophecy.[66] It is not primarily an "objective" map of future events, least of all one which, in the words of Bernard McGinn, "took a holiday for almost two thousand years (the dispensation of the Gentiles) between the fall of the Second Temple of Jerusalem in 70 C.E. and the restoration of the Jewish state in 1948," and then predicted the political history of Europe, Syria, the Middle East, and what was earlier called the Soviet Union or the Eastern bloc.[67] Such a definition of "prophecy" sits at odds with how the great theologians and biblical exegetes of the Church have regarded it. Prophecy is not primarily prediction (although it may include this), but primarily draws out the practical implications of the gospel for those who stand in need of assurance or rebuke as *participants*.

True, it remains partly correct to call the author of Revelation an apocalyptist. But he also calls his book "the prophecy" (Rev. 1:3), says that he is concerned with what must "soon take place" (Rev. 1:1), and is testifying to "the word of God" (Rev. 1:2). This fits with the Fathers' and the Reformers' definition of "prophecy." Athanasius asserts that it takes the form of *biblical* exposition.[68] Chrysostom and Augustine see prophecy in the context of expounding *Scripture*.[69] Thomas Aquinas observes, "Prophesying may be understood as divine doctrine. . . . Those who explain divine doctrine are called prophets . . . preachers."[70] John Calvin comments, "'Prophecies' mean the art of interpreting Scripture. . . . Prophetic teaching

66. Documentation appears below.

67. Bernard McGinn, *Antichrist: Two Thousand Years of the Human Fascination with Evil* (San Francisco: Harper, 1994), 253.

68. Athanasius, *Commentarius ad Thessalonicenses prima*, 232.

69. Augustine, *On the Psalms*, Ps. 77:4; *NPNF* ser. 1, vol. 8, 361.

70. Aquinas, *Commentary on 1 Thessalonians* (New York: Magi, 1969), 52.

is for edification, exhortation. . . . [It means] the interpretation of Scripture properly applied to the people present."[71] Quite explicitly he states in the *Institutes* that prophecy is to reconcile man with God, not speculate about the future.[72] Matthew Henry asserts, "By prophesyings here understand the preaching of the word."[73] John Wesley writes, "Prophesyings . . . that is, preaching, for the apostle is not speaking of extraordinary gifts."[74] In our generation, the notion of "prophecy" as applied, practical, pastoral preaching has been defended by David Hill, Ulrich Müller, Thomas Gillespie, and in my commentary on 1 Corinthians.[75]

When these historical and modern accounts of the work of prophets are applied to the book of Revelation, we can no longer be uncertain whether it functions primarily to produce an "observer" map of future events or a "participant" address concerning gospel truth. This helps us to think more clearly about belief in a literal, chronological millennium. We may doubt that Rev. 20:1-10 demands it, and it does not feature clearly elsewhere in the New Testament. Again, we discuss the symbolism, purpose, and understanding of the book of Revelation mainly in Chapter 11, in sections 11.3 and 11.4 of that chapter.

71. John Calvin, *Commentary on 1 and 2 Thessalonians* (Wheaton: Crossway/Good News, 1999), 60.

72. John Calvin, *Institutes of the Christian Religion* (2 vols.; London: James Clarke, 1957), 4.3.4 and 1.9.3.

73. Matthew Henry, *Concise Commentary on the Whole Bible* (C.D., Gospel Forum, n.d.), on 1 Thess. 5:20.

74. John Wesley, *Notes on the New Testament* (C.D., Gospel Forum, n.d.), 694.

75. David Hill, *New Testament Prophecy* (London: Marshall, Morgan & Scott, 1979), 111-40; U. B. Müller, *Prophetie und Predigt im Neuen Testament* (Gütersloh: Mohn, 1975), 47-108; Thomas W. Gillespie, *The First Theologians: A Study in Early Christian Prophecy* (Grand Rapids: Eerdmans, 1994); and Anthony C. Thiselton, *The First Epistle to the Corinthians: A Commentary on the Greek Text* (Grand Rapids: Eerdmans and Carlisle: Paternoster, 2000), 956-70 and esp. 1087-98.

CHAPTER 6

The Return of Christ

6.1. The Central Teaching of Paul

In spite of those who underestimate the central importance of the Return of Christ in the New Testament, the concept remains central from the earliest New Testament writings to the latest. The earliest, apart from the teaching of Jesus himself, comes in 1 Thessalonians 4, where Paul declares, "The Lord himself, with a cry of command, with the archangel's call and with the sound of God's trumpet, will descend from heaven, and the dead in Christ will rise first. Then we who are alive, who are left, will be caught up in the clouds together with them to meet the Lord in the air; and so we will be with the Lord forever" (1 Thess. 4:16-17).

The notion of Christ as "the man from heaven" (1 Cor. 15:49) and the future experience of Christians after death are both inextricably bound up with resurrection, both with Christ's resurrection and the resurrection of the dead. Indeed, if theological importance, rather than possible sequence, were the only concern, it would be tempting to discuss resurrection before turning to the Return of Christ. Further, although Paul uses the imagery of the sounding of the trumpet elsewhere (1 Cor. 15:52), the trumpet is a metaphor for rousing a sleeping army, and "caught up in the clouds" is a physical metaphor for the gathering together of all believers with Christ, which remains a constant feature of language about the Return of Christ, while Paul seems to leave behind some of the more pictorial geographical or physical imagery. Much of this language serves primarily to call to mind the language of the Old Testament, which, after all, was the Bible of earliest Christians. Thus Daniel speaks of "one like a human being [or Son of

Man] coming with the clouds of heaven. . . . To him was given dominion and glory and kingship" (Dan. 7:13-14).

It is not only radical scholars, such as Rudolf Bultmann, who comment negatively, even caustically, on "caught up in the clouds of heaven," but scholars who belong to a much more orthodox tradition, such as George Caird and Tom Wright, who insist on the metaphorical status of this eschatological language. Commenting explicitly on what he calls the "tricky verses" of 1 Thess. 4:16-17, Tom Wright insists, "They [these verses] are *not* to be taken as literal description of what Paul thinks will happen [his italics]. They are simply a different way of saying what he [Paul] is saying in 1 Corinthians 15:23-27 and 51-54, and in Philippians 3:20-21."[1] G. B. Caird acknowledges that frequently we find in such language "a curious interplay between the metaphorical and the literal," especially in the apocalyptic discourses of the Gospels.[2] But he also insists, "Luke and Paul did not expect their language about life after death to be taken with flat-footed literalness."[3] Caird believes that a careful and right understanding of metaphor forms a condition for a careful and right understanding of the Last Things.

We may add that whether or not Caird and Wright are right about 1 Thessalonians 4, Christians would still meet the Lord clothed in their postresurrection "bodies." We discuss the nature of these "bodies" in our chapter on resurrection. This would also contribute to a less literalistic or "physical" meaning. The furthest that we can go is to consider the resurrection mode of existence of Christ, perhaps as seen in the ascension. Nevertheless, the manifestation of Christ's raised body occurred *within the conditions of this world*. We still cannot have a *comprehensive* view of this "body," which is *more than* "physical" but *not less than* "physical." We consider this more fully in Chapter 7. On the whole, however, Caird and Wright offer the best exposition so far.

To understand the full impact of these statements by Caird and Wright we need to understand the meaning of Paul's terms for the Return of Christ from heaven before we examine the special reasons for the spatial and pictorial language in 1 Thessalonians 4 and in 1 Corinthians 15. Paul's main word for the Coming of Christ in the last days is the term *Parousia*. This Greek noun normally means "the state of being present," connected

1. Tom (N. T.) Wright, *Surprised by Hope* (London: S.P.C.K., 2007), 143.

2. G. B. Caird, *The Language and Imagery of the Bible* (London: Duckworth, 1980), 246.

3. Caird, *Language and Imagery*, 248.

with the verb *pareimi*, "I am here."[4] In a Roman or Hellenistic context the word may denote not only the presence or "coming" of ordinary people but also especially a visit by the emperor or of a person of high rank. In 1 Thessalonians, Karl Donfried and others argue, Paul consciously uses the word *Parousia* to refer to the public and victorious Coming and Presence of Christ, in contrast and opposition to the use of *Parousia* in imperial language (1 Thess. 2:19; 3:13; 4:15; 5:23).[5] It provides an extension to the idea of the eventful arrival of the emperor, king, or dignatory, to the arrival of the King of kings in visible and final glory. It may also indicate the "putting to rights" in sovereign judgment which we shall examine in our chapter on the Last Judgment under judgment as vindication. The term is by no means confined to 1 Thessalonians. Paul uses it of the Return of Christ in 1 Cor. 15:23 and 2 Thess. 2:8; and uses the same word to denote the "presence" or "arrival" of Titus in 2 Cor. 7:6, and his own apostolic presence in Phil. 1:26; 2:12. In 1 Thessalonians Paul has already acknowledged the faith and love of the Church (1 Thess. 1:3; 2:13), but he also recognizes that an inadequate confidence in the certainty of the *Parousia* will lead to declining hope.

Alongside the nuance of a royal, sovereign, and vindicatory "Coming" or "Presence," as suggested by *parousia*, Paul also uses the Greek word *epiphaneia* (with *parousia* in 2 Thess. 2:8; and in 1 Tim. 6:14; 2 Tim. 1:10; 4:1; Tit. 2:13), meaning "appearance" or "public appearance."[6] In religious literature it may be used of the sudden manifestation of a hidden deity, often as a personal appearance (e.g., Diodorus Siculus 1.25.3 and 4.2.47.7, of the appearance of Apollo; Diodorus Siculus 3.62.10 of Dionysius; first century B.C.). In 1 Tim. 6:14 Paul (or arguably a Pauline disciple) associates the appearance of Christ with judgment; in Tit. 2:13 he speaks of "the manifestation of the glory of our great God and Savior Jesus Christ." The term *apokalypsis*, also used of the *Parousia* of Christ, primarily denotes "revelation" or "full disclosure," often of that which has been largely hidden until the last days. Paul sometimes uses it of "revelation," as opposed to human discovery (Gal. 1:12; 2:2; 2 Cor. 12:7); sometimes of the visible manifestation

---

4. Frederick W. Danker (ed.), *A Greek-English Lexicon,* known as BDAG (3rd ed. 2000), 780-81; cf. 773-74; and A. Oepke, *TDNT,* vol. 5, 861-65.

5. Karl P. Donfried, "The Imperial Cults and Political Conflict in 1 Thessalonians," in *Paul and Empire: Religion and Power in Roman Imperial Society,* ed. Richard Horsley (Harrisburg, PA: Trinity Press International, 1997), 215-23. On *Parousia* as apostolic presence, see Robert W. Funk, *Parables and Presence* (Philadelphia: Fortress, 1982), 81-110; cf. 67-80.

6. Danker, *A Greek-English Lexicon* (BDAG), 385-86.

of the children of God at the last day (Rom. 8:19); sometimes of the revelation of God's final, righteous, definitive judgment (Rom. 2:5). But he also uses it of the full and final revelation of Christ at his Return (1 Cor. 1:7; 2 Thess. 1:7). This accords with other writings in the New Testament.

Some writers mistakenly write off such terminology as mere survivals of Jewish apocalyptic thought which Paul eventually means to eliminate or at least to reinterpret. One such writer was R. H. Charles, who detected, he claimed, four stages of development in Paul, of which he saw as the first "the Pauline apocalypse" of the two Epistles to the Thessalonians.[7] This material included reference to a final apostasy, the Day of the Lord, and allegedly the Antichrist (though Paul does not explicitly write of such a figure under that name), the *Parousia*, final judgment, and the final resurrection. Charles then calls 1 Corinthians the "second period of development."[8] This material also insists on the importance of the *Parousia*, the Day of the Lord, judgment, and especially the resurrection of the dead. Allegedly Paul's writings take a turn with "the third period of development," namely, 2 Corinthians and Romans, a turn which C. H. Dodd more broadly replicates later.[9] Here, according to Charles, Paul has a conscious change of view, and now focuses on the universal spread of Christ's kingdom, almost as an emerging growth. He especially focuses on the different perspectives of 1 Corinthians 15 and 2 Cor. 5:1-8 on eschatology. Finally, he sees a fourth stage in Philippians, Colossians, and Ephesians, in which Christ becomes the principle of the present cohesion of the universe (Col. 1:17) and the goal of its development. Ulrich Simon has been heard daily to remark that it is a puzzle why Charles should have produced a massive book on eschatology (some 500 pages) when he found the subject so uncongenial and primitive.

Two death blows befell the claim of Charles, and by implication those of C. H. Dodd. One was a careful reappraisal of Paul's references to the Last Things by John Lowe; the other is a recent assessment of the value and importance of apocalyptic both for Paul throughout his life and for the New Testament as a whole.[10]

---

7. R. H. Charles, *A Critical History of the Doctrine of a Future Life in Israel, in Judaism, and in Christianity* (also entitled *Eschatology*; London: Black, 2nd ed. 1913), 438; cf. 438-45.

8. Charles, *A Critical History/Eschatology*, 445; cf. 445-54.

9. C. H. Dodd, "The Mind of Paul: I" (1933) and "The Mind of Paul: II" (1934), in *New Testament Studies* (Manchester: Manchester University Press, 1953), 67-127.

10. John Lowe, "An Examination of Attempts to Detect Developments in St. Paul's Theology," *JTS* 42 (1941): 129-42.

Dodd's comments on 1 Corinthians are surprising. Paul, he claimed, faced the troubles at Corinth "in a passion of resentment" and wrote a letter "full of caustic sarcasm and indignant self-vindication."[11] But by the time he wrote 2 Corinthians he wrote in a chastened and accepting mood. J. Lowe addresses the problem of the chronology of Paul's letters, especially the fact that all spring out of a period of his life when he had enjoyed time for thought and already had the maturity of an older man. Moreover, on the basis of most dating "there is a constant oscillation between the two emphases" of "now" and "not yet" of Pauline eschatology.[12] Philippians, for example, speaks of pressing on toward the goal (Phil. 3:12, 14) and of the future transformation of our bodies (Phil. 3:21). Galatians (which is early) uses apocalyptic language about "set us free from the present evil age" (Gal. 1:4); while Colossians (which is late) uses similar language: "He has rescued us [Greek, *errysato hēmas*] from the power of darkness and transferred us into the kingdom of his beloved Son" (Col. 1:13).

Whether or not we find Lowe's argument convincing (and I certainly do), the question about a positive or negative verdict on apocalyptic in Paul is far more important. Since about 1962, with Ernst Käsemann's decisive and influential essay "On the Subject of Primitive Christian Apocalyptic," published in his *New Testament Questions of Today,* the tide has turned against Charles, Dodd, and W. L. Knox.[13] He writes, "I speak of primitive Christian apocalyptic to denote the expectation of an imminent Parousia," with universal categories, and more emphasis on acts of God than on existential human plight (as with Bultmann).[14] Especially he rejects "eschatological enthusiasm" or an "over-present" eschatology at Corinth, in favor of a more realistic sharing of Christ's cross and resurrection in preparation for the Last Day. If we think that "complete redemption" has "already been effected, . . . [t]his is the root of all that has gone wrong at Corinth."[15] In the present period both bodily life and the struggle of the pilgrim are vital to understanding both justification by grace and obedience to Christ's

11. Dodd, "The Mind of Paul: I," in *New Testament Studies,* 80.

12. Lowe, "An Examination of Attempts," 132-34.

13. Ernst Käsemann, "On the Subject of Primitive Christian Apocalyptic," in his *New Testament Questions of Today* (London: S.C.M., 1969), 108-37.

14. Käsemann, "Primitive Christian Apocalyptic," in *New Testament Questions of Today,* 109, 113, and 117-24.

15. Käsemann, "Primitive Christian Apocalyptic," in *New Testament Questions of Today,* 126.

lordship.[16] Käsemann concludes, "I describe apocalyptic as the mother of Christian theology."[17]

Since Käsemann, Klaus Koch (1972), J. Christiaan Beker (1980 and 1982), J. L. Martyn (1967 and 1985), Alexandra R. Brown (1995 and 2000), and several others have rightly urged the positive importance of apocalyptic for Paul and for the New Testament.[18] Apocalyptic not only makes God and his purposes for the whole world central to Paul and the New Testament, rather than human existential attitudes or even "religion"; it also depicts the reign of Christ, which makes Paul seem less remote from Jesus' language about the kingdom, or reign, of God. It stresses God's "righteous judgment," which, we shall see in our chapter below on the Last Judgment, bears closely on the meaning of justification by grace through faith as more than a legal transaction, let alone a legal fiction. It takes seriously the forces of evil without falling into dualism, as we discuss in our chapter on "Hell." It concerns epistemology and revelation, as Martyn makes clear. It is "part of a larger discourse on the theme of knowing the 'glory of God.'"[19] It stresses the embodiedness of the Christian life. Alexandra Brown quotes some memorable comments from David Tracy. Tracy urges that it is "the genre most frequently employed to articulate the sense of expectancy of the Parousia."[20] Tracy also argues that it challenges any purely "private" understanding of the gospel, and gives scope to vindication of the poor and oppressed. Above all, it stresses resurrection and new creation, which constantly emerges as at the heart of our present subject.

16. Käsemann, "Primitive Christian Apocalyptic," in *New Testament Questions of Today,* 135.

17. Käsemann, "Primitive Christian Apocalyptic," in *New Testament Questions of Today,* 137.

18. Klaus Koch, *The Re-Discovery of Apocalyptic* (London: S.C.M., 1972); J. Christiaan Beker, *Paul the Apostle: The Triumph of God in Life and Thought* (Edinburgh: T&T Clark, 1980); J. Christiaan Beker, *Paul's Apocalyptic Gospel: The Coming Triumph of God* (Philadelphia: Fortress, 1982); J. Louis Martyn, "Epistemology at the Turn of the Ages," in *Christian History and Interpretation: Studies Presented to John Knox,* ed. W. R. Farmer et al. (Cambridge: Cambridge University Press, 1967), and J. Louis Martyn, "Apocalyptic Antinomianism in Paul's Letter to the Galatians," *NTS* 31 (1985): 410-24; Alexandra R. Brown, *The Cross and Human Transformation: Paul's Apocalyptic Word in 1 Corinthians* (Minneapolis: Fortress, 1995), and A. R. Brown, "Paul and the Parousia," in John T. Carroll with Alexandra Brown and J. S. Siker, *The Return of Jesus in Early Christianity* (Peabody, MA: Hendrickson, 2000), 47-76. The long subtitle of Koch's book is *A Polemical Work on a Neglected Area of Biblical Studies and Its Damaging Effects on Theology and Philosophy.*

19. Brown, *The Cross and Human Transformation,* 8; cf. 8-12.

20. David Tracy, *The Analogical Imagination* (New York: Crossroad, 1981), 265.

6.2. Further Questions on Paul's Teaching

We must consider several further questions in Paul's work on the Return of Christ. First, does his phrase, "We who are left," imply his belief in the Coming of Christ in his own generation? Second, what are the pastoral dimensions of Paul's theology of the Return of Christ?

There can be no doubt that the vast majority of twentieth- and twenty-first-century commentators and New Testament specialists believe that Paul's utterance, "We who are left [Greek, *perileipomenoi*] until the coming of the Lord [Greek, *eis tēn parousian*]" (1 Thess. 4:15), implies that Paul thought that the *Parousia* would occur during his lifetime. Ernest Best comments, "This imminence is clear. . . . Judaism already had attached some importance to being in the generation of the End (Dan. 12:12-13; *4 Ezra* 13:24; *Ps. Sol.* 17:50). Many attempts have been made to evade what appears to be the plain meaning of the phrase. We have to reject outright any attempt to allegorize the words (cf. Origen), or to weaken their meaning (cf. Calvin)."[21] Similarly Earl J. Richard asserts, "Paul includes himself within the group that will survive until the end. . . . Paul, along with his contemporaries, believed in the imminent Parousia."[22] Abraham Malherbe uses almost exactly the same words. He writes, "Paul includes himself with those who will still be living at the Parousia."[23] In the early Church, however, and up to the very end of the nineteenth century, many held a contrary view. John Chrysostom (347-407) was one of the first to engage with the problem, arguing that "we" did not signify Paul himself, but "the faithful" who remain alive when the *Parousia* occurs. This might be "ten thousand years" away.[24]

It is doubtful whether sheer linguistic exegesis will entirely solve this problem, for it is a subsidiary point within the main pastoral point of the passage. On the other hand, the reception of the text over the centuries shows how many followed Chrysostom's view. Among these we may include Theodore of Mopsuestia (350-428), Rabanus Maurus (780-856), Thomas Aquinas (1225-74), John Calvin (1509-64), Johann Bengel (1687-

21. Ernest Best, *The First and Second Epistles to the Thessalonians* (London: Black, 1972), 195.

22. Earl J. Richard, *First and Second Thessalonians,* Sacra Pagina 11 (Collegeville, MN: Glazier/Liturgical Press, 1995 and 2007), 241.

23. Abraham J. Malherbe, *The Letters to the Thessalonians,* AB 328 (New Haven and London: Yale University Press, 2000 and 2004), 270.

24. John Chrysostom, "Homily 7 on 1 Thessalonians," in *NPNF,* ser. 1, vol. 13, 353.

1752), and others.[25] Rather than follow the blind alley of repetitive exegesis, we need to ask two questions raised by philosophers and linguisticians. If, indeed, "meaning as choice" is a universal maxim of linguisticians, what would Paul's choice of "those who remain" have implied, and what is the difference in logic between an explicit proposition and an implicit presupposition? First, the only alternative to "we" is "those" or "they" (third person). But this distances Paul from those Thessalonians about whom anxiety has been expressed, and it is no "dogmatic" argument to stress Paul's deliberate solidarity with those who have died before the *Parousia*. "We" places all believers in the same category, which is the very point of Paul's argument, as we shall see shortly. Second, the philosopher P. F. Strawson has clearly demonstrated that while a proposition or statement has an explicit truth-value, a presupposition has only a *conditional* truth-value, which may depend on varied circumstances or revision.[26] Strawson formulates a "theory of presuppositions" in contrast to propositions.[27] As I concluded in my commentary on 1 and 2 Thessalonians, "'We' shows *solidarity* with all Christians who are open to expect the *Parousia* at any moment; not *necessarily* (by logical necessity) those who firmly expect to be *alive* at the *Parousia*."[28]

The appeal to Strawson and logical theory may be unique to this book. But I am not alone among recent commentators in supporting the view of Chrysostom, Aquinas, Calvin, and others. The most important of these is Arthur L. Moore, who argues this case both in his commentary on 1 and 2 Thessalonians and in his detailed book on the *Parousia*.[29] Moore explains that the grief of the Thessalonians was not caused by the nonarrival of the

25. Theodore of Mopsuestia, *Commentarii in Epistolas B. Pauli*, vol. 2, ed. H. B. Swete (Cambridge: Cambridge University Press, 1880), 29; Rabanus Maurus, *Opera Omnia*, in *Patrologia Latina*, ed. J.-P. Migne, vol. 112, part 6, 555; Thomas Aquinas, *Commentary on 1 Thessalonians* (New York: Magi, 1969), 36; John Calvin, *Commentary on 1 Thessalonians* (Wheaton: Crossway/Good News, 1999), 49; and Johann Bengel, *Gnomon Novi Testamenti* (Stuttgart: Steinkopf, 1866), 801-2.

26. P. F. Strawson, *Individuals: An Essay in Descriptive Metaphysics* (London: Methuen, 1959), 190-92 and 199-204; and P. F. Strawson, *Introduction to Logical Theory* (London: Methuen, 1963), 175-79.

27. Strawson, *Individuals*, 201.

28. Anthony C. Thiselton, *1 and 2 Thessalonians through the Centuries* (Oxford: Blackwell-Wiley, 2011), 117-19.

29. Arthur L. Moore, *1 and 2 Thessalonians*, New Century Bible (London: Nelson, 1969), 69-71; and A. L. Moore, *The Parousia in the New Testament*, NovTSup 13 (Leiden: Brill, 1966), 108-10.

Parousia, but over whether Christian dead would experience the first festive phase of the *Parousia.* He adds, "Although Paul is not here speaking of the time of the *Parousia's* arrival, he does go on to discuss this in 5:1-11, and there he affirms explicitly that the *Parousia* will come suddenly, and all must watch (5:2ff.) and implies that 'we' (5:9:10) might either 'watch' *(grēgorōmen)* or 'sleep' *(katheudōmen);* i.e. the possibility is held out that Paul and his readers might live to the *Parousia* but also that they might die prior to it."[30]

All in all, Moore cites at least five distinct reasons for holding this view. For example, he claims that the composition of the group who are alive and are left remains open, and 2 Cor. 5:9 ("whether we are at home or away") and especially Phil. 1:23-24 ("I am hard pressed between the two . . . to depart and be with Christ . . . to remain in the flesh . . .") "still reckons with the dual possibility."[31] In his commentary Moore concludes (surely rightly) that the certainty of the idea supported by many recent scholars "arises more through its frequent assertion than its sound evidence."[32] Again he cites such references as 2 Cor. 5:9, Phil. 1:20-21, and Rom. 14:8 to underline that Paul remained open to two possibilities: either that the *Parousia* would come during his lifetime, or that it would not.

Yet Moore is not alone in putting forward this view among recent scholars. Joost Holleman considers the view that the Thessalonians did not expect any Christian to die before the *Parousia,* and rejects such a conclusion.[33] Béda Rigaux, whose commentary on 1 and 2 Thessalonians in French is still the most detailed and magisterial of works on these Epistles (750 pages), supports the view advocated later by Moore.[34] Ben Witherington also supports this view, arguing, "Paul did not know in advance when he would die," and that the timing or date of the *Parousia* would be unexpected.[35] Against most New Testament specialists, we find five who dissent: Rigaux (1956), Moore (1966 and 1969), Holleman (1996), Witherington (2006), and the present writer, not to mention the work by Strawson and other commentators, who include Leon Morris and Howard

---

30. Moore, *The Parousia in the New Testament,* 110.

31. Moore, *The Parousia in the New Testament,* 110.

32. Moore, *1 and 2 Thessalonians,* 70.

33. Joost Holleman, *Resurrection and Parousia,* NovTSup 84 (Leiden: Brill, 1996), 24.

34. Béda Rigaux, *Saint Paul: Les Épitres aux Thessaloniciens* (Paris: Gabalda, 1956), 538-39; cf. also 195-234.

35. Ben Witherington, *1 and 2 Thessalonians: A Socio-Rhetorical Commentary* (Grand Rapids: Eerdmans, 2006), 133-34.

Marshall, making seven, along with P. F. Strawson on logic and many specialists in linguistics who expound the key principles of meaning as choice, and of paradigmatic relations.[36]

Finally, at the end of this long section, we may summarize Paul's pastoral concern in stressing the *Parousia*. Broadly, in 1 and 2 Thessalonians it is to provide grounds of *hope*. In Galatians it assures believers of Christ's sovereign *liberation and vindication* over evil. In 1 Corinthians it is to remind Christians that they have *not yet arrived,* and that full redemption will be experienced in every way at the *Parousia* and resurrection. 2 Corinthians, Romans, and Philippians present a combination of all three elements.

1 Thessalonians, however, contains a comment on the dead in Christ and their status, and many claim also about a supposed "rapture." It is not necessary to assume that the deaths of believers before the *Parousia* caused shock and consternation. Nevertheless the Thessalonian Christians were anxious that those who died before Christ's return would miss out on any final triumphant event. Paul replies that they should not grieve, for "God will bring with him those who have died through Jesus" (1 Thess. 4:13-14), and the living and dead will share equally in the glorious events of the *Parousia* and resurrection. For Paul invokes the Lord's word "that we who are alive, who are left until the coming of the Lord, will by no means precede those who have died" (4:15). The emphasis in many of the major passages on the *Parousia* is that all Christians will be "gathered together," just as in a preliminary way the presence of Christ at the Eucharist or Lord's Supper similarly "gathers together" all believers (*Did.* 9:4; probably very early second century). This is probably the key point behind the spatial metaphor of "meet the Lord in the air" (4:17); both the living and the dead will meet in the resurrection between heaven and earth. To quote Caird again, there is "a curious interplay between the metaphorical and the literal" which should not be understood "with flat-footed literalness" (quoted above, nn. 2 and 3).

These quotations about metaphor also apply to some overly elaborate theories about "the rapture." Paul does say, as part of his imagery or metaphor of meeting, that "we . . . will be caught up in the clouds together with

---

36. Leon Morris, *The First and Second Epistles to the Thessalonians* (Grand Rapids: Eerdmans, 1959), 142, and I. Howard Marshall, *1 and 2 Thessalonians: A Commentary* (Vancouver: Regent College Publishing, 1983), 127-28. Cf. also John Lyons, *Introduction to Theoretical Linguistics* (Cambridge: Cambridge University Press, 1968), 70-81 and 400-443; and Stephen Ullmann, *Semantics: An Introduction to the Science of Meaning* (Oxford: Blackwell, 1967), and *The Principles of Semantics* (Oxford: Blackwell, 2nd ed. 1957 and 1963); and John Lyons, *Semantics* (2 vols.; Cambridge: Cambridge University Press, 1977).

them to meet the Lord" (4:17). The Church of England clergyman John Nelson Darby (1800-1882) provided the inspiration for a "Dispensationalist" approach which was popularized by the *Scofield Bible* (1909), which uses passages in Daniel and Revelation to elaborate notions of a "rapture" in accordance with certain supposed prophecy. The "rapture" becomes a physical ascent to heaven, and is associated with a theory known as "premillennialism." It is highly doubtful that Paul interpreted events (even the conversion of Israel) in this way, and as we have seen does not even mention "Antichrist," which bulks large in this theory. Paul is not describing a history of the world or of prophecy, or a spatio-physical cosmology, but simply a meeting together as one at the *Parousia*. In spite of their popular influence, such works as *The Late Great Planet Earth* are a distraction from the serious and scholarly study of Paul.[37]

As a tailpiece to our study of Paul we must explode the long-standing myth of Paul's alleged inconsistency about the timing of the Return of Christ. For the most part, he portrays the time as unknown. It will come as a surprise, "like a thief in the night" (1 Thess. 5:2). Yet certain events must precede the event. He writes, "That day will not come unless the rebellion comes first and the lawless one is revealed, the one destined for destruction" (2 Thess. 2:3). For those who doubt the Pauline authorship of 2 Thessalonians this may not cause a problem. But the arguments for its genuineness are convincing. The clue to resolving any inconsistency comes in 1 Thess. 5:3. Paul compares the coming of the *Parousia* to a pregnant woman's experience of labor pains. Of course the birth pains must come first; but this does not mean that exact date of the birth is always predictable. In fact, Paul derives the whole tradition of labor pains, signs, and surprise from the teaching of Jesus: "Keep alert, for you do not know when the time will come. . . . Keep awake" (Mark 13:33). "About that day or hour no one knows, neither the angels in heaven, nor the Son, but only the Father" (Mark 13:32).

6.3. The Teaching of Jesus and the Book of Acts

In the first three Gospels, we recall in section 1 of our chapter below on judgment, that many of the parables of Jesus point to an End-time. For ex-

---

37. Hal Lindsey, *The Late Great Planet Earth* (Grand Rapids: Zondervan, 1970). Cf. John F. Walvoord, *Armageddon: Oil and the Middle East* (Grand Rapids: Zondervan, 2nd ed. 1990), on one side; and Christopher Rowland and Judith Kovacs, *Revelation* (Oxford: Blackwell-Wiley, 2004), on the other side.

ample, the hidden will become manifest (Matt. 10:26); the poor will become rich (Luke 6:20); the hungry will be filled (Luke 6:21); the blind will receive their sight (Matt. 11:5); and so on. Jeremias provides many examples.[38] In the Parable of the Wheat among the Weeds (Matt. 13:24-30) and of the Seine Net which catches good and bad fish (Matt. 13:47-48), the whole logic depends on a time of hiddenness and ambiguity in the present as contrasted with a decisive "reversal" and openness in the future. There can be no doubt that the central teaching of Jesus looks to a decisive moment of vindication and sovereign intervention of God in the future.

But we have considered such material under the Last Judgment because the emphasis lies more upon vindication and truth, and less upon the Return of Christ as such. Certainly this will be a time when God's rule or "kingdom" will bring peace and liberation. The ministry of Jesus, the cross, and the resurrection bring victory over evil forces, but although that victory is decisive, it will not become complete and comprehensive until the end of time. Oscar Cullmann's now dated analogy of the difference between "D" day and "V" day in the Second World War is often invoked to illustrate this point.[39]

The most specific and explicit references to the Return of Christ occur in what are usually called the "apocalyptic" discourses of much of Mark 13, and parallels in Matthew 24 and Luke 21. What is often missed, however, is that not all of this material is about the *Parousia* or Return of Christ. The whole discourse is introduced with the rural Galilean disciples being stunned by the impressive nature of the temple buildings in Jerusalem: "Look, Teacher, what large stones and what large buildings!" "Then Jesus asked him, 'Do you see these great buildings? Not one stone will be left upon another; all will be thrown down.'" This was a clear allusion to the historical destruction of Jerusalem, which came about in A.D. 70. The end of Israel's "world," however, became intertwined with the prediction of Christ's coming and the end of "the world," as G. B. Caird and others have rightly pointed out.[40]

If we read through the whole of Mark 13:1-37, it quickly becomes apparent that Jesus intertwines *two* issues which may seem entirely distinct

38. Joachim Jeremias, *The Parables of Jesus* (London: S.C.M., 1963), 224-27 and 221-22.

39. Oscar Cullmann, *Christ and Time: The Primitive Conception of Time and History* (London: S.C.M., 1951), 39-49.

40. Caird, *The Language and Imagery of the Bible*, 265-68; cf. John T. Carroll (with Alexandra Brown et al.), *The Return of Jesus*, 9-15; G. R. Beasley-Murray, *Jesus and the Last Days* (Peabody, MA: Hendrickson, 1995).

to us, but were less clearly separate to the immediate audience: one concerns the historical fall of Jerusalem; the other has to do with the final Return of Christ. Clearly, for example, the section which begins "In those days . . . the sun will be darkened, and the moon shall not give its light, and the stars will be falling from heaven . . ." (Mark 13:24-27) refers to the final Coming of the Lord as Son of Man. These cosmic events seem to go beyond simply poetic imagery.[41] But the next passage from v. 28 to v. 32, which contains the famous saying, "This generation will not pass away until all these things have taken place" (13:30) (unless its original context was misplaced or different), seems to refer to the fall of Jerusalem or even possibly, some claim, to the resurrection of Christ or even to Pentecost. This wording is identical to the parallel passage in Matt. 24:32-35. R. T. France explains, "These verses consist of a collage of Old Testament apocalyptic language, which to modern ears sounds like a description of the 'parousia and the close of the age.' . . . Yet the events . . . are explicitly dated 'within this generation' (24:34), whereas the parousia cannot be so dated (24:36), and 24:27 has just explicitly distinguished the parousia from the events of the siege of Jerusalem."[42]

France is still more emphatic in his more recent commentary on the Greek text of Mark. If it were not for those who mistakenly think that Jesus is talking about the *Parousia* in Mark 13:30 and who therefore "got it wrong!" the language of this passage would be understood as a "clear, definite . . . straightforward statement" referring to historical events concerning the fall of Jerusalem.[43] France links this with earlier verses in the chapter. He writes, "The events described in vv. 14-22 [of Mark 13] are a description of the period of distress which will lead up to the fall of the city."[44] If it refers to something else, it would fail as an answer to the disciples' question. William Lane also believes that these verses (13:30-32) refer to the destruction of Jerusalem, with its Old Testament background of prophecy.[45]

The least that we can say is that these verses find "partial fulfillment"

41. See Morna D. Hooker, *The Gospel according to Saint Mark* (London: Black and Peabody, MA: Hendrickson, 1991), 318.

42. R. T. France, *Matthew* (Leicester: Inter-Varsity Press and Grand Rapids: Eerdmans, 1985), 343.

43. R. T. France, *The Gospel of Mark: A Commentary on the Greek Text*, NIGTC (Grand Rapids and Cambridge: Eerdmans and Carlisle: Paternoster, 2002), 538.

44. France, *The Gospel of Mark*, 538.

45. William L. Lane, *The Gospel according to Mark* (Grand Rapids: Eerdmans and London: Marshall, Morgan & Scott, 1974), 480.

in the reference to historical events and partial fulfillment in eschatol-ogy.[46] For Craig Evans the verses are "ambiguous," and for Charles Cranfield "paradoxical." Cranfield writes, "The Incarnation-Crucifixion-Resurrection-Ascension, on the one hand, and the Parousia, on the other, belong essentially together and are in a real sense one Event, one divine Act, held apart only by the mercy of God who desires to give men the op-portunity for faith and repentance."[47] It is not usual for a prophecy of the future to have more than one level of fulfillment, as in Revelation. When, however, we proceed to the next section, Mark 13:32-37, clearly "about that day or hour no one knows, neither the angels in heaven, nor the Son, but the Father . . ." (v. 32), we have moved entirely to the expectation of the *Parousia.* It returns to the central theme: "Keep awake, for you do not know when the master of the house will come" (13:33; cf. v. 37). "It is like a man going on a journey, when he leaves home and puts his slaves in charge" (13:34). We have noted that R. T. France finds these two themes both distinct and intertwined in the parallel discourse in Matt. 24:29-36. Luke offers a third parallel in Luke 21:25-33. The wording is similar in the three traditions. On the Luke passage Joel B. Green contrasts the "im-plicit" sign of the destruction of the temple with the "explicit" signs of the coming of the End. Green appeals to the term "fulfillments" and the Old Testament language concerning the Last Days as an example of "intertextuality." This uses "meaning-laden details for this eschatological portrait" drawn from a reservoir of scriptural texts.[48] Similarly Luke T. Johnson asserts that Jesus talks of both "the fall of the city" and "a glimpse at the last days of the Son of Man."[49]

The simile of a man going on a long journey also appears in the parables (Matt. 25:14-30; Mark 13:34; Luke 19:12-27). Other parables make a similar point about looking toward the End (the Tares among the Wheat, Matt. 13:24-30; the Seine Net, Matt. 13:47-48; perhaps the Man without a Wedding Garment, Matt. 22:11-14; the Burglar, Matt. 24:42-44; the Man in Charge of a Household, Matt. 24:45-51; the Ten Virgins, Matt. 25:1-13; and perhaps the Servant's Reward, Luke 17:7-10). Even if Jeremias can argue that some applied

46. Craig A. Evans, *Mark 8:27–16:20,* WBC 34B (Nashville: Nelson, 2001), 334-37.

47. C. E. B. Cranfield, *The Gospel according to Mark,* Cambridge Greek Testament (Cambridge: Cambridge University Press, 1963), 408.

48. Joel B. Green, *The Gospel of Luke,* NICNT (Grand Rapids and Cambridge: Eerd-mans, 1997), 739-40.

49. Luke T. Johnson, *The Gospel of Luke,* Sacra Pagina 3 (Collegeville, MN: Glazier/Li-turgical Press, 1991), 324.

originally to the ministry of Jesus, we cannot exclude a further reference to the *Parousia* from all of these. Moreover, in our later chapter on judgment, we include more "parables of reversal," which Jeremias explicitly categorizes under the theme "the consummation," when the hidden will be revealed, the hungry will be filled, and so on.[50] Matthew, incidentally, is the only Gospel to use the term "Parousia" (Matt. 24:3, 27, 37, 39), and he distinctively associates the Return of Christ with the Last Judgment (see below). Like Mark and Luke, he sees the public, climactic, and complete fulfillment of what began in the ministry and work of Jesus, namely, the public, sovereign reign (or kingdom) of God. All the Evangelists stress watchfulness; Matthew also especially stresses accountability, and is at home with apocalyptic language. Since he sees the cross and resurrection as apocalyptic and cosmic events, he sees even the crucifixion and resurrection in these terms (Matt. 27:45-53).

It is sometimes said that Luke is less "eschatological" than Matthew and perhaps Mark. It is true that he has greater interest than the others in the continuing history of the Church and the coming of the Holy Spirit. After all, it constitutes the second part of the two-part Luke-Acts. At the same time he retains such material as that of the nobleman who went to a distant country and gave his servants resources to do business "until I come back" (Luke 19:11-27), and he includes a parallel to the apocalyptic discourse of Matthew 24 and Mark 13 (Luke 21:5-36). Luke clearly refers to both the fall of Jerusalem (21:20-24) and to "signs in the sun, the moon, and the stars" when "They will see the Son of Man coming in a cloud with power and great glory" (21:27).

Stephen G. Wilson is among the most convincing of writers on Luke's eschatology. He identifies both a "delay strand" which takes account of the history of the Church and the delay of the *Parousia* and an "imminent expectation" strand.[51] Luke 18:8, "He will vindicate them speedily," and Luke 12:45-48, "If that slave says to himself, 'My master is delayed in coming,' . . ." are examples of the "imminent expectation" strand. Wilson concludes, "Both strands in Luke's eschatology are well attested. . . . Both strands are motivated essentially by practical, pastoral problems which faced Luke in the Church of his day. . . . By treading a deliberate path via media he both avoided and corrected two false extremes."[52]

50. Jeremias, *The Parables of Jesus,* 221-26.

51. S. G. Wilson, *The Gentiles and the Gentile Mission in Luke-Acts,* SNTSMS 23 (Cambridge: Cambridge University Press, 1973), 67-85.

52. Wilson, *The Gentiles and the Gentile Mission in Luke-Acts,* 85. Cf. also Carroll, *The Return of Jesus in Early Christianity,* 26-45.

Acts, as Carroll reminds us, has little or no mention of the *Parousia* after chapter 3, because its main purpose concerns the expansion of the Church. But Acts 1:11 asserts, "This Jesus, who was taken up from you into heaven, will come in the same way as you saw him go into heaven." Acts 1:7 forbids speculation about the time of this Return: "It is not for you to know the times or periods that the Father has set. . . ." Peter's sermon in Acts 2 uses apocalyptic imagery ("The sun shall be turned to darkness . . ."; 2:19-20) of the moment "before the coming of the Lord's great and glorious day" (Acts 2:20). In chapter 3 Peter speaks of Jesus as remaining "in heaven until the time of universal restoration" (Greek, *achri chronōn apokatastaseōs pantōn*, 3:21). Danker renders this: "until the time for restoring everything to perfection . . . or to their starting-points."[53]

6.4. Hebrews, John, and Revelation, and the Postbiblical Church

We must glance briefly at the two other major theological traditions of the New Testament, namely, Hebrews (which was not written by Paul) and John. The Epistle to the Hebrews is the only writing of the New Testament explicitly to speak of the "second" Coming of Christ, but it does so in the context of stressing the once-for-all (Greek, *hapax*) nature of the ministry, crucifixion, and resurrection of Christ: "Christ, having been offered once to bear the sins of many, will appear a second time . . . to save those who are eagerly waiting for him" (Heb. 9:28). Believers, Hebrews urges, are to meet together and encourage one another "all the more as you see the Day approaching" (Heb. 10:25).

Whereas Paul speaks of reconciliation, Hebrews speaks of "approach" or "access" to God through Christ as perfect High Priest and Sacrifice (e.g., Heb. 4:14-16, "since we have a great high priest who has passed into the heavens, Jesus, the Son of God, . . . let us approach the throne of grace with boldness. . . ." Hebrews sees the importance of "completion," whether it is need for the qualifications of Jesus Christ as High Priest and Sacrifice to be comprehensive and complete (Heb. 5:1–8:6; 9:11–10:18), or looking ahead to the completion of the history of salvation or salvation history (1:1–4:13). Christ is the "exact imprint of God's very being" (1:3) and surpasses even the ministry of prophets and angels (1:1-14; 2:5-18); he supersedes even the priestly and prophetic or mediatorial ministry of Moses (3:1-19); he espe-

---

53. F. W. Danker, *A Greek-English Lexicon* (BDAG), 112.

cially won for us the "rest" which Joshua (Greek, *Iēsous* or Jesus) could not provide when he led Israel to the Promised Land (4:1-11). Hebrews declares, "If Joshua had given them rest [Greek, *katepausen*], God would not speak later about another day. So, then, a Sabbath rest still remains for the people of God" (4:8-9).[54]

Hebrews emphasizes the many promises of God and responses of faith which are fulfilled in certain decisive ways in the work of Christ but which still look for "complete" fulfillment at the End, with the "second" Coming of Christ. Certainly in the Old Testament all believers "died in faith without having received the promises, but from a distance they saw and greeted them" (Heb. 11:13). They were "strangers and foreigners on the earth" (11:13), and sought a "homeland" (11:14). Christians enjoy fulfillments brought about by the work of Christ, but still must "run with perseverance the race that is set before us" (12:1). Now is a time of trials and discipline (12:4-11). But the pilgrim journey will end in victory. As C. K. Barrett comments, "The only true rest from work is to be sought and found in the completion and perfection of the work. . . . The rest . . . is the complete fulfilment of God's work."[55] Hence Barrett compares Hebrews with John Bunyan's *Pilgrim's Progress*, the story of Christian's journey from the City of Destruction to the Celestial City. The present Jerusalem is merely a copy of the heavenly Jerusalem which lies ahead: "Here we have no abiding city" (13:14). Ernst Käsemann, too, declares that this Epistle "calls to a way, the goal of which it points out by way of promise. . . . It follows that form of existence in time . . . that of wandering" or pilgrimage.[56]

The climax is the heavenly or eschatological temple and New Jerusalem which lies not so much above, as it would in Alexandrian thought, but ahead. Hebrews may use Platonic or Alexandrian terminology, but its thought is profoundly eschatological.

This provides a link with the book of Revelation, with its imagery of the New Jerusalem (Rev. 21:1-2). But Hebrews and especially Revelation emphasize the importance of the future end of the *Parousia* more than

---

54. H. W. Attridge, "Let Us Strive to Enter That Rest," *HTR* 73 (1980): 279-88; and Otfried Hofius, *Katapausis: Die Vorstellung vom endzeitlichen Ruheort in Hebräerbrief* (Tübingen: Mohr, 1970).

55. C. K. Barrett, "The Eschatology of the Epistle to the Hebrews," in *The Background of the New Testament and Its Eschatology,* ed. W. D. Davies and D. Daube, Studies in Honour of C. H. Dodd (Cambridge: Cambridge University Press, 1958), 371; cf. 363-93.

56. Ernst Käsemann, *The Wandering People of God: An Investigation of the Letter to the Hebrews* (Minneapolis: Augsburg, 1984), 19.

does the Gospel of John. It is generally accepted that John emphasizes the present: Christian believers receive eternal life now, in the present. This has often been called "realized eschatology." Yet this picture can be one-sided and overly simple. John twice uses the phrase "The hour comes and now is" (John 4:23; 5:25), and partly in 5:25 and fully in 5:28-29 declares, "The hour is coming when all who are in their graves will hear his voice and will come out — those who have done good, to the resurrection of life, and those who have done evil, to the resurrection of condemnation."

A number of New Testament specialists, including W. F. Howard, C. K. Barrett, and Raymond Brown, ensure the balance. Brown insists, "There are . . . passages in John which reflect a future element."[57] He cites John 5:28-29, which we have noted; 6:39-40, " . . . raise them up on the last day" (also repeated in 6:44 and 54, making four repetitions); and 12:48, " . . . on the last day . . . the word . . . will serve as judge." It remains true, however, that John includes little on the final *Parousia*. This shows not that it was unimportant, but that the degree of attention which it should occupy depends very much on pastoral needs and practical circumstances.

The book of Revelation presents a different picture. We shall address the question of its use of symbols, their Old Testament allusions, and the purpose and interpretation of the book in much fuller detail in Chapter 11. What is said here is provisional on further discussion in that later chapter. However, we may offer some preliminary comments. Much of Revelation draws on the language of the Old Testament and Jewish apocalyptic, which looks forward to the consummation of history. These allusions include mainly Ezekiel, but also Daniel, the Psalms, Isaiah, Zephaniah, and probably 2 *Esdras* (or 4 *Ezra*) and *Enoch* among postcanonical writings. It includes a vision of resurrection and judgment (Rev. 14:14–15:4; 16:1-21; 17:1–19:8); heavenly worship (Rev. 4:1–5:14), including the four living creatures (Rev. 4:6; 5:8; 6:1; cf. Ezek. 1:5-21); the new song (5:9); the four apocalyptic horsemen: the white horse of conquest (6:2); the red horse of violence (6:4); the black horse of famine and economic collapse (6:5); and the pale green horse of Death and Hades (6:8). These are discussed further in Chapter 11. The book then unfolds the seven seals and earthquakes, with cosmic disruption in the skies (6:12-17), trumpets and woes (8:13; 9:1-19), and the ministry of angels at the End-time (10:1–11:13; cf. 2:8–3:3). After all this cosmic revolution, there are further passages on the sovereignty of

---

57. Raymond Brown, *The Gospel according to John (I–XII)* (New York: Doubleday and London: Chapman, 1966), cxviii.

God and the final subduing of evil, including the Dragon and the beasts (12:3–13:18); and the "sealing" of those who belonged to God, called symbolically the one hundred and forty-four thousand. The number may symbolize completeness since elsewhere this is a vast number, which no one can calculate. We discuss this symbolism further in Chapter 11. The converse image is used of those who worship the beast and receive *his* mark of ownership on their foreheads (14:9-11). All this is to encourage "the endurance of the saints" (14:12), who are undergoing struggle and persecution.

Visions of the final state, a consolation in time of trial, are interdispersed with other material: "They will rest from their labors, for their deeds follow them" (Rev. 14:13). Some seek to restrict the message of Revelation to John's own time, and see virtually all of it in terms of resistance to the claims of Rome and the Imperial Cult and perhaps to any who oppressed the first-century Church, claiming a rival loyalty to that of Christ. This approach is generally known as "praeterist" interpretation. Others go to the opposite extreme, and see the book as a coded panorama of the history of the Church and the world with its struggles and difficulties, identifying the Antichrist with either the Pope, Mohammed, or any force of evil that opposes the "true" Church. This approach is said to derive in part from Nicholas of Lyra (d. 1340). But in line with the function of apocalyptic, many see it as a vision of the sovereignty of God that applies to every era of the Church, although also having partial fulfillment in the events of the first century. "Fallen, fallen, is Babylon the great!" is seen to refer to an oppressive pagan or secular power in which "the merchants of the earth have grown rich from the power of her luxury" (Rev. 18:2-3). "God has remembered her iniquities" (18:5), and "the merchants of the earth weep and mourn for her" (18:11). Robert Mounce discusses these various approaches, and we consider them further, with some assessment, in Chapter 11.[58]

When the worshipping multitude cries, "Hallelujah! Salvation and glory and power to our God, for his judgments are true and just" (Rev. 19:1-2), the heavenly host celebrate the ultimate victory of God in Christ. The climax of that act of vindication comes in 20:1–22:5. Cycles of events occur in symbolic form rather than a single, linear history. The book concludes with an assurance about the Return of Christ: "See, I am coming soon; my reward is with me" (Rev. 22:12). The "reward" will be that Christ's

---

58. Robert H. Mounce, *The Book of Revelation* (Grand Rapids: Eerdmans and London: Marshall, Morgan & Scott, 1977), 39-45.

sovereign presence and coming will put everything right. The suffering and oppressed will be vindicated, and God's sovereignty will be public and absolute.

Apocalyptic reveals that things are not what they seem: the Beast seems to be victorious, but in fact God is sovereign. "The entire universe will have to acknowledge the righteous character of all God's sentences."[59] Many of the symbols and visions, Hendriksen rightly claims, are not in chronological sequence but in repetitive cycles. Much of the symbolism is not code, but transparently reflects their use in the Old Testament. Gog and Magog, for example (20:7-10), comes from Ezekiel. Even in his work on the notorious chapter 20, Hendriksen carefully demonstrates the *parallels* between chapter 20 and 12:5-12; 11:2-6; 11:17-18; and 14:14-20.[60] He writes, "It should be clear immediately to anyone who carefully reads Revelation 20 that the 'thousand years' precede the second coming of our Lord."[61] The people of God sigh at the forces of oppression, asking "Will this condition never change?" The partial but decisive fall of Satan came with the work of Christ: "I beheld Satan falling as lightning from heaven" (Luke 10:17-18). Hence, "the binding of Satan . . . begins with that first coming. . . . The thousand years indicates that throughout this present gospel age the devil's influence on earth is curtailed. . . . A dog securely bound with a long and heavy chain can do great damage within the circle of his imprisonment. Outside that circle, however, the animal can do no damage."[62]

The purpose of this chapter is not to expound Revelation as such, but to show the significance of Christ's Return within it. We shall revisit Revelation again in Chapter 11. Here the primary point is that the *Parousia* vindicates the sovereignty of God publicly and absolutely. The literature on Revelation is vast, but we select some sources below.[63] In the light of these studies and John's use of Old Testament imagery, we have cause to quote

---

59. William Hendriksen, *More than Conquerors: An Interpretation of the Book of Revelation* (Grand Rapids: Baker and London: Tyndale, 1962 [1940]), 160.

60. Hendriksen, *More than Conquerors*, 184-85 and 186-95.

61. Hendriksen, *More than Conquerors*, 185.

62. Hendriksen, *More than Conquerors*, 188 and 190.

63. George B. Caird, *The Revelation of St. John the Divine* (London: Black, 1966); Mounce, *The Book of Revelation*; G. K. Beale, *The Book of Revelation: A Commentary on the Greek Text*, NIGTC (Grand Rapids: Eerdmans and Carlisle: Paternoster, 1999); David E. Aune, *Revelation 1–5, 6–16, and 17–22*, WBC (3 vols.; Nashville: Nelson, 1998); and J. Estlin Carpenter, *The Johannine Writings: A Study of the Apocalypse and the Four Gospels* (London: Constable, 1927).

Caird's key comment that to compile neatly packaged catalogues of Revelation's symbols "is to unweave the rainbow."[64]

The importance of the hope of the *Parousia* continued after the New Testament period. At the beginning of the second century it appears in the *Didachē*. In its Eucharistic prayer (which we note again) the writer asks God to "gather [his people] together . . . from the four winds to your kingdom. . . . For yours is the power and glory forever. Let grace come, and let this world pass away. . . . Maranatha" (*Did.* 10:5-6). It also draws the main lesson from the hope of the *Parousia,* which we find in Jesus and in Paul: "Watch [Greek, *grēgoreite,* as in the New Testament] over your life; let your lamps be not quenched . . . be ready [Greek, *hetoimoi*]; for you know not the hour at which our Lord comes" (*Did.* 16:1). *1 Clement* (A.D. 96) warns its readers against skepticism concerning the Return of Christ, as in the case of the false teachers against whom 2 Peter writes (2 Pet. 3:4-5). It quotes from Isa. 13:22 and Mal. 3:1: "He shall come quickly and shall not tarry, and the Lord shall come suddenly to his temple" (*1 Clem.* 23:5).

The *Epistle of Barnabas,* probably in the second century, seems to be among the first to speculate that "the Lord will make an end of [Greek, *syntelesei*] everything in six thousand years, for a day with him means a thousand years" (*Barn.* 15:4). He argues his point from the six "days" of creation, and Irenaeus later takes up this idea. The early Christian apologist Justin Martyr (c. 100–c. 165) speaks explicitly of "two advents of Christ" (*Apology* 1.52). Irenaeus (c. 130–c. 200), whom many call the first biblical theologian of the Church, and who grew up in the East but later became presbyter at Lyons in the West, clearly speaks also of "the two advents . . . the second in which he will come in the clouds, bringing the Day . . . and smiting the earth" (*Against Heresies* 4.32.1).

The hope of the *Parousia* is now on a firm footing. Tertullian (c. 160–c. 235) stresses it especially in connection with the resurrection of the body, the judgment of the world, and the new creation. He quotes much of 1 Thess. 4:13-18 almost verbatim, as well as 1 Thess. 1:9-10, "to wait for his Son from heaven" (Tertullian, *On the Resurrection of the Flesh* 4; or *ANF,* vol. 3, 562; and *Against Marcion* 5.15 and 20; or *ANF,* vol. 3, 462 and 473; and *On Prayer* 29; or *ANF,* vol. 3, 691). Origen (c. 185-253) similarly quotes much of 1 Thess. 4:13-17 (Origen, *Against Celsius* 2.65 and 5.17; *ANF,* vol. 4, 458 and 550). Lactantius (c. 250–c. 325) alludes to 1 Thess. 4:14, 16, in *The Divine Institutes* 2.13 (*ANF,* vol. 7, 61).

64. Caird, *The Revelation of St. John,* 25.

We now enter the period of the ecumenical creeds and councils. The Return of Christ becomes a fixed article of faith in them, with explicit comments from Basil the Great (330-75), Cyril of Jerusalem (315-87), Gregory of Nazianzus (328-90), Ambrose (338-97), Ambrosiaster (c. 380), John Chrysostom (c. 347-407), Jerome (c. 345-420), and of course Augustine (354-430; *City of God* 20:20; *NPNF,* ser. 1, vol. 2, 439). It is firmly established in the medieval and Reformation periods, and up to the late nineteenth century. Thereafter it becomes more controversial among some, but not in Church formularies. In official Church documents it remains an integral part of "the Last Things," together with resurrection and the Last Judgment.

CHAPTER 7

The Resurrection of the Dead

7.1. Do Our Conclusions Represent a New or Distinctive Approach?

The proportion of material in this particular chapter which represents a genuinely "new" approach may perhaps be less than in some, but this is not the case if "new" is taken to mean what is widely ignored and requires more significant rediscovery. For example, it is crucial to Paul's argument not only in 1 Corinthians 15 but also in Rom. 4:16-25, 2 Cor. 1:9 and 5:1-10, and 1 Thess. 4:14-17 that resurrection from the dead constitutes a sheer *gift* of *God's sovereign, creative grace,* and not the fruition of latent capacities in the human soul.[1] The view that immortality derives merely from human capacities has more in common with Plato and with other religions than with the New Testament and its teachings on the foundations of the resurrection of Christ (e.g., Rom. 8:11). In a sovereign creative act *God raised Christ,* and will in the future raise those who share in Christ's death and resurrection.

Yet some aspects of this chapter go further to establish a "new" approach. Provisionally we may select four features which we discuss fully below, to which a fifth generally accepted feature is added. (1) If the resurrection, as we believe, is initiated by *God* as a gift of grace and sustained through the agency of Christ and the *Holy Spirit,* we must exclude any notion of resurrection existence as *static* perfection. It will reflect the character of the *living, ongoing God,* and of the dynamic, ever fresh movements of

1. Cf. Jürgen Moltmann, *Theology of Hope* (London: S.C.M., 1967), 165-72 and 190-216; and Jürgen Moltmann, *The Coming of God: Christian Eschatology* (London: S.C.M., 1996), 25-29.

the Holy Spirit. We shall not be like those forever "frozen" in the last shot of a film or movie. Believers will not be "bored" with "perfection," let alone with worship, for this and other reasons.

(2) Too often the question of the resurrection of the "body" becomes posed as a debate about "immaterial" or "*physical*" existence. This is almost marginal to Paul's concerns. In effect, only Ernst Käsemann seems to have seen that the real point of *bodiliness* is *not its physicality as such* (even if this is usually included) but the mode of God's creation of us, first in the world, as those who count as precious individuals, each with his or her own unique *identity* and ability to *communicate* with others and to be *recognizable* as the people we are.[2] Again, in contrast to adherents of many Eastern religions, Christian believers do not hold that they will be assimilated with some divine "All," but God will raise them as the individuals they are. The resurrection will vindicate belief in the preciousness of each person to God.

(3) On the other hand, the resurrection is not just an individual-centered event. When we consider the Coming of Christ, or *Parousia,* we shall note that whereas today people think of postmortal existence largely in individualist terms, in the New Testament age "the Last Things" denoted the three last *corporate and cosmic* events of the resurrection, the *Parousia,* and the Last Judgment. The Deist assumption that God has created the world, only to view it thereafter idly from a distance, is a wicked travesty of the Bible's portrait of God in Christ. By choosing to create the world, God has chosen to go forth out of himself to engage with, and commune with, his creatures in love. He wills to form relationships with humankind, and wills that humans should relate to one another. Why should we imagine that this relationality will not characterize the resurrection state? Closeness with God may take most of our attention, but will human relationships suddenly be excluded? Most of the promises of resurrection appear with the plural: "*We* will all be changed" (1 Cor. 15:51).

(4) Our three considerations above shed new light on the notion of a "*spiritual body,*" or better, "Spiritual body" (1 Cor. 15:44). This may or may not be "immaterial"; this is the Greek, or Platonic, way of using the word *spiritual.* In the biblical writings the adjective *spiritual* (Greek, *pneumatikos*) nearly always denotes the quality of being animated, led, and sanctified by the Holy Spirit. Since Paul has already specifically defined

2. Ernst Käsemann, *New Testament Questions of Today* (London: S.C.M., 1969), 135; cf. Moltmann, *The Coming of God,* 126-28.

spiritual in this way several times in 1 Corinthians (1 Cor. 3:1-4), and since he clearly sees the Holy Spirit as the causal agent of the resurrection (Rom. 8:11), we must conclude that he is using the term "spiritual body" (1 Cor. 15:44) in exactly this sense. Since the Holy Spirit witnesses to Christ (1 Cor. 12:3), this also suggests how believers might be without sin in the postresurrection state, and also choose freely to be so, and underlines the dynamic, progressive character of the postresurrection state.

(5) The fifth point is not "new," but it should be included in our thinking. Resurrection, we shall see, is always marked by three features: (i) *contrast* (1 Cor. 15:36; i.e., with the "old" body); (ii) *continuity* (1 Cor. 15:49; i.e., involving accountability, identity, recognition, and so on); and (iii) *transformation* (1 Cor. 15:51-54; i.e., involving full openness to the Holy Spirit). The reason why this emphasis is not "new" is that it constitutes an inescapable conclusion from a sound exegesis of 1 Corinthians 15 and other passages.

Paul argues that the basis of belief in the resurrection is twofold: belief in testimony to the resurrection of Christ as the "firstfruits" of the resurrection of believers (1 Cor. 15:1-34); and belief in the Creator God, who showed his power and wisdom in creating diverse species, each for a particular environment. In the case of the Gospel accounts, we find a strange ambiguity about the identity and recognizability of Jesus Christ. In Luke 24:16 the two disciples who were going to Emmaus "were kept from recognizing him" during their extended walk and conversation, and even while Jesus expounded the Scriptures to them (Luke 24:17-30). But as soon as Jesus "took bread, blessed [God], and gave it to them," then "their eyes were opened, and they recognized him" (24:30-31). In the Upper Room or elsewhere, Jesus "stood among" his disciples, and at first they imagined that they had seen a ghost. But then he "showed them his hands and his feet," and they recognized him (24:37-40). He ate broiled fish, expounded the Scriptures, and walked with them to Bethany (vv. 41-50). He was sufficiently in recognizable bodily form to begin an ascent to heaven, in their sight, but sufficiently different to ascend "into heaven" (v. 51).

The Johannine account bears the same two features of recognizable identity or continuity, and contrast or difference. Mary at first thought that Jesus was the gardener: "she saw Jesus standing there, but she did not know that it was Jesus . . . supposing him to be the gardener" (John 20:14-15). He even spoke to her, but it was only when he said, "Mary!" that she fully recognized him as Jesus, her Teacher. Similarly, when the disciples were hiding behind locked doors (20:19), Jesus entered the locked room, and, again, "showed them his hands and his side. . . . Then the disciples rejoiced when they saw the Lord" (20:20). Thomas later joined the other disciples, and Jesus again passed through locked doors (20:26). When he had placed his finger on the nailprints of the hands and side of Jesus, Thomas no longer doubted, but fully recognized "My Lord and my God" (20:27-29).

Matthew and Mark telescope the scene, but it has the same outcome (Matt. 28:4-10, 16-18; Mark 16:1-8). The "longer ending" of Mark, which is a textual variant, includes the appearance to Mary Magdalene (Mark 16:9-11) and the appearance of Jesus "in another form" (16:12; cf. 16:14-20).

We cannot doubt that according to all four Evangelists Jesus was identifiable and recognizable, and according to Paul "the firstfruits" (Greek, *aparchē*, or first *sample* of the harvest sheaves) to be raised (1 Cor. 15:20).[3] But Christ represents a sample of the resurrected mode of existence *as it appears in this world*. The raised body of Christ does not represent the raised mode of existence *comprehensively*. But the difference represents both continuity and contrast. Few would dispute this fifth feature. But very recently Jonathan Moo has endeavored to apply this principle to the renewal and transformation of the material creation. He repeats Jürgen Moltmann's well-known claim that "there is no fellowship with Christ without fellowship with the earth: love for Christ and hope for him embrace love and hope for the earth."[4] But Moo offers no crudely materialist hope for the earth, as some millennialists may portray it. Paul, he argues, formulates a continuity between present creation and the future new creation in Romans 8. Although "the same creation . . . is now groaning" until it is released from bondage, when it is "renewed" there will be a contrast with the old.[5] In addition to Rom. 8:18-25, Moo cites 2 Pet. 3:5-13 and Revelation 21–22 as pointing in the same direction. We must "care for the earth," he argues, because it will be transformed but not destroyed.[6]

The second basis on which belief in the resurrection is urged also suggests continuity and contrast. In 1 Cor. 15:35-44 Paul turns to an argument from creation, or from God's creative power. He declares, "What you sow does not come to life unless it dies" (15:36). He adds, "As for what you sow, you do not sow the body that is to be" (v. 37). Paul sees *contrast* here. But

---

3. On *aparchē*, see Frederick W. Danker, *A Greek-English Lexicon* (BDAG), 98; with Rev. 14:4 and 2 Thess. 2:13, "the emphasis is less on chronological sequence than on quality" (98).

4. Moltmann, *The Coming of God*, 279.

5. Jonathan Moo, "Continuity, Discontinuity, and Hope," *Tyndale Bulletin* 61, no. 1 (2010): 29; cf. 21-44.

6. Moo, "Continuity, Discontinuity, and Hope," 44.

God gives "to each kind of seed its own body" (v. 38). There are also *continuity* and *identity*. If we buy a particular seed or bulb at the nursery, we expect *that* seed or bulb to be transformed into a flower. But there is also a contrast: we do not expect that bulb to reappear on the top of its stalk. The point of Paul's language about God's multi-faceted skill in creation is God's capacity to transform each entity into a form which is suitable or appropriate for its environment. If God could create "bodies" for land, air, water, or space (animals, birds, fish, and stars), God can surely create recognizable forms appropriate for entering heaven. Thus Paul declares "a mystery! We . . . will all be changed, in a moment, . . . at the last trumpet" (1 Cor. 15:51-52). We must return, however, to look at Paul's chapter and our four "new" points in more detail.

7.2. An Exegesis and Exposition of 1 Corinthians 15

As with the whole of this study of "the Last Things," the promise of God is the fundamental presupposition of 1 Corinthians 15. I am taking care to avoid repeating what I have already said in my 150 pages or so on the resurrection in the chapter in my larger commentary on 1 Corinthians. I cannot refrain, however, from repeating Karl Barth's comment that 1 Corinthians 15 sheds light on the whole Epistle, and exhibits the sheer grace or gift of the sovereign God on the basis of promise.[7] H. Moxnes and J. Moltmann compared the creative gift of the resurrection with God's calling into being things that are not in Rom. 4:15, 17.[8]

(1) 1 Cor. 15:1-11 embodies the apostolic tradition which goes back earlier than Paul, and which Paul received and transmitted as authentic, agreed, common apostolic teaching, which was not peculiar to Paul (15:1-3).[9] "In accordance with the scriptures" (v. 3) refers not to some single verse, but to the pattern of divine vindication of suffering in the Old Testament. These first eleven verses embody part of the premise or *narratio* on which the remainder of the chapter is based, namely, that God raised

7. Karl Barth, *The Resurrection of the Dead* (London: Hodder & Stoughton, 1933), 11; cf. Anthony C. Thiselton, *The First Epistle to the Corinthians,* NIGTC (Grand Rapids: Eerdmans and Carlisle: Paternoster, 2000), 1169-1313.

8. H. Moxnes, *Theology in Conflict: Studies of Paul's Understanding of God in Romans,* NovTSup 53 (Leiden: Brill, 1980), 231-82; and Moltmann, *Theology of Hope,* 145.

9. See A. Eriksson, *Traditions as Rhetorical Proof: Pauline Argumentation in 1 Corinthians* (Stockholm: Almqvist & Wiksell, 1998), 86-97 and 232-78.

Christ, to which Paul cites various witnesses. Hence, as we read in Rom. 8:11, "He who raised Christ from the dead will give life to your mortal bodies also." Without the sovereign power and agency of God through the Holy Spirit, the Pauline logic is destroyed. Only if God raised Christ will he also raise all who are "in Christ." Only on this basis does God "*give* [Greek, *didōsin*] it a body as he wills" (1 Cor. 15:38; cf. Rom. 4:16-25). But "as he wills" (NRSV) is strictly an aorist tense or mode (Greek, *ēthelēsen*) signifying God's past decree in creation. Here NIV's "as he has determined" seems better. Kennedy and Edwards, both older but perceptive writers, retain the stress on God's sovereignty.[10] Barth repeats the point.[11]

The most controversial clause may be v. 5, "that he appeared" (NRSV, REB, NJB, NIV; Greek, *ōphthē*). The AV/KJV has "was seen," and this is indeed the aorist passive of *horaō*, "I see." Danker follows Grimm-Thayer in giving as the first meaning of this verb "to perceive by the eye, catch sight of." But he places 1 Cor. 15:5-8 under the heading "passive in the active sense, become visible, appear," as when God "appeared" to Abraham (Gen. 12:7; 17:1).[12] But Willi Marxsen and Hans Conzelmann are more comfortable with the rendering "to see with the mind," as when one has wrestled with a problem, and exclaims, "I see!"[13] On the other hand, Wolfhart Pannenberg more recently asserts that the tradition, found in 15:5, is *"decisive for confidence in the facticity of the resurrection of Jesus,"* including *"the primitive Christian testimonies to the appearances of the risen Lord . . . along with the discovery of the empty tomb of Jesus in Jerusalem"* (his italics).[14] Pannenberg rightly insists that we consider the "appearances" tradition alongside the "empty tomb" tradition. He argues that we "cannot question the age of the account from a man who knew personally the witnesses cited, or most of them."[15] He still speaks of a "factual core" in the accounts.[16] We should not

---

10. H. A. A. Kennedy, *St. Paul's Conception of the Last Things* (London: Hodder & Stoughton, 1904), 243; T. C. Edwards, *A Commentary on the First Epistle to the Corinthians: Greek Text* (London: Hodder & Stoughton, 1885), 434.

11. Barth, *Resurrection of the Dead*, 18.

12. F. W. Danker, *A Greek-English Lexicon* (BDAG), 719; cf. Thiselton, *The First Epistle*, 1197-1205.

13. W. Marxsen, *The Resurrection of Jesus of Nazareth* (Philadelphia: Fortress, 1970), 72 and 81; and Hans Conzelmann, "On the Analysis of the Confessional Formula in 1 Cor. 15:3-5," *Interpretation* 20 (1966): 15-25.

14. W. Pannenberg, *Systematic Theology* (3 vols.; Grand Rapids: Eerdmans and Edinburgh: T&T Clark, 1991, 1994, and 1998), vol. 2, 352-53.

15. Pannenberg, *Systematic Theology*, vol. 2, 353.

16. Pannenberg, *Systematic Theology*, vol. 2, 354.

underrate visionary experiences, such as that of Acts 9:3 or perhaps Gal. 1:16, but they are more than this. The "empty tomb" tradition is in process of being taken much more seriously than it used to be. The appearance to Peter and to the Twelve takes place in the public domain.

The original apostolic tradition which Paul receives places the death and burial of Jesus alongside the resurrection as an early common creed (1 Cor. 15:3-4). The resurrection is more than a source of faith; on the contrary, as a public event it gives rise to faith. Walter Künneth, like Pannenberg, stresses God's action in Christ in the resurrection.[17] N. T. Wright similarly declares, "Not only was Jesus' resurrection in principle a datable event. . . . It was always something that took place, not immediately upon his death, but a short interval thereafter."[18] The time lag of the "three days" is significant for this. The use of *ōphthē*, Wright concedes, is varied and of itself indecisive, but the many witnesses must be taken seriously.[19] Paul insists that of the witnesses "most [Greek, *hoi pleiones*] . . . are still alive" (v. 6). Richard Hays observes that the gallery of witnesses shows that for Paul the resurrection was not "some sort of ineffable truth beyond history; rather it was an event . . . for which historical eyewitness testimony was readily available."[20] E.-B. Allo explicitly argues that 1 Cor. 15:6 refers to the same observable events as Matt. 28:16-20.[21] In 15:8 Paul considers his own witness to the raised Christ as authentic (cf. 1 Cor. 9:1), but as "a prematurely born dead fetus" whom God brought to life (Greek, *ektrōma*).[22] It is no accident that Paul concludes this first section on the basis of resurrection with "By the grace of God I am what I am . . . not I, but the grace of God" (15:10). Grace is also the basis of resurrection.

(2) The second section, 15:12-34, concerns the dreadful consequences of denying the resurrection. In rhetorical terms, a first *Refutatio* and *Confirmatio* follow the *Narratio*. Some have seen this section as also "deliberative rhetoric," appealing to good or bad outcomes and consequences. If

---

17. W. Künneth, *The Theology of the Resurrection* (London: S.C.M., 1965), 117; cf. 97 and 111-49.

18. N. T. Wright, *The Resurrection of the Son of God* (London: S.P.C.K., 2003), 322.

19. Wright, *The Resurrection*, 323-26.

20. Richard B. Hays, *First Corinthians* (Louisville: John Knox, 1997), 257.

21. E.-B. Allo, *Saint Paul: Première Épitre aux Corinthiens* (Paris: Gabalda, 2nd ed. 1956), 396; cf. 394-98.

22. Johannes Munck, "Paulus Tanquam Abortivus, 1 Cor. 15:8," in *New Testament Essays: Studies in Memory of T. W. Manson*, ed. A. J. B. Higgins (Manchester: Manchester University Press, 1959), 180; cf. 180-95.

resurrection were to be denied in principle, how could Christ himself have been raised? But if Christ had not been raised, the consequences are dire: (a) apostolic proclamation is in vain (v. 14); (b) the apostles have misrepresented God (v. 15); (c) the faith of Christians is futile (v. 17a); (d) Christians are still in bondage to sin (v. 17b); and finally (e) Christians are pitiful people (v. 19).

But this leads on to the second part of section two, vv. 20-34, the first *Confirmatio*, in positive terms, of the resurrection. In reality, Christ has been raised (v. 20a). Moreover, he is the "firstfruits" [Greek, *aparchē*] of the harvest of the dead" (v. 20b). We have already considered the word "firstfruits." Hamilton calls it "the beginning of the harvest proper which will occur in the new creation of the future age."[23] M. C. de Boer considers this verse pivotal for the whole chapter.[24] It is more than a sample of the future crop to come; it constitutes a *pledge or promise* of the remainder of the harvest, to which it will be *similar in kind*. Holleman calls it "a representation of the rest."[25]

Paul repeats the metaphor of firstfruits in 15:23. Each (Christ, order 1; and those in Christ, order 2) "in his own order: Christ the firstfruits, then at his coming those who belong to Christ" (v. 23). This declaration follows Paul's assertion, "As all die in Adam, so all will be made alive in Christ" (v. 22). Without v. 23, many might assume that the "making alive" occurred when they became Christians. But v. 23 clarifies the point that (1) there is a "making alive" when a believer becomes united with Christ; and (2) there will be a "making alive" in the general resurrection from the dead at the Coming of Christ in the future. The brief Adam-Christ section (vv. 21-23) underlines the contrast between the corporeity "in Adam," which faces only death; and the corporeity or community "in Christ," for whom the destiny is both death and resurrection. The passage runs parallel with Rom. 5:12-21, where again typology between Adam and Christ controls the argument. We have corporate solidarity either with Adam or with Christ.

The next subsection from 1 Cor. 15:24 to 15:28 includes an apocalyptic perspective on the transference of the reign of God from that of the intermediate messianic reign on God's behalf to Christ's complete victory over

---

23. N. Q. Hamilton, *The Holy Spirit and Eschatology in Paul*, SJT Occasional Paper 6 (Edinburgh: Oliver & Boyd, 1957), 19; cf. 19-25.

24. M. C. De Boer, *The Defeat of Death: Apocalyptic Eschatology in 1 Corinthians 15 and Romans 5* (Sheffield: J.S.O.T. Press, 1988), 109.

25. J. Holleman, *Resurrection and Parousia: A Traditio-Historical Study of Paul's Eschatology in 1 Corinthians 15*, NovTSup 84 (Leiden: Brill, 1996), 49.

evil forces and death (vv. 25-27). The passage is expounded in particular by Christiaan Beker, de Boer, and Holleman, who see apocalyptic as central to Paul's thought.[26] In *4 Ezra*, similarly, death is the "all-embracing reality of the aeon," while in *2 Baruch* "the world is determined by a sentence of death."[27] But we can say only that these ideas are in the air in Jewish apocalyptic, because these two writings should probably be dated after Paul. The final verse, v. 28, seems to subordinate Christ ultimately to God, when he hands back his reign, and God will be "all in all." But this is doubtless because hellenistic cults or worship groups tended to focus on their "Lord," but perhaps to give more superficial attention to a more remote "God." James Moffatt and Neil Richardson detect such a tendency, especially in the "Christ group" of 1 Cor. 1:12.[28] Death in v. 26 is described as "the last enemy to be destroyed." Christians still die before the End, but thereafter Christ's victory over death becomes apparent and decisive. Present death in no way calls resurrection into question.

Indeed, the third section of Part 2 expounds the necessity for death before resurrection. First it alludes to baptism on behalf of those who are now dead (15:29). This verse is so obscure that F. Godet counts thirty explanations, and Rudolf Schnackenburg even more.[29] But, depending on our view of the scope of the preposition *on behalf of* (NRSV; Greek, *hyper*), this verse probably alludes to pleas of either a close relative or an intimate friend, for the person concerned to become a Christian, that he or she may be raised with Christ, and perhaps join them in the resurrection event. Paul's attitude to the sacraments excludes the notion of "vicarious baptism" in spite of those who advocate it.[30]

Paul then explains that he would not constantly risk death, if it were not the case that resurrection would follow. He is "in danger every hour" (v. 30); he "dies every day" (v. 31); he fought with wild beasts at Ephesus (v. 32a). Without a firm belief in the resurrection, he may as well live the

---

26. J. C. Beker, *Paul the Apostle* (Edinburgh: T&T Clark, 1980), 100; cf. 135-81; de Boer, *Defeat of Death,* 32-35; Holleman, *Resurrection and Parousia,* 53.

27. De Boer, *Defeat of Death,* 75 and 81.

28. James Moffatt, *The First Epistle of Paul to the Corinthians,* Moffatt Commentary (London: Hodder & Stoughton, 1938), 250; and Neil Richardson, *Paul's Language about God,* JSNTSup 99 (Sheffield: Sheffield Academic Press, 1994), 114-19; cf. Larry W. Hurtado, *One God, One Lord* (London and New York: T&T Clark and Continuum, 2nd ed. 1998), 96.

29. R. Schnackenburg, "Baptism for the Dead," in his *Baptism in the Thought of St. Paul* (Oxford: Blackwell and New York: Herder, 1964), 95-103.

30. Cf. Thiselton, "Baptism for the Dead," in *First Epistle,* 1240-49.

life of a self-indulgent pagan materialist (v. 32b). He advises Christians in Corinth not to be corrupted and seduced by "bad company" (v. 33). Nevertheless, Paul sustains his main point: belief in the resurrection depends on "knowledge of God" (v. 34). It is appreciation of God's generous grace and sovereign power that nurtures belief in the credulity and conceivability of the resurrection.

(3) Paul now reaches Part 3 of his argument (1 Cor. 15:35-58). He addresses the question: How can the resurrection of the body be intelligible and conceivable? This constitutes, in rhetorical terms, a second *Refutatio* and *Confirmatio*. Eriksson comments, "The question concerns the nature of the resurrection, the . . . quality signalled by [Greek] *pōs* (how?) and *poiō sōmati* (with what kind of body?)."[31] This section, too, begins with a negative *Refutatio:* "Fool!" (v. 36). Supposedly a thickheaded addressee suggests that the resurrection body would be unintelligible and inconceivable by assuming that it is mere continuation of the present body. Such an argument ignores the creative role, and runs counter to all common sense about the putrefaction of the present body. In more positive terms Paul sets out the power and versatility of God in already having shown his ingenuity in creation. Do we need "bodies" for an environment of the sea? God created fish. Do we need "bodies" for an environment of the air? God created birds. Do we need "bodies" for the vacuum of space? God created planets and stars (vv. 38-41). Do individuality and identity disappear? "Star differs from star in glory" (v. 41). Is "body" primarily physical? "There are both heavenly bodies and earthly bodies" (v. 40).

The third section of Part 3 speaks directly of the resurrection body, without even analogy (1 Cor. 15:42-49). "What is sown is perishable, what is raised is imperishable. It is sown in dishonour, it is raised in glory. It is sown a 'physical' body [NRSV, REB; but 'physical' is misleading]; it is raised a spiritual body" (vv. 42b-44). Every one of these terms, however, deserves close examination if we are fully to understand Paul's argument. The first contrast is represented by the Greek *en phthora* and *en aphtharsia,* where the "a" is an "alpha privative" or negative, like the English prefix "non-" or "un-." But "incorruption" or "imperishability" convey too static a meaning. In my *Shorter Commentary* I proposed "decay" and "decay's reversal."[32] The Greek *phthora* represents the Hebrew *shāchat* and *chebel,*

31. Eriksson, *Traditions as Rhetorical Proof,* 267.

32. Anthony C. Thiselton, *1 Corinthians: A Shorter Exegetical and Pastoral Commentary* (Grand Rapids: Eerdmans, 2006), 281.

meaning not only "vanity" or "emptiness," but in the Niph'al form of the verb, "to be spoiled." Its opposite is "flourishing," "abundance," and "fullness of life."[33] The reversal of a decrescendo is a *crescendo*, not *fortissimo*. Hence the negative "imperishable" (NRSV, REB, NIV, NJB) is simply not good enough to convey a dynamic, ever-increasing condition.

The second contrast, "dishonour . . . glory" (v. 43), is more adequate. But the Greek *atimia,* while it can mean "dishonour" or "shame," also means "in a lowly position," and may be associated with "misery" and "pitifulness." Pannenberg shows that "misery" constitutes a master word for the human condition under the power of sin and not reconciled with God.[34] He refers to Rom. 7:24, "Wretched man that I am . . . ," and comments, "The root of this misery lies in death's opposition to our destiny of fellowship with God. . . . To speak of human misery is better than using the classical doctrine of sin. . . . The term 'misery' sums up our detachment from God."[35] The opposite of this misery is the glory or radiance of one suffused with joy. The Greek *doxa* ("glory") translates the Hebrew *kābôdh,* which means what makes someone impressive or weighty; but we must bear in mind that this *splendor* derives from the experience of the total expulsion of misery, and of finding all that we long for in God.

The third contrast, namely, of "weakness" and "power," is a correct translation of the Greek words, except that, again, "weakness" also implies here the *decreasing* and *declining* capacities that come with old age. In some sense our bodies begin to decline almost as soon as we have been born. "Power" (Greek, *dynamis*) often means "effectiveness." Hence here it means the full command of all capacities, to do all that we seek to do. The climax of all this is the fourth contrast. It is so important that we shall reserve a special section of this chapter to discuss it.

The remainder of this third section of Part 3 concerns the Christlike character of the resurrection mode of existence. It takes up the Adam-Christ parallel of 1 Cor. 15:21-23, and argues that just as we shared with Adam the spoiled image of God, so we shall share the image of Christ, "the man from heaven" (v. 49). The reference to the "first" and "second" Adam may be a reference to the thought of Philo of Alexandria, but is also Christological.

The fourth section of Part 3 traces the implications of resurrection with Christ in 1 Cor. 15:50-58. Joachim Jeremias produced an important ar-

---

33. Thiselton, *First Epistle,* 1271-72.
34. Pannenberg, *Systematic Theology,* vol. 2, 178-80.
35. Pannenberg, *Systematic Theology,* vol. 2, 178-79.

ticle confirming that "flesh and blood cannot enter the kingdom of God" (v. 50). This is directed *not* toward the idea that the *physical or material* cannot enter heaven, but is addressed to the problem of how *the sinful* can approach and encounter God.[36] The answer to this "mystery" is that "we shall all be changed . . . at the last trumpet" (vv. 51-52). Through the agency of the Holy Spirit (1 Cor. 15:44; Rom. 8:11), death loses its sting, because "the sting of death is sin," and Christ has won the victory over sin and death (vv. 54-57). On this basis, Christians may remain "steadfast . . . always excelling in the work of the Lord, because you know that in the Lord your labor is not in vain" (v. 58). Moltmann rightly concludes that resurrection involves "not a mere return to life . . . but a conquest of the deadliness of death . . . a conquest of God-forsakenness."[37] It is "annihilation of the total *nihil.*"[38]

7.3. The Nature of the Spiritual Body as the Ongoing Work of the Spirit

We promised to discuss in a separate section the fourth and most important contrast in 1 Cor. 15:44. We also questioned the translation, "It is sown a *physical* body; it is raised a spiritual body" (NRSV, REB). The AV/KJB, New King James Version (1995), and New American Standard Bible retain the AV "natural." The problem with "physical" is that this closes the question of whether its opposite (spiritual) means "immaterial" or "nonphysical." The Greek might include this meaning on occasion, but it is inadequate here. The Greek phrase is *psychikon sōma*, which Joseph Fitzmyer translates "animated," and I have translated "ordinary human body."[39]

The correct logical step is to note what the same word *psychikos* means in 1 Cor. 2:14 and 15:46, and how *psychē* translates the Hebrew *nephesh*. In 1 Cor. 2:14 the NRSV translates the word "unspiritual," in contrast to "receiving the gifts of God's Spirit." In 1 Cor. 2:14 the Vulgate rendered the phrase *animalis homo*, and R. F. Collins and NJB translate it "the natural

---

36. Joachim Jeremias, "Flesh and Blood Cannot Inherit the Kingdom of God (1 Cor. 15:50)," *NTS* 2 (1955): 151-59.

37. Moltmann, *Theology of Hope*, 211.

38. Moltmann, *Theology of Hope*, 198; cf. 201.

39. Joseph A. Fitzmyer, *First Corinthians*, The Anchor Yale Bible 32 (New Haven and London: Yale University Press, 2008), 595; Thiselton, *1 Corinthians: A Shorter Exegetical and Pastoral Commentary*, 283; and Thiselton, *First Epistle*, 1279.

person."[40] *Psychē* means either "life" or "soul," just as *nephesh* means either in Hebrew (cf. Mark 8:36-37; Matt. 16:26). *Psychikos* "stands in contrast to what is animated and motivated by God's Spirit."[41]

The contrast in 1 Cor. 15:44 is precisely parallel with 1 Cor. 2:14 and earlier allusions in 1 Corinthians. Hence spiritual body *(sōma pneumatikon)* denotes a mode of existence or form animated, motivated, and controlled by the Holy Spirit (Greek, *pneuma*). But the contrast with *psychikos* ("unspiritual") contributes *only partially* to the solution. We must examine what *pneumatikos* and *pneuma* denote in Paul and 1 Corinthians. *Pneumatikos*, the adjective "spiritual," occurs in 1 Cor. 2:13, 15; 3:1; 9:11; 10:3; 12:1; 14:1, 37; as well as 15:44 and 46. The adverbial form *pneumatikōs* occurs in 1 Cor. 2:13-14. The noun "Spirit" *(pneuma)* occurs some thirty-six times in 1 Corinthians, of which references in 1 Corinthians 2, 3, 6, 12, and 14 are among the most significant. In the vast majority of these occurrences the word refers to the Holy Spirit, or, in the case of the adjective *pneumatikos*, that which pertains to the work of the Holy Spirit.

Clearly in 1 Cor. 2:10-16 Paul discusses revelation by the Holy Spirit (v. 10), and in v. 12 he specifically uses the phrase "the Spirit who [proceeds or issues] from God" (Greek, *to pneuma to ek tou theou*) to emphasize the Holy Spirit's transcendence, not primarily here his immanence. This harmonizes with the Old Testament background, where "Spirit" (Hebrew, *rûach*) is similarly transcendent. The Spirit "came upon" the Judges (e.g., Jephthah, Judg. 11:29) or "rushed upon" Samson (Judg. 14:6), and "he tore the lion apart barehanded" (with 14:6 cf. 14:19, where Samson killed thirty Philistine men). In Isa. 63:14 the Spirit protects cattle from marauders. Paul has said that the Holy Spirit witnesses to the lordship of Christ (1 Cor. 12:3; cf. John 16:13-14). The widespread modern popular meaning of "spirituality" to denote a vague human religious aspiration is entirely foreign to Paul and to the New Testament. It is that which is produced by, and accords with, the Christ-centered work of the Holy Spirit.

Hence *spiritual body* can mean only a form of postresurrection existence which is animated by, and characterized by, the Holy Spirit, who comes not from humankind, but from God.[42] N. T. Wright defines *spiritual body* as "a body animated by, enlivened by, the Spirit of the true God,

---

40. R. F. Collins, *First Corinthians* (Collegeville, MN: Glazier/Liturgical Press, 1999), 135.

41. Thiselton, *First Epistle*, 267.

42. Thiselton, *First Epistle*, 1275-81; Thiselton, *1 Corinthians*, 283-84.

exactly as Paul has said more extensively in several other passages. . . . The new body is the *result* of the Spirit's work" (his italics).[43] Rom. 8:9-11 provides confirmatory evidence. In view of the popular, non-Pauline understanding of spiritual, however, the comment of Joseph Fitzmyer seems at first sight to carry some weight. He writes: "The real problem . . . is the meaning of *sōma pneumatikon*, which seems to attribute to *sōma* a meaning that is diametrically opposed to 'body.'"[44] This may seem at first the case if we follow Fitzmyer (in spite of James Barr's warnings about "basic meaning" in seeing "the basic meaning" of *pneuma* as "breathing, blowing, air in movement," hence "wind." But Barr, among others, warns us in detail about confusing word history or etymology with word meaning.[45] It is doubtful whether Paul saw this as the "basic" meaning, but rather that which signified the Holy Spirit, even if we may concede that the word is also pluriform.

Fitzmyer himself concludes that *spiritual body* "must mean a human body as transformed by God through Christ for a new mode of existence, under the influence of *Pneuma*, 'Holy Spirit.'"[46] But he continues, more controversially, that this "really tells us nothing about a 'spiritual body' *in se*; hence the oxymoron remains." But this depends on an equally questionable meaning of "body," which we shall shortly discuss. There are too many hints of the older Platonic notion of "physical nonphysical" thinking in this general approach, in spite of its incisive rejection by Rudolf Bultmann and other writers as un-Pauline.[47] The Holy Spirit is both transcendent and immanent, or, as one writer has termed this, "The Beyond Who is Within." But throughout the biblical writings the transcendent is always there. Isaiah writes in a classic statement, "The Egyptians are men [Hebrew, *'ādām*], not God [*'ēl*], and their horses flesh [*bāśār*], not Spirit [*rûach*]" (Isa. 31:3). The Spirit transforms a wilderness into a paradise (Isa. 32:15-17). The Psalmist declares, "When you send forth your Spirit, they are created" (Ps. 104:30). Moltmann calls the Spirit "the Divine energy of life."[48] He empowers the

43. Wright, *The Resurrection of the Son of God,* 354.

44. Fitzmyer, *First Corinthians,* 596.

45. James Barr, *The Semantics of Biblical Language* (Oxford: Oxford University Press, 1961), 107-10 and throughout.

46. Fitzmyer, *First Corinthians,* 596.

47. Rudolf Bultmann, *Theology of the New Testament* (vol. 1; London: S.C.M., 1952), 153-64, 203-8, and 232-35.

48. Jürgen Moltmann, *The Spirit of Life: A Universal Affirmation* (London: S.C.M., 1992), 40.

Messiah (Isa. 42:1; Hos. 9:7). He brings together Ezekiel's "dry bones" into a single, living body (Ezek. 37:9).

In Paul the "spiritual" is not only all this, but is also Christological or even Christocentric (Rom. 8:9-11; 1 Cor. 12:3; Gal. 4:6). Reception of the Spirit both causes, and also flows from, the relation of a person or a community with Christ (Gal. 5:25; 1 Cor. 12:13; 2 Cor. 5:5). Oscar Cullmann observes, "The Holy Spirit is nothing else than the anticipation of the end in the present."[49] In summary, Paul places the work of the Holy Spirit in a threefold context: it is transcendent (i.e., holy, other, and *from* God); Christological (i.e., witnesses to Christ and activates union with Christ); and eschatological (i.e., reaches its climax in the resurrection).

Fitzmyer's "oxymoron" seems to be only an oxymoron if we imagine that "body" means primarily *physicality* as such, and that "spiritual" means primarily *nonphysicality*. But we have seen that this is only a partial meaning in Paul and in many of the biblical writings. Ernst Käsemann has the key to the meaning of "body" *(sōma)* for Paul. He is discussing early Christian apocalyptic, for which the present process of world history is important. The Christian life is not limited to "interior piety" and to specific acts of worship or liturgy. In this context, he argues, "body" signifies "that piece of the world which we ourselves are and for which we bear responsibility because it was the earliest gift of our Creator to us."[50] For Paul "body" signifies a human person or part of the world, "and therefore in his ability to communicate . . . the reality of our being in the world." Hence, *the body* provides "visible expression" and "personal shape" to the Christian's living out of obedience to Christ as Lord. As existence takes this personal shape and visibility, the "Gospel message" becomes "credible"; by "bodily obedience."[51]

Käsemann points out that this is not individualism. We are bound together in the situation of creatureliness, visible and communicable testimony and obedience, and in due course resurrection. Käsemann's emphasis on credulity, visibility, and identity is parallel with Ludwig Wittgenstein's emphasis on "public" criteria of meaning.[52] Wittgenstein

---

49. Oscar Cullmann, *Christ and Time* (London: S.C.M., 1951), 72.

50. Käsemann, "Primitive Christian Apocalyptic," in his *New Testament Questions of Today*, 135.

51. Käsemann, *New Testament Questions*, 135.

52. Ludwig Wittgenstein, *Philosophical Investigations* (Oxford: Blackwell, 1958), sects. 243-349.

remarks, "What people accept as a justification — is shown by how they think and live."[53]

It is worth taking a short digression to see how Wittgenstein clarifies the importance of this point. Public actions can give currency and credibility to what we say. I may say, "I am in terrible pain. . . . Oh, it's all right, it's gone off now!" That may sound credible. But if I say, "I love you deeply. . . . Oh, it's gone off now!" my hearer will not only be puzzled, but also doubt the credibility of what I said. Wittgenstein uses this example in his *Zettel*.[54] Faithfulness and repentance become credible and make sense if one lives through time and intervals of time.[55] Without bodily life, lived as a human being along with other people, Wittgenstein points out, much would become meaningless. He asks, tongue in cheek, "Why can't my right hand give my left hand money?"[56] It could go through the motions of transferring money from one palm to the other, but it would not make sense as a financial transaction because identities and life are not involved. Without concrete life and the community, Wittgenstein urges, it is "as if someone were to buy several copies of the morning paper to assure himself that what it said was true," or saying, "But I know how tall I am, and laying his hand on top of his head to prove it."[57]

We may finally, on this point, cite Wittgenstein's famous example of "the beetle in the box." We might call the hidden entity, Wittgenstein observes, anything we like. But if the box conceals the object, "it would be quite possible for everyone to have something different in the box. . . . The thing in the box has no place . . . in [this] language."[58] This would apply to postresurrection existence, unless we can conceive of the resurrection "body" as in some sense a transformed counterpart to what Käsemann has identified as the primary meaning and significance of "body," as Paul understood this. This is all part of Paul's "anti-enthusiastic argument," which avoids seeing Christian commitment as an "inner state."[59] "Spiritual body," then, cannot be an oxymoron; the Holy Spirit was active at creation in animating the earthly body; the Holy Spirit will be similarly active in animating and fully controlling the resurrection "body."

53. Wittgenstein, *Philosophical Investigations*, sect. 325.
54. Ludwig Wittgenstein, *Zettel* (Oxford: Blackwell, 1967), sect. 504.
55. Wittgenstein, *Zettel*, sect. 519.
56. Wittgenstein, *Philosophical Investigations*, sect. 268.
57. Wittgenstein, *Philosophical Investigations*, sects. 265 and 279.
58. Wittgenstein, *Philosophical Investigations*, sect. 293.
59. Käsemann, *New Testament Questions*, 133.

Martin Luther comes near to this approach. He writes of the *spiritual body:* "It is really the work of God. . . . It will not be a body that eats, sleeps, and digests, but . . . lives solely of and by the Spirit."[60] It is only by being born of the Holy Spirit that a person may "become completely spiritual."[61] Other writers have progressed toward Käsemann's understanding of "body" on the basis of 1 Cor. 6:13-20. Paul states here "The body belongs to the Lord, and the Lord to the body" (6:13). M. E. Dahl rightly speaks of somatic continuity, while also making a contrast between *body* and the spiritual *sōma,* partly by refusing to use the word "body" rather than *sōma.*[62] James Dunn sees 1 Cor. 15:44 as "the most revealing passage" about *sōma,* with the double emphasis on transformation (contrast) and creatureliness or belonging to the world (continuity).[63] J. A. T. Robinson also expounds the various nuances of "body," especially the corporate one.[64]

One point, however, remains to be explored. We have noted that *pneuma,* the Spirit, is, in Moltmann's words, "the Divine energy of life." Moltmann also speaks of the Spirit's "vitality as love of life."[65] He rejects the static dualism of Gnosticism and Platonism as a denial of eschatology.[66] He declares, "True spirituality will be the restoration of the love for life — that is to say, *vitality* [his italics]. The full and unreserved 'yes' to life, and the full and unreserved love for the living are the first experiences of God's Spirit . . . the well of life."[67] When the Holy Spirit is at work, we see "the rhythm of movements, the shining of eyes, the embraces, the feelings . . . of all this . . . creation."[68] The Spirit liberates, so that "the hitherto unexplored creative power of God is thrown open in men and women."[69] This also brings *"communicative freedom,"* and freedom in "the creative passion for the possible."[70]

If this is the case, and we have already seen that *spiritual body* consti-

---

60. Martin Luther, *LW,* vol. 28 (St. Louis: Concordia, 1973), 189 and 192.

61. Luther, *LW,* vol. 28, 192.

62. M. E. Dahl, *The Resurrection of the Body* (London: S.C.M., 1962), 51-126.

63. James D. G. Dunn, *The Theology of Paul the Apostle* (Edinburgh: T&T Clark, 1998), 71; cf. 55-73.

64. J. A. T. Robinson, *The Body: A Study of Pauline Theology* (London: S.C.M., 1952 and Philadelphia: Westminster, 1977), 31 and throughout.

65. Moltmann, *The Spirit of Life,* 86.

66. Moltmann, *The Spirit of Life,* 90.

67. Moltmann, *The Spirit of Life,* 97.

68. Moltmann, *The Spirit of Life,* 98.

69. Moltmann, *The Spirit of Life,* 115.

70. Moltmann, *The Spirit of Life,* 118 and 119 (his italics).

tutes a mode of existence characterized by the Holy Spirit, the post-resurrection mode of being will be *ongoing, moving ahead, dynamic, and on-the-move*. It will be more like a flowing stream or river than a lake or a canal. We cannot dream of what the Holy Spirit will yet do, in us and through us, in the mode of existence characterized by the Holy Spirit of Christ. We may discover new experiences and new heights of contemplation and worship. This will be discussed further in Chapters 11 and 12, on the wonder, satisfaction, joy, and glory of the postresurrection existence. In 1 Cor. 15:45 "the life-giving Spirit" is associated or identified with Christ. Eduard Schweizer comments on this passage, "Christ, like Adam, encloses a whole humanity within Himself. . . . Continuity between the earthly and heavenly body rests on miracle."[71] Hence we may also speak of "the consubstantiality of the believer with Christ." The notion of a "static" future postmortal life is a tragedy, and is nowhere implied by the New Testament.

We must add a brief postscript to this chapter. We have consistently urged that the resurrection is a creative, sovereign act of God, and does not at all arise from human capacities or religious aspirations. It is a sheer gift of God's grace. In this respect, resurrection is parallel with justification by grace, which comes as God's sheer gift. Part of God's gift is the gift of righteousness, not only in justification, but also through the fullness of the Holy Spirit. Only in the Spirit will Christian believers *freely choose to do the right*. Moltmann, once again, writes, "God is *wholly* present, and present as *himself*. . . . There can be no question of half a revelation, let alone a merely fragmentary revelation."[72] God will be "all in all" (1 Cor. 15:28). "Death has been swallowed up in victory" (15:54). Sin will be abolished; hence death has lost its sting (15:55-56). Hence in the present Christians may fearlessly "excel in the work of the Lord" (15:58). In the next chapter we shall inquire how it is possible for the Holy Spirit to convey holiness to the Christian in the resurrection itself, rather than in a long process of purification in Purgatory.

---

71. Eduard Schweizer, "*pneuma, pneumatikos*," *TDNT*, vol. 6, 419 and 421; cf. 415-55.
72. Moltmann, *The Spirit of Life*, 302.

CHAPTER 8

Is Holiness Given at Once in the Resurrection, or Gradually in Purgatory? What Does "Eternal" Mean?

8.1. Gradual Purification in Purgatory?

We have already considered briefly Thomas Aquinas on Purgatory in the thirteenth century, and the official promulgation of the doctrine by Pope Benedict XII in 1336. We noted, however, the objection of the Protestant Reformers that for them it compromised, or seemed to compromise, the all-sufficiency of Christ's work of atonement. We considered these arguments briefly in Chapter 5. Jürgen Moltmann, for example, gives a broadly sympathetic account of the Catholic and medieval doctrine of Purgatory, including its role in Dante's *Divine Comedy* (1319), but then concludes, "The idea of purgatory seems to be incompatible with the experience of the unconditional love with which God in Christ finds us, accepts us, reconciles us, and glorifies us."[1]

The doctrine of Purgatory arose, Moltmann argues, neither from Scripture nor from tradition, but from the medieval Church's practices of prayer and penance. Prayer for the dead all too often is intended to help the dead on their way, for which we see no biblical warrant. But if those who pray for the dead enjoy a glad confidence that God has already honored his promises, we might sometimes pray for the departed, on the ground that sometimes we do pray for what God has already promised to grant, for example, "Grant your blessing on our Church." But Aquinas makes it clear that for him such prayers ease the punishment of the dead, and assist, or add to, the atoning work of Christ. He first argues, "The pun-

---

1. Jürgen Moltmann, *The Coming of God: Christian Eschatology* (London: S.C.M., 1996), 98.

ishment of purgatory is intended to *supplement* [my italics] the satisfaction which was not yet completed."[2] Hence Aquinas next argues, "One person [can] be purified by another satisfying for him."[3]

This leads to the practice of prayer for the "advancement" of the dead, to penance, and to indulgences. Martin Luther, as is well known, denounced the "ungodly doctrine" of "the great sums that have been spent in their fallacious indulgences and other frauds."[4] The sixth of his Ninety-Five Theses (Oct. 1517) reads: "The Pope can remit no guilt, but only declare and confirm that it has been remitted by God."[5] "Those preachers of Indulgences are wrong when they say that a man is absolved . . . by the Pope's Indulgences."[6] "It is mere human talk to preach that the soul flies out [of Purgatory] immediately, the money chinks in the collection box."[7]

Luther and other Reformers also point out that the Latin word *poenitentia* had falsely given rise to the "sacrament" of penance.[8] This was often regarded as meaning "repentance" as well as "penance." But the New Testament word for "repent" does not even mean what the Greek word *metanoeō* is alleged to mean (namely, to have an "after-mind"), but looks back to the Hebrew *shûb* or *shûbh*, meaning "to turn from" and "to turn to." This represents a highly personal act and attitude. In the early Church the baptismal vows were sometimes accompanied by the physical act of turning from the West (to represent renouncing evil) to the East (to represent pledging allegiance to Christ), which today is perhaps reflected in "turning for the (baptismal) creed" in many churches. But we cannot do it as a "work" of merit accounted to someone else's credit. John Calvin also opposed Indulgences, which he called "transferred satisfactions," and Purgatory. They are all considered in his chapter headed "The Modes of Supplementary Satisfaction — Viz., Indulgences and Purgatory."[9] Prayer for

2. Thomas Aquinas, *Summa Theologiae* (London: Eyre & Spottiswoode, 1963), II:2, Q. 71, art. 6.

3. Aquinas, *Summa Theologiae*, II:2, Q. 71, art. 6, reply to obj. 3.

4. Martin Luther, "Letter to Justus Jonas" (1530), in *Luther: Letters of Spiritual Counsel*, ed. Theodore G. Tappert, LCC 18 (London: S.C.M., 1955), 153.

5. "The Ninety-Five Theses," in *Martin Luther: Documents of Modern History*, ed. E. G. Rupp and Benjamin Drewery (London: Arnold, 1970), 19.

6. "The Ninety-Five Theses," no. 21, in *Martin Luther*, 20.

7. "The Ninety-Five Theses," no. 27, in *Martin Luther*, 20.

8. "The Sacrament of Penance," in *Martin Luther: Selections from His Writings*, ed. John Dillenberger (New York: Doubleday, 1961), 314-24.

9. John Calvin, *Institutes of the Christian Religion*, trans. H. Beveridge (London: James Clarke, 1957), 3.5 (vol. 1, 571-82).

the dead, he says, "ought not to be despised," but Scripture makes "no such assertions about purgatory." "Blessed are the dead that die in the Lord." Purgatory "produces many grievous offences. . . . Assuredly it is not to be connived at . . . [it is] without any authority from the word of God, it was devised . . . by the wiles of Satan."[10]

In terms of biblical exegesis the doctrine cannot possibly be defended on the basis of 1 Cor. 3:11-15. Paul is there constructing a careful analogy of the "fireproof" permanence of the work of faithful ministers. The passage is about faithfulness in ministry, and the "fire" represents an analogy probably drawn from the actual incidence of a destructive fire at Corinth.[11] Any "loss" is probably the loss of ministerial trust. Paul's thrust is that "Prior to the last judgement all human evaluations remain corrigible; they depend on unknown factors . . . human motivations and long-term effects. . . . God pronounces a definitive verdict at the last judgement."[12] To be saved "as through fire" (Greek, *hōs dia pyros*) means coming through the fire intact like "a brand plucked from the burning" (Amos 4:11), or "saved by the skin of one's teeth."

After a broadly sympathetic account of the Catholic and medieval doctrine of Purgatory, including its role in Dante's *Divine Comedy* (1319), Moltmann concludes, "The idea of purgatory seems to be incompatible with the experience of the unconditional love with which God in Christ finds us, accepts us, reconciles us, and glorifies us."[13] The doctrine cannot possibly be defined, he repeats, on the basis of 1 Cor. 3:11-15. It is more than possible, however, to attempt a defense of the condition of Purgatory which does not so explicitly depend on arguments about "supplementary" atonement. Geoffrey Rowell, in his careful book *Hell and the Victorians*, argues from the need, not for justification, but for continuing sanctification or holiness.[14] Rowell insists that the Tractarians saw the necessity of sanctification. Many of them, however, explicitly rejected the *Roman Catholic* idea of "the celestial treasury of merits." Yet E. B. Pusey, working intensively in the Church Fathers, told Samuel Wilberforce, "I could not . . . refuse my belief in an intermediate state of cleansing, in some cases through

10. Calvin, *Institutes*, 3.5.6, 9, and 10.

11. Cf. Anthony C. Thiselton, *The First Epistle to the Corinthians: A Commentary on the Greek Text*, NIGTC (Grand Rapids: Eerdmans and Carlisle: Paternoster, 2000), 307-15.

12. Thiselton, *The First Epistle*, 323.

13. Moltmann, *The Coming of God*, 98.

14. Geoffrey Rowell, *Hell and the Victorians* (Oxford: Clarendon, 1974), 90-115 and 153-79.

pain."[15] By 1867, Pusey "considered that it was inconceivable that men who had shown little love to God on earth would be brought immediately to the Beatific Vision, and he was prepared to characterize . . . the time of waiting as purgatory."[16]

When he was fully converted from Anglicanism to Catholicism, John Henry Newman spoke of Purgatory as a punishment, but as a punishment which constituted a purification actually welcomed by the Christian in the presence of Christ.[17] *The Dream of Gerontius* portrayed its bitter-sweet character. Rowell writes, "Purgatory is a place of preparation for heaven, not a lesser hell."[18] The condition involves progress, but not succession of time as we know it. The issue turns upon the rejection of the Protestant idea that holiness, as well as justification by grace, can be experienced at or after the resurrection (critics would say), "ready-made." If sanctification means a growth in holiness, how can this be given or acquired in a moment, instantaneously, especially to those who still enter the heavenly kingdom with little contemplation of God or Christian obedience? Even if "being right with God" may be God's instantaneous gift, how can the raised community of resurrection *suddenly* become holy in desire, character, and habit?

8.2. The Nature of Holiness in the Immediate Power of the Spirit and Presence of God

It is a profound mistake to equate holiness with good moral character, even if it includes this. In the biblical writings the vast proportion of references to "holy" or "holiness" (Hebrew, *qādôsh*; Greek, *hagios*) derive their force or significance from their closeness to God.[19] If we were for a moment to cut through complex arguments, the line of the well-known hymn sums it all up: "When I see Thee as Thou art, I'll praise Thee as I ought." Holiness under the conditions of this world, where God can be seen only by faith, and where temptations abound, differs from holiness when we come face to face with God, leave temptations and earthly attractions behind, see the interconnectedness of all things and their true significance,

---

15. Rowell, *Hell and the Victorians*, 103.
16. Rowell, *Hell and the Victorians*, 104.
17. Rowell, *Hell and the Victorians*, 159.
18. Rowell, *Hell and the Victorians*, 161.
19. Jackie A. Naudé, "*q-d-sh*," in *NIDOTTE*, vol. 3, 878-83.

and are totally open to the power of the Holy Spirit, overshadowed by divine glory and the resurrection side of the cross.

It is helpful to draw especially on one book, amid the numerous studies of holiness, which has been unduly neglected: O. R. Jones, *The Concept of Holiness*.[20] Jones first establishes the logical distinctiveness of holiness, in contrast to the nature of physical or empirical objects. Holiness, he asserts, involves a vision that transcends the physical or moral. Holiness belongs to God alone; all other meanings are derivative from this. Hence, if it is set apart for God, or belongs in a special way to him, a mountain becomes a holy mountain; a people becomes a holy people; a table becomes a holy table; a land becomes a holy land; and so on.

Fear of the holy, Jones urges, may sometimes find expression as an emotion, though an emotion of a distinctive sort. Isaiah experienced God as holy; but his reaction was to exclaim, "Woe is me! I am lost, for I am a man of unclean lips" (Isa. 6:5). "Awesome is God in his sanctuary, the God of Israel" (Ps. 68:35). "Holy and awesome is his name. The fear of the LORD is the beginning of wisdom" (Ps. 111:9-10). With many others, Jones cites Rudolf Otto on the numinous: on God the *mysterium tremendum et fascinans*.[21] Yet his discussion of Otto is rightly not without criticism. Sometimes Otto goes too near to equating the holy with the weird or the spooky.

Yet the emotional response does not exhaust human response. The response is *also dispositional*.[22] It constitutes a constant disposition to behave in a certain way when certain conditions are present or absent. For example, an attitude of reverence or respect toward the Ark of the Covenant in the Old Testament is expected. An analogy here would be an electrician's fear or respect for live wires in a circuit. He does not *consciously* experience fear all the time, any more than belief always remains a conscious process. As Ludwig Wittgenstein and H. H. Price point out, a believer does not become an unbeliever when he or she falls asleep.[23] An electrician becomes aware of the danger of a live wire only when particular situations of investigating malfunctions arise. Helmer Ringgren asserts

20. O. R. Jones, *The Concept of Holiness* (London: Allen & Unwin, 1961).

21. Rudolf Otto, *The Idea of the Holy*, trans. J. W. Harvey (London: Oxford University Press, 1928).

22. Jones, *The Concept of Holiness*, 39-50.

23. H. H. Price, *Belief* (London: Allen & Unwin, 1969), 20, 29-31; L. Wittgenstein, *Zettel* (Oxford: Blackwell, 1967), sect. 85; and Anthony C. Thiselton, *The Hermeneutics of Doctrine* (Grand Rapids: Eerdmans, 2007), 19-34.

that the holy "should be handled in the right way. . . . He who approaches it should be well prepared to do so."[24] Jones speaks of "precautions such as changing, washing clothes, taking off shoes."[25]

Moses took off his shoes when he approached holy ground (Exod. 3:5). Uzzah provoked God to anger when he touched the holy ark (2 Sam. 6:6-7). Holy days and holy times offer another example. A person may respond differently to the same situation when it is a holy day, such as the Sabbath (Isa. 58:13-14). There is danger in "profaning the holy name" (Lev. 20:3). Augustine asserts that God gives us grace in such a way that we have both the capacity and will to persevere in holiness. He writes, "Because by the Holy Spirit their *will* is so much enkindled that they therefore *can* (i.e., have the ability or capacity for holiness), because they so *will*; and they therefore so *will*, because *God* works in them to will."[26] This, Augustine insists, is compatible with true freedom, because no external compulsion is involved, and the human agents in question remain free to express themselves in action or thought as they will. They freely choose to obey the will of God.

O. R. Jones clarifies both the certainty and freedom in two distinctive ways, among others. First, according to the dispositional view which he, Wittgenstein, and Price advocate, the holy expression of a holy will would become apparent in terms of behavior where appropriate conditions apply. It might founder if the earthly conditions of the attractiveness of sin and seduction of temptations were to apply to the heavenly state after the resurrection, but they no longer apply. Conditions of glory, service, and worship offer appropriate conditions for holiness. Second, the holy, Jones insists throughout his book, derives directly from God. After the resurrection God knows, "even as he has been fully known" (1 Cor. 13:12). Faith will have been overtaken by sight: "Now we see in a mirror dimly, but then we shall see face to face" (1 Cor. 13:12a). "We know only in part . . . , but when the complete comes, the partial will come to an end" (1 Cor. 13:9-10). Alongside this, we behold "the perfect vision." Jones writes, "It involves grasping or seeing interconnections between certain things done and the results that follow."[27]

If we saw not only the whole universe, but also God's purposes behind

---

24. Helmer Ringgren, *The Prophetical Conception of Holiness* (Uppsala: Lundequistka, 1948), 10.

25. Jones, *The Concept of Holiness*, 41.

26. Augustine, *On Rebuke and Grace* 38 (my italics; also in the *NPNF*, ser. 1, vol. 5, 487).

27. Jones, *The Concept of Holiness*, 158.

every chain of events and the consequences that follow either self-willed or divinely willed actions, should we still choose sin? Could sin or disobedience still remain *attractive*? If Athanasius is right (and he surely is) in defining sin as lack of contemplation of God, not primarily as this or that particular action, should we wish contemplation of God to suffer distraction through self-willed disobedience? But this is not servitude in the sense of bondage or compulsion. Should we deny the adjective "free" of God himself because he is always only righteous, good, and loving? Is he a prisoner to his own chosen will for himself and others?

Divine self-consistency is no more a denial of freedom than the holiness of the raised community in Christ. Even more wonderfully and awesomely, experience of sin and self in the afterlife may enhance this. We have personal knowledge of where sin leads, and of its deceitful seductions. On earth we have a saying, "Once bitten, twice shy." Shall we ever see anything good, productive, or satisfying to have arisen from past sins or from lack of contemplating God? Wittgenstein often talks about "the stage setting" of language. Human experience of right and wrong can provide stage setting for a life of holiness. He often refers to it as "training," after which we have the capacity to say, "Now I can go on."[28]

Jones follows F. Waismann in explaining the value of "vision," and especially "perfect vision." This does not arise out of previous experience, as if merely by inference or by extrapolation. It is "the flashing of a new aspect which is non-inferential."[29] "The perfect vision (would be) quite beyond even the highest we can conceive of. In its light, everything, every state of affairs, all facts, would be perfectly intelligible; no inconsistency could arise within it, for working out its implications would be perfectly logical."[30] This perfect vision, however, is not the timeless perfection of Plato; it still lies open before the future. Like a creative work of art, it does not become "finished" in the sense of reaching a dead end or full stop. It is simply that when the perfect vision finds expression, we no longer climb up to God on the basis of past deeds (like being under Law), but simply keep pace with the perfect Architect or Designer (as those under grace).

There remains a difference between the wonder of seeing the interconnectedness of all things and seeing this interconnectedness in the light of

---

28. Wittgenstein, *Philosophical Investigations,* sect. 257 (on stage setting) and sects. 150-54 (on "Now I can go on").

29. Jones, *The Concept of Holiness,* 165.

30. Jones, *The Concept of Holiness,* 168.

God's immediate presence and creative will. Even knowledge of the whole might remain baffling without the presence of the interpreter Holy Spirit; or without the presence of the Son, in whom "all things hold together" (Col. 1:17, NRSV; or "come into focus," or "cohere"; Greek, *ta panta en autō synestēken*). It would equally remain baffling without the presence of the Father, who is the source and purposive goal of all things. Paul writes, "For from him and through him and to him are all things" (Rom. 11:36).

In the light of these varied factors, there is nothing *prima facie* implausible about the notion of "being transformed" at the resurrection of the dead, in such a way that the Holy Spirit not only raises us in and with Christ, but also makes us always choose freely to be holy and to contemplate God. This would not seem to be a greater miracle than the unquestioned fact that many may grow in holiness at a time when the evidence for the presence of God is ambiguous; when we cannot see him (in the everyday sense of "see"); and when we cannot hear him (in the everyday sense of "hear"). Wittgenstein observes, "You can't hear God speak to someone else; you can hear him only if you are being addressed."[31] He explains that this is a logical or "grammatical" remark about the distinctive logic of "hear" in relation to God. Holiness indeed requires a long period of growth and time *within the conditions of this world*. But the perfect vision, the presence of God, and the dispositional character of holiness, suggest that it is otherwise *within the conditions of the postresurrection world*. As A. G. Hogg suggests, "There is . . . a wide kingdom . . . , in which the world lies like a foolish, wilful dream in the solid truth of the day."[32]

8.3. Eternity as Timelessness, Everlasting Duration, Simultaneity, or Multidimensional and Transformed Reality?

Time is far more complex than we easily imagine. Even in everyday life not all time is *chronological* time, measured by the sun and the calendar. If we read a detective story or a crime novel, a straightforward chronological sequence would tell us at the beginning who committed the crime, and in that case we could not enter into the detective's puzzlement, tension, examination of clues, discovery, and resolution. Hence authors introduce "*narrative* time." Gérard Genette and others put this concept on a sound

---

31. Wittgenstein, *Zettel*, sect. 717.
32. A. G. Hogg, *Redemption from This World* (Edinburgh: T&T Clark, 1924), 26.

theoretical basis. We are given flashbacks and variations from the chronological sequence of events. Clock time may be measured by the sun, but sociologists know that clock time is not the only experience of time. Whether we wait to see someone, or whether others wait to see us, depends on our respective status in employment or in professional esteem. "Sociological time" is neither narrative time nor clock time. Martin Heidegger urges that time to give the dog a walk, or time to perform a task, is seldom measured strictly by the clock, but by our more subjective experience of time.

In philosophy, the question of whether time is "real" has a long history of debate. Immanuel Kant saw it mainly as a mechanism or category which allows us to find order and intelligibility. In response to F. H. Bradley's claim that time is unreal, G. E. Moore asked why it should matter whether we have lunch before breakfast. Plato saw time as something that belonged to our contingent, imperfect world but not to the eternal realm of Form or Ideas.

Mathematicians and physicists ask questions about the beginning of the universe and the "beginning" of time. Stephen Hawking suggests, in David Wilkinson's words, "that as we move closer to the origin of the Universe, the nature of time changes. Indeed, as one goes back the notion of time eventually melts away. . . . The Universe is such that once upon a time there was no time."[33] Hawking's theory is complex for the layman to understand, involving the mathematics of a quantum theory of gravity and the model of "imaginary time." Calculations presuppose that "any distinction between time and space disappears."[34] Indeed, prior to Hawking, especially in the light of Albert Einstein's theory of relativity work, it was customary to speak of "space-time" in the context of physics or astronomy.

In theology most agree with Augustine's aphorism that God created the universe *with* time, not *in* time. Given the conditions of this world, however, most followed Oscar Cullmann and others in stressing that the biblical writers understood time primarily in a linear way, allowing for purposive goals in God's interaction with the history of the world. Cullmann insists that linear time is the presupposition behind "the redemptive plan" and "stages of the redemptive history."[35] Continuous linear time (Greek, *chronos*) may also allow for special terms of opportunity

33. David Wilkinson, *Christian Eschatology and the Physical Universe* (London: Continuum and T&T Clark, 2010), 122-23.

34. Wilkinson, *Christian Eschatology and the Physical Universe,* 121.

35. Oscar Cullmann, *Christ and Time* (London: S.C.M., 1951), 77.

(Greek, *kairos*).[36] But a minority of theologians insist that Christian theology must also make room for "cyclical time." The cycles of nature and of the Christian year with their seasons allow the observance of festivals, such as Christmas, Easter, and Pentecost. Indeed, several writers criticize Cullmann's approach as too generalizing, squeezing all time within one model.

Without question the linear concept of time remains dominant, and forms the frame within which cyclical time may be considered as important but secondary. Jürgen Moltmann recently has carefully qualified Cullmann's work, but even his view of time is said to be unduly simple by Richard Bauckham and David Wilkinson. His distinctive contribution is to stress the openness of the future, in contrast to the "closed" past. He writes that the essence of God's time of promise is "futurity."[37] In this earthly life, he points out, the experience of time brings aging and death. By contrast, "hope looks . . . to the future of 'a new time', the abiding aeon of an 'everlasting life' (1 John 1:2) in which *chronos* will enjoy more efficacy (Rev. 10:6)."[38] Like Wilkinson, Moltmann sees Entropy as a confirmation of the directional and irreversible nature of time: "All temporal happening is irreversible."[39] Like Augustine and Paul Ricoeur, he traces human experience from memory to expectation. Above all, he asserts, "Eternal life has nothing to do with timelessness . . . but is *full-filled life*" (his italics).[40] Rom. 13:12 looks to both the past, "when you first believed," and to the future, to when "the day of the Lord will dawn" and drive out the night of earthly life: "The temporal creation will then become an eternal creation . . . 'the restoration of all things.'"[41] Space will end because "earth and sky fled away" (Rev. 20:11). Hence, Moltmann argues, God will no longer restrict himself by creating a sphere for the world. God will be "all in all."

Wolfhart Pannenberg helpfully comments, "The future or consummation is the entry of eternity into time."[42] Eternity, he argues, is not opposed to time, but positively related to it. Although time, as we now know it, tends to fragment life in terms of a succession of events, eternity gathers

36. Cullmann, *Christ and Time*, 39-44.
37. Moltmann, *The Coming of God*, 283.
38. Moltmann, *The Coming of God*, 284.
39. Moltmann, *The Coming of God*, 286.
40. Moltmann, *The Coming of God*, 291.
41. Moltmann, *The Coming of God*, 294.
42. Wolfhart Pannenberg, *Systematic Theology*, vol. 3 (Grand Rapids: Eerdmans and Edinburgh: T&T Clark, 1998), 603.

up points of time in a totality and unity, so that only in eternity does a person's full identity, seen as a unified totality, actually emerge.[43] His view of time comes closer to that of Plotinus and Boethius, whose views we shall consider shortly.

Cullmann, Moltmann, Wilkinson, and Pannenberg together resist Plato's understanding of eternity as timelessness, or of time as a contingent "moving image" of a "timeless" eternity. Thus by implication they oppose the parallel in Eastern philosophy, such as the *Advaita Vedanta* of Śaṅkārā (788-820) and other *advaita* (nondualist) themes in Hindu philosophy. In practice, theologians have adopted one or more of three or four views of eternity: (1) eternity as timelessness; (2) eternity as an everlasting duration; and (3) eternity as simultaneity. This was the view of Plotinus, and its best-known form of Boethius (c. 480-525), that eternity denotes "the complete possession all at once [Latin, *totum simul*] of the illimitable life." (4) Some are dissatisfied with all of the three best-known theories. In view of the varied notions of time in human life, and in view of considerations of physics and mathematics, a minority suggest that time with more dimensions than ordinary human or clock time brings us nearer to a solution concerning eternity than any other approach.

(1) Most theologians acknowledge that eternity suggests a complete termination of time as we know it. Does this mean, as Plato suggests, timelessness? At first sight "time" seems to be at odds with perfection, as if to suggest that the perfect can make room for improvement. Further, most thinkers agree with Augustine that God created the universe not *in* time, but *with* time. Moreover if space-time is one entity, as Einstein's theory of relativity suggests, would not the transcending of space imply the cessation of time? Among modern philosophers who are also committed Christians, Paul Helm holds this view. Helm speaks of "the eternally timeless God."[44] He confronts counterarguments about God's foreknowledge, or of God's "remembering," as "the proper and inevitable expressions of someone in time who wishes to speak of his relation to a timeless being."[45] Helm couples with this a bold emphasis on the sovereignty of God, who is omniscient and who knows the future.

Some argue, in the words of Brian Leftow: "A timeless God does not

---

43. Pannenberg, *Systematic Theology,* vol. 1, 404 and 408-9.

44. Paul Helm, *Eternal God: A Study of God without Time* (Oxford: Clarendon, 1988), 37.

45. Helm, *Eternal God,* 37.

remember, forget, feel relief, or cease to do anything. For a timeless God has no past, and one can remember [or] forget . . . only what is past. A timeless God does not wait . . . hope, foreknow . . . or deliberate. For a timeless God has no future . . . if timeless, God does not change . . . His attitudes or plans."[46] These seem to be "biblical" qualities. Richard Swinburne, Oxford philosopher, also argues: "If God had thus fixed his intention 'from all eternity' he would be a very lifeless thing; not a person who reacts to men with sympathy or anger, pardon or chastening, because he chooses there and then. . . . The God of the Old Testament . . . and Christianity . . . is a God in continual interaction with men."[47]

Nevertheless Helm carefully considers God's foreknowledge in a substantial chapter, and shows how his case relates to human freedom. He urges, "What God foreknows is something that is capable of being expressed in a tenseless form, for that is how he [God] knows it. The timelessness of God's knowledge is ontologically prior to any recognition of his knowledge by time-bound creatures. The crucial assumption . . . is the centrality of timeless truths."[48] Helm adds that this view of God seemed to reign from Augustine to Aquinas, thinkers of no mean stature. Helm makes one of the best and strongest cases for this "timelessness" approach. However, unlike the participants in the Continental European debate, Helm does not seem to allow for a more complex, multidimensional view of time, or what Martin Heidegger called "temporality" (Zeitlichkeit), namely, conditions for the possibility of time. The most serious criticism of Helm, however, is that he writes entirely as a philosopher, appealing to philosophical works, while the biblical material clearly takes second place, with little careful exegesis of relevant passages.

(2) The second view, according to which eternity involves temporal sequence and everlasting duration, at least appeals to the Old Testament notion of "the living God," where the word "living" (Hebrew, chay; Greek, zōn, from zaō) in such phrases as "living water" (John 4:10) denotes running water, in contrast to stagnant water from a pool or jug. As applied to God, it denotes onward-moving. The symbolism of moving cloud and fire in the desert, or of the moving tabernacle and ark (Exod. 23–40) represents the living God of Israel better than the static temple. God revealed his

46. Brian Leftow, "Eternity," in A Companion to the Philosophy of Religion, ed. Philip L. Quinn and Charles Taliaferro (Oxford: Blackwell, 1999), 257.

47. Richard Swinburne, The Coherence of Theism (Oxford: Clarendon, 1977), 214.

48. Helm, Eternal God, 140; cf. 126-43.

Name to Moses in the Hebrew imperfect, best translated, "I will be what I will be" (Exod. 3:14; Hebrew, *'ehyeh 'ăsher 'ehyeh*). This stands in contrast with the Greek Septuagint's mistranslation of the Hebrew, "I am what I am" (Greek, *egō eimi ho ōn,* present indicative and present participle; also NRSV, "I am who I am"). In Isa. 9:7 "forever" occurs in parallel with "there shall be no end."

The New Testament words for "eternity" and "eternal" (Greek, *aiōn* and *aiōnios*) may refer to ages or to the life of the new age. The noun varies from denoting "world" to an "indefinite time," or to a new quality of life derived from Christ. Yet this cannot be said to mean temporal succession in all contexts. Sometimes the phrase "forever" or "the same" is popularly misunderstood, as in Heb. 13:8: "Jesus Christ is the same yesterday, today, and forever." The context is not that of immutability of God in Christ; it is that whereas there is a perpetual succession of Aaronic priests, Christians may always approach Jesus, who has no successor and is unsurpassable. Swinburne cites the Revelation of St. John as saying that "God is Alpha and Omega, the beginning and the end"; and that God is he "who was and is and is to come" (Rev. 1:8, 17; 21:6). But he adds that this does not imply "the doctrine of divine timelessness."[49]

Many see this as the mainstream view before Augustine, and believe that Duns Scotus and William of Ockam rejected a "timeless God" approach. Hegel viewed God as in process, and explicitly argued that eternity is not timelessness. Paul Tillich seems to have shared this view. Some argue that the resurrection of "the body" means the continuance of location and space, although Paul asserts: "You do not sow the body that is to be" (1 Cor. 15:37).

In the end, there are enormous difficulties in placing God among the temporal and contingent entities he has created. Augustine and Aquinas are surely right to accord to God a special status different in kind from the creatures which he has created. Paul Helm, in spite of problems which his view faces, at least seeks to preserve the transcendence, otherness, and sovereignty of God as creator.

(3) This leads us to a strong modification of the "timeless" view, which some would see as a third approach. Following Plotinus, Boethius discussed eternity in two places. His classic and widely known definition comes in his *Consolation of Philosophy:* "Eternity, then, is the complete possession all at once of the illimitable life [Latin, *totum simul*]."[50] Crea-

---

49. Swinburne, *The Coherence of Theism,* 217.
50. Boethius, *The Consolation of Philosophy* (London: J. M. Dent, 1902), bk. 5:6.

tures of time, he urges, are transient. What lives in time "proceeds as something present from the past into the future, and there is nothing placed in time that can embrace the whole extent of its life equally." It has already "lost" yesterday, and does not yet grasp "tomorrow." The present is a mobile, transitory moment. Earlier, in his *On the Trinity* Boethius declares that God signifies a unity: what he has been in the past is all in the present, and will totally endure into the future.[51] Henry Chadwick uses an analogy. He comments, "Boethius suggests . . . that as time is to eternity, so the circle is to the centre. . . . For us, events fall into past, present and future time. God is outside time. For him knowledge of temporal events is an eternal knowledge . . . all is a simultaneous present."[52]

The distinction between this and the "timeless" view may be difficult to distinguish, and sometimes Aquinas and Helm may seem to be defending this view. Nevertheless Aquinas (and perhaps Helm) believes that this view suggests "immutability" in a way which does not seem to be entirely compatible with Scripture.[53] Moreover, Boethius speaks of the eternal not only as "fullness" but also as "enduring"; and we have already noted that it is "illimitable" or without limits. It has no beginning, it is endless, and it therefore has duration. On the one hand, "the complete possession all at once" (Latin, *totum simul*) seems to suggest timelessness; while "illimitable life" seems to suggest duration. Eleonore Stump and Norman Kretzmann declare, "Eternity is a mode of existence that is, on Boethius' view, neither reducible to time, nor incompatible with the reality of time."[54] This facing both ways probably encounters least difficulties compared with the other two approaches, but suffers from some ambiguity and oversimplification. Some, therefore, prefer to explore a fourth model.

(4) Why did we spend so long in exploring the complexity of time in everyday situations? We aimed to show that time is *not one thing*. What time is depends decisively upon context. We can now speak of a postresurrection, non-earthly context. David Wilkinson leans toward Boethius's definition: "God experiences all time at once and knows every moment of the future as well as the past simultaneously."[55] Moreover, "eternity is where God dwells."

51. Boethius, *On the Trinity*, 4.

52. Henry Chadwick, *Boethius* (Oxford: Clarendon, 1981), 242 and 246.

53. Aquinas, *Summa Theologiae*, 1a, Q. 10, art. 2.

54. Eleonore Stump and Norman Kretzmann, "Eternity," in *Philosophy of Religion: The Big Questions*, ed. Eleonore Stump and Michael J. Murray (Oxford and Malden, MA: Blackwell, 1999), 44.

55. Wilkinson, *Christian Eschatology and the Physical Universe*, 124.

But he then adds, "The four dimensions of space-time are laid out as a sheet before God. . . . God has both eternal and temporal poles to his nature. . . . We need to see time as a fundamental part of eternity. . . . [But we need] the notion of multiple dimensions."[56] It is easy to imagine a two-dimensional world in spatial terms, like *Flatland,* in which a visitor arrives from a three-dimensional world, unlimited in the way that two-dimensional creatures have been limited. He sees and understands more than they do. If we now extend the analogy, we can think of a one-dimensional world in time, with an irreversible and one-directional flow. Now let us imagine a world in which a visitor from a reality with two or more dimensions in time enters the one-dimensional temporal world. The visitor's interaction with that world "could be both describable but inexplicable to the inhabitants. . . . Our experience of time in the physical universe is a small and limited part of an ontologically real time that we might call eternity."[57] God, Wilkinson asserts, inhabits these higher dimensions of time.

My close agreement with Wilkinson arises from the fact that for forty years I have been convinced that the discussion founders because writers talk of "time" rather than of *"our"* time, *social* time, *clock* time, and *God's* time as something quite different from each other. That is why I earlier explained how different "narrative time" often was from chronological time. Paul Ricoeur is one of those who have further explained this phenomenon.[58] David Wilkinson, however, takes us further by arguing, "Such an analogy receives support from the claim that certain models for quantum gravity require ten or even 26 dimensions for the physical universe."[59] Our three dimensions of space and one of time, he suggests, crystallize out in the early stages of the emergence of the Universe from the Big Bang. This early crystallization reflects God's purposive and creative action.

Wilkinson cites E. M. Conradie on depth dimension, and his contention that "higher dimensions would, by definition, be inaccessible to scientific investigation."[60] To repeat an old aphorism in the face of positivism, "Our everyday experience of the universe is not all there is."[61] To be fair,

---

56. Wilkinson, *Christian Eschatology and the Physical Universe,* 124 and 125.

57. Wilkinson, *Christian Eschatology and the Physical Universe,* 126.

58. Paul Ricoeur, *Time and Narrative* (3 vols.; Chicago: University of Chicago Press, 1984-88), vol. 2, 5-94, and esp. vol. 3, 12-98.

59. Wilkinson, *Christian Eschatology and the Physical Universe,* 126.

60. E. M. Conradie, "Resurrection, Finitude and Ecology," in T. Peters, *Assessments* (Grand Rapids: Eerdmans, 2002), 290; cf. 277-96.

61. Wilkinson, *Christian Eschatology and the Physical Universe,* 126.

Swinburne insists that there cannot be more than three dimensions. But relativity and quantum theory may suggest otherwise, and even "dimension" may stimulate imagination of the possible, even if the term were to be used analogically. We are on speculative ground.

Perhaps further support comes indirectly from the moving volume of essays edited by John Polkinghorne under the title *The Work of Love: Creation as Kenosis*.[62] Keith Ward, for example, rejects the classical idea of a flawless perfection of the immutable God who bears no relation to time. God realizes possibilities that are eternally present. "When God gives up pure bliss, he obtains in return many new sorts of values that could only be actualized in a cosmic process from which finite beings emerge. . . . By self-limitation . . . God not only suffers new things, God also enjoys and delights in new things." Ward continues, "If we can speak of *kenosis* in God, a renunciation of his absolute and unmixed perfection, we must also speak of a *plēroma* or fulfilment in God, by which new forms of perfection are added by creatures to the divine being. . . . This is in accordance with the continuation of the passage in Philippians 2:5-11. . . . God wills to realize the divine nature in creation, relationship, and co-operation."[63]

Various other writers in this volume have discussed kenosis in very positive and moving terms. Arthur Peacocke regards suffering as a key to progress; why should we regard it as a negative quality, divorced from the "timeless" God?[64] Holmes Rolston speaks of nature providing regeneration by labor pains, whereby all creation "travails until now" (Rom. 8:22); thus God created "a cruciform nature." Jürgen Moltmann sees the very creation of the world as God's "self-humiliation." He does not stand isolated from suffering and time, because "it is not God's power that is almighty. What is almighty is his love."[65] The nature of God is not timeless perfection and isolation, but choosing to go out of himself in love to engage with a temporal creation. All approaches to "eternity" seek to guard some particular truth. But what we have listed as a fourth approach seems to offer the most comprehensive account of "eternity," even if the third commands respect.

62. John Polkinghorne (ed.), *The Work of Love: Creation as Kenosis* (Grand Rapids: Eerdmans and London: S.P.C.K., 2001).

63. Keith Ward, "Cosmos and Kenosis," in *The Work of Love*, ed. Polkinghorne, 158, 160, and 161; cf. 152-66.

64. Arthur Peacocke, "The Cost of New Life," in *The Work of Love*, ed. Polkinghorne, 31.

65. Jürgen Moltmann, "God's Kenosis in the Creation and Consummation of the World," in *The Work of Love*, ed. Polkinghorne, 146; cf. 137-51.

CHAPTER 9

Claims about "Hell" and Wrath

This chapter has demanded more reading and reflection than others. Yet students have tended to express greater appreciation for considering the Last Judgment and kindred questions than many other themes in systematic theology or doctrine. Perhaps this is partly because many treatments of doctrine, and even sermons, simply sidestep these issues as if it is somehow unnecessary or bad taste to explore them. Certainly James P. Martin shows that the subject has rapidly declined in the light of liberalism, especially on the part of Schleiermacher and Ritschl toward the end of the nineteenth century. He writes that Ritschl refused to admit "any attribute of God save that of love. . . . Ritschl rejects wrath in the New Testament. . . ."[1] Yet it is not difficult to understand why. *Love* remains a *permanent* feature of God's character; *wrath* is not permanent. Moltmann thinks that "hell" denies God's sovereign grace. However, we begin by showing that three different views were already prominent in the early Church: annihilation, universal restoration, and everlasting torment.[2]

9.1. The Nature of "Hell": Everlasting Punishment in Christian Thought

(1) It is a mistake to be seduced into thinking that "hell" has always denoted *everlasting punishment in "orthodox" theology,* just as it is equally

---

1. J. P. Martin, *The Last Judgement in Protestant Theology from Orthodoxy to Ritschl* (Edinburgh: Oliver & Boyd, 1963), 203.
2. At the time of writing, I. Moreira and M. Toscanano, *Hell and Its Afterlife* (Aldershot: Ashgate, 2011), was not yet available.

misguided to relegate the notion to only a premodern era of the Church, or to fundamentalism. Helpfully David Powys has looked carefully at historical questions as well as biblical thought.[3] He concedes on his first page that Origen was condemned at the Council of Constantinople in 553 for his doctrine of the restoration of all things (Greek, *apokatastasis*), in spite of the presence of the word in the New Testament (Acts 3:21). But he insists that from the very beginning of the Church three different views were in circulation, none of which could be called "orthodox" until later. Irenaeus (c. 130–c. 200) stressed the importance of the unitary nature of people and the centrality of corporeal resurrection. Because resurrection of the dead depends on union with Christ in his resurrection, he tended to endorse the view which today is called "conditional immortality." Quite rightly he saw that resurrection and immortality is not a natural, intrinsic property of humans. It constitutes *a gift of God*. His general view of the fate of the wicked is that they will inherit ruin or loss of life, since they become separated from God, who is the *giver of life*. After quoting, "Know you not the unrighteous shall not inherit the kingdom of God?" and kindred passages (1 Cor. 6:9-11; Gal. 5:19), he comments, "He shows in the clearest manner through what things it is that a man goes to destruction" (*Against Heresies* 5.11.1; also *ANF*, vol. 1, 537).

(i) In *Against Heresies* 4.39, according to Powys, Irenaeus discusses choosing between good and evil. He observes, "How can man be immortal, who in his mortal nature did not obey his Maker?" (*Against Heresies* 4.39.2; also in *ANF*, vol. 1, 523). In discussing the nature of Christ, he says of unbelievers: "They are deprived of His [God's] gift, which is eternal life," and they cannot attain to "incorruptibility and immortality" (*Against Heresies* 3.19.1; also *ANF*, vol. 1, 448). Elsewhere he declares, "God alone . . . is without beginning and without end" (*Against Heresies* 2.34.2; also *ANF*, vol. 1, 411). Irenaeus also tells us that "those who separate themselves from God" partake of the calamities of the world (*Against Heresies* 5.18.1; *ANF*, vol. 1, 556). Admittedly here he also calls this "eternal fire," but the fire (which is eternal) leads only to "deprivation." Irenaeus sums up the point: "Life does not arise from us, nor from our own nature, but is *bestowed* according to the grace of God" (*Against Heresies* 2.34.3). Powys insists that Irenaeus represents one of three possible views in the Patristic Church.[4]

---

3. David Powys, *"Hell": A Hard Look at a Hard Question* (Milton Keynes and Waynesboro, GA: Paternoster, 1997), with a Foreword by Graham Stanton.

4. Powys, *"Hell": A Hard Look*, 2-4.

Irenaeus also inherited views from Polycarp of Smyrna and the East, and from Lyons, Rome, and the West. He is therefore well grounded in the apostolic tradition of the whole Church.

(ii) Powys next turns to Gregory of Nyssa (c. 330–c. 395) the younger brother of Basil of Caesarea. He was a Christian and theologian of some originality, stressing the view of the Trinity found in the Cappadocian Fathers and taking part in the Council of Constantinople (381 and 394). Unlike Irenaeus, he believed that all humanity was destined to enjoy immortality. Unlike Plato, he rejected a dualist view of human nature, and rejected his view of cyclical time. This also distinguishes him from Origen. But like Origen, he believed in the restoration of all things (Acts 3:21), and today he would be classed as *universalist.* He argues in the Great Catechism: "It is the peculiar effect of light to make darkness vanish, and of life to destroy death. . . . cleansing reaches those who are befouled with sin; and life, the dead. . . . Error may be corrected, and what was dead [is] restored to life" (Gregory of Nyssa, *Catechism* 24; also in *NPNF,* ser. 2, vol. 5, 494). The Deity penetrates the universe; all things depend on him who is: "Therefore all things are in him, and he in all things. . . . His [Christ's] return from death becomes to our mortal race the commencement of our return to immortal life" (Gregory, *Catechism* 25; also in *NPNF,* ser. 2, vol. 5, 495).

Gregory is still more explicit in his philosophical work *On the Making of Man.* He asserts, "Now the resurrection promises us nothing else than the restoration of the fallen to their ancient state . . . bringing back again to Paradise him who was cast out from it" (Gregory, *On the Making of Man* 17.2; also in *NPNF,* ser. 2, vol. 5, 407). In case it is objected that this referred to once-fallen believers, Gregory elsewhere argues, "The LORD is good to all" (Ps. 145:16, LXX; *Catechism* 40; also *NPNF,* ser. 2, vol. 5, 508). If sin is punished at all, it is "removed by some remedial process, the medicine which virtue supplies . . . to the healing" (*Catechism* 8; also *NPNF,* ser. 2, vol. 5, 483). Later notions of Purgatory owe much to Gregory. Evil is deceptive and in the present mixed with good, but it cannot continue forever (Gregory, *On the Making of Man* 20.1, 2). Some may need to experience a period of purification, but in the end, all will enjoy salvation.

(iii) Powys further argues that Augustine of Hippo (354-430), the greatest theologian of the Western or Latin Church, taught "unending physical torment."[5] He is considering the Fall of humankind and the finality of

---

5. Powys, *"Hell": A Hard Look,* 6; cf. 6-10.

death when he writes: "The death of the soul takes place when God forsakes it. . . . The soul . . . is tormented. For in that penal and everlasting punishment . . . the soul is justly said to die, because it does not live in connection with God. . . . It could not otherwise feel the bodily torments which are to follow the resurrection. . . . In the last damnation, though man does not cease to feel. . . . this feeling is . . . painfully penal; it is called death rather than life" (Augustine, *City of God* 13.2; also *NPNF*, ser. 1, vol. 2, 245).

In his doctrinal "Handbook" Augustine declares, "Whoever are not liberated from that mass of perdition . . . will also rise again . . . but only that they may be punished, together with the devil and his angels. . . . *This damnation is certain and eternal.* . . . Where an unhappy being is not allowed to die, then death itself, so to say, does not. . . . Pain perpetually afflicts, but never destroys; corruption goes on endlessly. This state is called, in the Scripture, 'the second death' (Rev. 2:11; 20:6, 14)" (*Enchiridion* 23.92; also in Augustine, *Confessions and Enchiridion*, ed. Albert C. Outler, LCC 7 [London: S.C.M. and Philadelphia: Westminster, 1965, 393]).

Augustine even paints this horrendous picture in darker colors by coupling eternal doom with predestination to that state. He explores the origin of two respective "cities," and comments, "This [human] race we have distributed into two parts, the one . . . those who live according to man; the other . . . those who live according to God. . . . One is predestined to reign eternally with God, and the other to suffer eternal punishment with the devil" (Augustine, *City of God* 15.1; also *NPNF*, ser. 1, vol. 2, 284).

David Powys does not compare enough evidence from the period of the Church Fathers to gauge the proportion of those who follow each of these lines of approach. His main, if not only, concern is to suggest that we should not characterize the Augustinian tradition of eternal torment as "the orthodox view." At least three very different views competed in the early Church, all of them seeking some support from Scripture. But even this is too simple. Augustine sees God as "All-creating and All-sustaining," and in his discussion of time nevertheless seemed, according to Geoffrey Rowell, to "hope" for universal salvation.[6] How, in any case, can Augustine see God as timeless, or at least above time, if an "eternal" condition is everlastingness, like time stretched out to infinity? Powys simply wishes to show that eternal punishment, rather than being "*the* orthodox view of the Church," simply covers its widespread acceptance first to the influence of

6. Augustine, *Confessions*, ed. Henry Chadwick (Oxford: Oxford University Press, 1991), bk. 11, ch. 13:15; cf. 11:5(7)-21(41).

Augustine, and second of Aquinas, as the dominant view of the Western Church, until perhaps the middle or late nineteenth century.

(2) We must consider further the case argued by Augustine and his tradition. We may first note, however, the situation from the nineteenth century until today. Geoffrey Rowell begins his study of hell with the bold statement, "Heaven, hell, death, and judgement are the traditional Four Last Things of Christian theology, but . . . twentieth-century theologians have, for the most part, been embarrassed at saying much about any of them. In this they stand in sharp contrast to the majority of nineteenth-century divines, who . . . regarded it as a central part of Christian teaching."[7]

The death rate before 1900 and 1935 was startlingly different from today, when it is easier to postpone indefinitely questions about death and the postmortal condition than when the death of children and friends was a regular experience. Debate about the fate of unbelievers dominated the nineteenth century, with Samuel Coleridge, F. D. Maurice, John Henry Newman, E. B. Pusey, and F. W. Farrar expressing views on the subject. As is well known, in around 1853 F. D. Maurice was dismissed from his Chair at King's College, London, for arguing against eternal or everlasting punishment, largely on the grounds that "eternal" did not denote an infinite extension of the temporal process. Rowell points out, however, that Maurice expressed universalism as a hope rather than as a dogma.[8] While Maurice found "deathbed moralism" repulsive, the evangelical Henry Venn urged parents to let their children have experience of Christian deathbeds.

The lynchpin of a biblical and historical view of hell is that hell denotes the absence of the presence of God. The greatest difficulty of the "everlasting punishment" view may be partly the relation between eternity and time; but even more fundamentally *how we can conceive of God eternally sustaining both the life of believers in fellowship with him, and also that of a group who are in every other sense "separate" from him.* Although it is usually unhelpful to speak of "-isms," does this flagrantly imply a *dualism* in reality, in which God gladly sustains the life of those in fellowship with him, and more reluctantly sustains the lives of those in torment, who are "separated" from him?

Yet if there is *no* "hell," as Nicholas Berdyaev and others insist, what are we to make of human freedom? Berdyaev observes that hell is neces-

---

7. Geoffrey Rowell, *Hell and the Victorians* (Oxford: Clarendon, 1974), 1.
8. Rowell, *Hell and the Victorians*, 76-89, esp. 88.

sary to save man from being forced to be compulsorily installed in heaven.[9] Rowell concludes his book, "We cannot do without a doctrine of hell, for it stands as a vitally important reminder of the reality and seriousness of the experience of alienation, isolation, and estrangement, and the consequences of evil. . . ."[10] He admits that hell may be expounded in a way which makes God morally "obnoxious and repellent," and that the theologian's path is perilous; but we must avoid distortions, confusions, and reductionism.

Yet in the Western Church the influence of Augustine and Aquinas was dominant. The Fourth Lateran Council of 1215 spoke of "perpetual punishment with the devil." Anselm encouraged the idea. Aquinas taught an endless "physical" punishment by fire, although his distinction between "venial" and "mortal" sin served to modify the Augustinian tradition. Yet he anticipates some of the most extreme Protestant Puritans. For example, he (or his close associate) cites Psalm 11:6: "Fire and brimstone and storms of winds shall be the portion of their cup."[11] Purgatory is intended not to punish, but to cleanse. He then quotes Matt. 22:13, "Cast him into the exterior darkness."[12] The breath of the Lord is "a torrent of brimstone kindling it [the fire]."[13] "Fire continues in that place for all eternity by the ordering of divine justice."[14] He further cites 1 Cor. 6:9-10 and James 2:10 to argue that "not all who have the Catholic faith will be freed from eternal punishment."[15] In spite of all these more speculative expositions of Augustine, Aquinas does see the fate of unbelievers most of all as "the loss of God."[16] We have considered Purgatory in Chapter 8.

Among the Reformers, no less a thinker than John Calvin argued for the Augustinian-Thomist view, but only on the basis of biblical passages which he saw as supporting that view. He spoke of "darkness, wailing and gnashing of teeth, inextinguishable fire, the ever-gnawing worm (Matt. 8:12; 22:13; Mark 9:43; Isa. 66:24) . . . and the breath of the Lord, like a

9. Nicholas Berdyaev, *The Destiny of Man* (London: Bles, 1937), 267; cf. Nicholas Berdyaev, *The Beginning and the End* (London: Bles, 1952), 229-54.

10. Rowell, *Hell and the Victorians*, 221.

11. Thomas Aquinas, *Summa Theologiae* (London: Eyre & Spottiswoode, 1963), Part 3 (Supplement), Q. 97, art. 1.

12. Aquinas, *Summa Theologiae*, Part 3 (Supplement), Q. 97, art. 4.

13. Aquinas, *Summa Theologiae*, Part 3 (Supplement), Q. 97, art. 6.

14. Aquinas, *Summa Theologiae*, Part 3 (Supplement), Q. 97, art. 7 (reply to obj. 2).

15. Aquinas, *Summa Theologiae*, Part 3 (Supplement), Q. 99, art. 5.

16. Aquinas, *Summa Theologiae*, Part 3 (Supplement), Q. 87, arts. 2-5.

stream of brimstone . . . (Isa. 30:33)."[17] Calvin quotes in full 2 Thess. 1:9, "punished with everlasting destruction from the presence of the Lord, and from the glory of his power."[18] Yet out of some 1200 pages of text, little explicitly concerns the fate of the wicked. Indeed, commenting on 2 Thess. 1:8-9, John Chrysostom asserts, "If we always think of hell, we shall not soon fall into it. . . . Do you fear the offensiveness of such words? Have you, if you are silent, extinguished hell? . . . Let it be continually spoken of that you may never fall into it. . . . No one of those who have hell before their eyes will fall into hell."[19] Tertullian similarly cites the "eternal destruction from the presence of the Lord" in 2 Thess. 1:8-9.[20] In the Reformation era the Roman Catholic writer Estius, and the Protestants James Arminius and later John Owen, followed this approach.

Thomas Vincent (1634-78) wrote one of the harshest accounts of the fate of unbelievers ever written. The fate of Sodom and Gomorrah, he wrote, is only a shadow of the fire and brimstone "which in hell shall burn the wicked eternally."[21] He cited Matt. 13:30, 25:41, on the unquenchable fire, and 2 Thess. 1:8-9 on everlasting punishment. He wrote, "You will be ready to tear yourselves to pieces for madness and vexation."[22] Only anguish of soul will exceed torture of body.

9.2. An Assessment of the Biblical Evidence

We must now assess the biblical evidence to which those in the Augustinian tradition appeal. "Gehenna" (the Latin term) was often cited. This was originally a place where Kings Ahaz and Manasseh of Judah condoned pagan worship, including child sacrifice (2 Kings 16:3; 23:10; Jer. 7:31; 32:35). But the term "Gehenna" does not appear in the Septuagint, and the Hebrew speaks only of "the valley of Hinnom." It is referred to three times in the Sermon on the Mount (Matt. 5:22, 29, 30); in Matt. 10:28; and twice in the passage of woes to the Pharisees (Matt. 23:15, 33). The NRSV translates

---

17. John Calvin, *Institutes of the Christian Religion* (2 vols.; London: James Clarke, 1957), 3.25.12 (vol. 2, 275).

18. Calvin, *Institutes,* 3.25.12 (vol. 2, 276).

19. John Chrysostom, *Homilies on 2 Thessalonians, Homily 2* (*NPNF,* ser. 1, vol. 13, 382-83).

20. Tertullian, *Against Marcion* 5.6 (also in *ANF,* vol. 3, 463).

21. Thomas Vincent, *Fire and Brimstone in Hell,* repr. *Gospel Truth Forum* C.D., 1.

22. Vincent, *Fire and Brimstone,* ch. 5.

it as "hell" or "hell of fire" (Greek, *geennē tou pyros*, or *geennan* in Matthew 5, *en geennē* in Matt. 10:28; and the genitive *geennēs* in Matthew 23). Mark 9:43, 45, 47 is parallel with Matthew 10, as is Luke 12:5. Proponents of the Augustinian tradition argue that this is about hell. Powys insists, however, "This utterance was not concerned with the fate of the unrighteous. . . . It was a call to holiness."[23] Mark adds, "where their worm never dies, and the fire is never quenched" (Greek, *to pyr to asbeston*), but C. E. B. Cranfield and Vincent Taylor suggest that this may well be "Mark's own explanatory comment, based on Isa. 66:24, for the benefit of his Gentile readers."[24] On the Lukan passage, Powys comments, "The fundamental thrust of Lk. 12:4, 5, is not so much that God casts anyone into Gehenna, [but] . . . that . . . God's power extends beyond death."[25]

Some might suggest that Powys has his own motive for this interpretation of Gehenna. But the Evangelical Alliance report *The Nature of Hell*, which is not opposed to the traditional view, admits, "None of the . . . verses specifically mentions the *duration* of Gehenna."[26] This report rightly stresses exclusion from the kingdom of God in the Synoptic Gospels. But one problem for the traditional view is that most or all of such references come from the parables of Jesus. The Parable of the Sheep and the Goats (Matt. 25:31-46) and the Parable of the Rich Man and Lazarus (Luke 16:19-31) are perhaps the most discussed. Is an "eternal postmortal state" central to what Jesus is saying, or simply stage setting of the parable? Admittedly not all of such warnings constitute part of parables. For example, those who choose to disobey Christ are told, "I never knew you; go away from me, you evil-doers" (Matt. 7:23). On the other hand, there is no reference to duration or even to permanency here. Yet "Go in through the narrow gate" (Luke 13:24) assumes that there is a broad way that leads to destruction.

The parables certainly do not have postmortal conditions as their primary content. Most are an existential or practical call to responsibility and accountability. Powys, again, reminds us that in response to the disciples' question, "Lord, will those who are saved be few?" Jesus did not answer that question, but urged, "Strive to enter the kingdom" (Luke 13:23, 24-30).[27] "Weeping and gnashing of teeth" (Luke 13:28; Matt. 8:12) is a power-

23. Powys, *"Hell": A Hard Look*, 277.

24. C. E. B. Cranfield, *St. Mark*, Cambridge Greek Testament (Cambridge: Cambridge University Press, 1963), 314.

25. Powys, *"Hell": A Hard Look*, 280.

26. Evangelical Alliance Commission, *The Nature of Hell* (London: Acute, 2000), 43.

27. Powys, *"Hell": A Hard Look*, 274.

ful image of remorse. Standing at the closed door is a more wistful and sorrowful one. Yet "there" (Greek, *ekei*) means "in that place" (not "there-shall-be"), even if it remains part of the imagery. The parabolic language about the fate of the Servant who received one Talent (Matt 25:30) simply means that if a person is unwilling to take responsibility (in the parable, of investment), that person deprives himself of opportunity (in the parable, of ruling over ten cities).

This language in Matthew, Mark and Luke certainly seems to underline the concept of some serious losses which those who advocate a universalist theory of salvation must face. But many argue, as Powys does, that this loss denotes not everlasting punishment, but sheer destruction. We shall consider shortly whether destruction must be instant, but it certainly is not everlasting. Meanwhile, Powys declares, "Destruction is the most common way of depicting the fate of the unrighteous within the Synoptic Gospels."[28] As to other references to "hell," he cites C. S. Lewis as observing, "The Dominical utterances about Hell, like all Dominical sayings, are addressed to the conscience and the will, not to our intellectual curiosity."[29]

Not everyone is convinced by this. The Evangelical Alliance Commission concludes, "The New Testament . . . implies some duration of punishment," though "John, Paul and the other letters refer mainly to perishing, destruction, and death."[30] On Paul, Powys similarly concludes, "Existential human experience rather than . . . prospective divine action" is the main point in such passages as Rom. 1:18-32.[31] Rom. 9:22 speaks of "objects of wrath that are made for destruction" (Greek, *skeuē orgēs katērtismena eis apōleian*). But here there appears to be no hint of eternal torment, only of destruction. The Fourth Gospel has no reference to Gehenna, torment, or fire. Usually, if John touches on the fate of unbelievers, it is said that willful refusal to recognize Christ results in (or is the fruit of) blindness and disobedience, and leads to perishing or death. Clearly the unbeliever will somehow participate in the resurrection, but will then be condemned (John 5:29). Believers, by contrast, "will not perish, but have eternal life" (John 3:16); will cross from death to life (5:24); will "never perish" (10:28); and will "never die" (11:26). 1 John is similar: believers "passed from death to life" in contrast to the loveless who "remain in death" (1 John 3:14). A

28. Powys, *"Hell": A Hard Look,* 284.

29. C. S. Lewis, *The Problem of Pain* (London: Bles, 1940), 107; cf. Powys, *"Hell": A Hard Look,* 295.

30. Evangelical Alliance Commission, *The Nature of Hell,* 51.

31. Powys, *"Hell": A Hard Look,* 310.

reference to "punishment" occurs in 4:17-18; but usually it is a matter of life or death (5:16).

A closer investigation of Paul shows that he never speaks of "hell," but regularly of death (Greek, *thanatos*): "The wages of sin is death" (Rom. 6:23); "The message about the cross is foolishness to those who are perishing" (1 Cor. 1:18; Greek, *apollymenois*). We shall consider "wrath" shortly, and in the next chapter "judgment" (Greek, *katakrima* and cognate terms). "Destruction" (Greek, *apōleia*), occurs in Rom. 9:22; Phil. 1:28; 3:19; 1 Thess. 5:3; 2 Thess. 1:9. Only one passage seems to support the traditional Augustinian view. In 2 Thess. 1:8-9, Paul (some would say a Pauline associate) declares, "Those who do not obey the gospel of our Lord Jesus Christ . . . will suffer the punishment of eternal destruction, separated from the presence of the Lord, and from the glory of his might." But "eternal destruction" (Greek, *olethron aiōnion*) still means "destruction," even if "eternal" refers to its quality.

Admittedly, as we have seen, John Chrysostom does understand the reference to refer to "hell," and argues, "It is not temporary" (*Homilies on 2 Thessalonians*, Hom. 2 and 3; *NPNF*, ser. 1, vol. 13, 384-85). Perhaps he means "not reversible." For although Frederick Danker interprets *aiōnios* to mean "pertinent to a period of time without beginning or end" or "without end," in this context *olethros*, he states, usually means "a *state* of destruction, ruin, death" (my italics), so that it is the *state* of destruction which will not end.[32] Abraham Malherbe translates it "eternal ruin," but adds, "It does not mean annihilation."[33] He relates it to 1 Cor. 5:5; Phil. 1:28; *Pss. Sol.* 2:31, 34; Heb. 6:2; and Matt. 18:8; 25:41. Many Patristic commentators, he notes, interpreted *apo-* temporally; others saw it as equivalent to *ek*. But Malherbe sees it as causal; bringing ruin by his presence. It seems to be more serious than a straightforward cessation of existence.

Such questions reintroduce more broadly theological ones. *If "hell" means separated from all that is good in the presence of God, can we conceive of the human entity still existing by virtue of its own life?* Paul Tillich, one of the most metaphysical theologians of the twentieth century, makes two comments about "hell." First, it underlines "the seriousness of the condemning side of the divine judgement, the despair in which the exposure

---

32. Frederick Danker, *A Greek-English Lexicon* (called BDAG), 33-34 on *aiōnios;* and 702 on *olethros.*

33. Abraham J. Malherbe, *The Letters to the Thessalonians*, AB (New Haven: Yale University Press, 2000), 402.

of the negative is experienced."[34] But, second, he cannot conceive of a dualism or split in the divine nature which allows for a realm of darkness, disobedience, and ruin to co-exist forever by his sustaining power. Splits in the nature of reality are for him demonic, and render the nature of an enduring hell absurd. This would not be a stark problem if "destruction" was thought to be the main description of the fate of unbelievers. Hebrews speaks of "those who are destroyed" (Heb. 10:39); 2 Pet. 3:7, 9, 16 also speak of "destruction." Revelation uses this term (Rev. 11:18); but it also refers to torment (14:9-11); "the second death" (2:11); torment forever (20:10); and the lake of fire or burning sulphur (21:8). Dan. 12:2 speaks of "everlasting contempt."

The Evangelical Alliance Commission, however, seems to label everyone who advocates the "cessation of life" view as a *"conditionalist."*[35] We must consider this problem. "Conditionalism" means the theory of *conditional immortality; i.e., immortality does not depend on innate human capacity, but is conditional upon God's gift of immortality or resurrection.* Although the Evangelical Alliance Commission and textbooks of this persuasion claim that the notion begins with the early Church Fathers, it was first a clear inference from Paul's teaching about the resurrection. Paul insists that resurrection is a gift of God, as much as justification by grace through faith alone. *It is a mistake to identify absolutely with annihilationism and the total nonexistence of hell,* as the Evangelical Alliance Commission and many traditional conservative writers suggest.[36] But *nowhere in the New Testament is resurrection due to innate capacity of human beings.* "Annihilationism" is widely taken to mean extinction or annihilation immediately after death. The unbeliever, on this basis, will know nothing of "the Last Things" except only this-worldly experience of dying, and "hell" would become an empty concept. Numerous books and debates offer only the two extremes of immediate extinction or everlasting torment. We reject both of these alternatives.

Many so-called universalists, like F. D. Maurice and others, hold to the *possibility* and *hope* of universal salvation on the grounds of the victory of love of God. Jürgen Moltmann bids us to remember three biblical verses: "If I make my bed in hell, thou art there" (Ps. 139:8); Christ alone has "the

---

34. Paul Tillich, *Systematic Theology,* vol. 3 (London: Nisbet, 1964), 435.
35. Evangelical Alliance Commission, *The Nature of Hell,* 52.
36. Evangelical Alliance Commission, *The Nature of Hell,* 60-67; L. Berkhof, *Systematic Theology* (London: The Banner of Truth, 1959), 690-92.

keys of death and hell" (Rev. 1:18); and Paul's exclamation, "Hell, where is your victory?" (1 Cor. 15:55).[37] He argues that if any creature were "lost," this would constitute *a defeat for the love of God*, especially since his ultimate purpose is that "God may be all in all" (1 Cor. 15:28), that "all things will be united in Christ" (Eph. 1:10), and that "all things will be reconciled to him, whether on earth or in heaven" (Col. 1:20).

Moltmann goes even further in his book *Sun of Righteousness, Arise!*, published in German in 2009 and in English in 2010. Anticipating our Chapter 10 on the Last Judgment, he insists that the central theme of God's judgment is not the Aristotelian concept of equivalent justice, but "putting things right, which saves and heals."[38] Often, he declares, the appeal to the God who "creates justice for those who suffer violence" finds expression in the protection of the weak. He rejects most of the medieval pictures of judgment. The universal glorification of God, he argues, necessitates "universal reconciliation."[39] Even "annihilation" does not constitute an option, for "death will be destroyed" (1 Cor. 15:26). Moltmann rejects Dispensationalist pictures of a cosmic battle between God and the forces of evil, and the interpretation of "snatched away" as a rapture. He concludes: "Every theology of grace tends towards universalism . . . in the triumph of grace." He contrasts this theology of grace with a theology of faith, "which starts from the decision of the believer, and hence issues in the separation of believers from the unbelieving: . . . 'God has consigned all men to disobedience that he may have mercy upon all'" (Rom. 11:32).[40] To end the world with a division into believers and unbelievers would, he says, be a defeat for the grace of God. If this occurred, "God would not be God."[41]

We may note that Tom Wright, former Bishop of Durham, also rejects the two extreme positions of "dogmatic universalism" and everlasting torment.[42] In fact we find several points of affinity with Wright in this chapter. He traces the doctrine of Purgatory, for example, through Aquinas, Dante, and Newman, and rejects it as a distinctly Roman Catholic doctrine. He shows how even Karl Rahner and the former Cardinal Ratzinger,

---

37. Jürgen Moltmann, *In the End — In the Beginning* (London: S.C.M., 2004), 148.

38. Jürgen Moltmann, *Sun of Righteousness Arise! God's Future for Humanity and the Earth* (London: S.C.M., 2010), 130.

39. Moltmann, *Sun of Righteousness*, 141.

40. Moltmann, *Sun of Righteousness*, 148.

41. Moltmann, *Sun of Righteousness*, 141.

42. Tom Wright (also N.T.), *Surprised by Hope* (London: S.P.C.K., 2007), 177-98.

now Pope Benedict XVI, modified this doctrine as "not . . . a long-drawn-out process, but in the moment of final judgement itself."[43] Similarly he rejects the usual significance of All Souls' Day (November 2nd), which he calls "a tenth-century Benedictine innovation."

Tom Wright rejects, as Moltmann does, the image of hell which uses medieval imagery rather than the earliest Christian writings. He makes broadly the points about Gehenna and parabolic imagery which can be found above. He concludes, "We cannot therefore look to Jesus' teaching for any fresh detail on whether there are really some who finally reject God."[44] He points out, further, that "hell" is not mentioned in Acts, which constitutes a crucial point for those who see it as an indispensable part of missionary preaching, or gospel preaching. He warns against the "double dogmatism . . . both of the person who knows exactly who is and who isn't 'going to hell', and that of the universalist who is absolutely certain that there is no such place (as hell) or that it will . . . be empty."[45] "Dogmatic" universalism, as an assured doctrine, was *not* held by F. D. Maurice, who adopted "universalism" only as a *hope*, and the "liberal optimism" of the 1960s and 1970s cannot speak in the face of the genuine evil of the Balkans, Rwanda, Darfur, the Middle East, and Zimbabwe, let alone Auschwitz, genocide, child prostitution, and so on. Wright stresses the special evil of "subhuman" behavior, and the idolatry of money, sex, and power. He concludes, "My suggestion is that it is possible for human beings so to continue down this road . . . that after death they become at last, by their own affective choice, beings that *once were human but now are not . . . ;* beyond hope, but also beyond pity."[46] Admittedly however, this is "territory that no one can claim to have mapped."[47] He adds, "I shall be glad to be proved wrong."[48] In the next chapter, on judgment, I suggest that if God's vindication of the oppressed includes *those weighed down with constraints imposed upon them,* by their race, gender, culture, or upbringing, who is to say how far God's act of vindication can or will reach? They may have experienced no gospel and no Church.

This gives a wonderful picture of the all-conquering love of God. Yet in the end it might be argued that human freedom is overcome by irresist-

43. Wright, *Surprised by Hope*, 179.
44. Wright, *Surprised by Hope*, 189.
45. Wright, *Surprised by Hope*, 190.
46. Wright, *Surprised by Hope*, 195 (his italics).
47. Wright, *Surprised by Hope*, 195.
48. Wright, *Surprised by Hope*, 196.

ible grace. Moltmann consciously distances from the 1995 Report of the Church of England Doctrine Commission, for example, which asserts, "It is our conviction that the reality of hell (and indeed of heaven) is the ultimate affirmation of the reality of human freedom. Hell is not eternal torment, but it is the final and irreversible choosing of that which is opposed to God so completely and so absolutely that the only end is total non-being."[49] The Commission even approves of John Burnaby's comment, "Dogmatic universalism contradicts the very nature of love. . . . Love cannot compel the surrender of a single heart that holds out against it. . . . Love never forces."[50] On one side, it is difficult to imagine obstinate resistance in the light of God's love; on the other, it is hard to imagine forces of ingrained self-absorption and narcissism choosing to yield control of their lives. For some, stubborn self-will is bound up with their very identity.

What we can be sure of is that many of these questions lie beyond our horizons in the present. On the one hand, we endorse C. S. Lewis's warning that these issues are written in the biblical writings not to satisfy intellectual curiosity, but to summon us to responsibility in solemn concern. On the other hand, we remain unconvinced by Rudolf Bultmann's valiant but mistaken attempt to "deobjectify" everything in the Bible that he chooses to regard as myth. We have discussed elsewhere in detail why we cannot accept Bultmann's proposals.[51] The darker side of language about "the Last Things" cannot all be hypotheses, designed to imply accountability, but with no clear indication of how, when, or to whom. Yet an overly objectified understanding of "the Last Things" sometimes goes beyond what we know for sure. The biblical writings contain less detail about the darker side than we may imagine.

It is not clear that we are free to dismiss this language as having no content. Yet we find so many different threads even within the biblical writings that it would be unwise to privilege or to prioritize some things over others. No one can reshape the Christian message as he or she pleases. On this subject, we can only commit our uncertainties to God in his sovereign love. Isaiah declares that the love of God cannot be measured by human standards. Perhaps this is partly what Moltmann means by an "anthropocentric eschatology" when he directs us to contemplate "the

49. The Doctrine Commission of the Church of England, *The Mystery of Salvation* (London: Church House Publishing, 1995), 199.

50. Doctrine Commission, *Mystery*, 198.

51. Anthony C. Thiselton, *The Two Horizons* (Grand Rapids: Eerdmans and Exeter: Paternoster, 1980), 205-92.

boundlessness of love," especially as conveyed by Karl Barth.[52] Isaiah writes, "God will abundantly pardon. For my thoughts are not your thoughts, nor are your ways my ways, says the LORD. For as the heavens are higher than the earth, so are my ways higher than your ways, and my thoughts than your thoughts" (Isa. 55:7-9). There are some things which even revelation does not yet make clear in specific detail.

9.3. The Wrath of God

"Wrath" has a distinctive peculiarity in the qualities shown by God. These qualities were formerly called his "attributes" when people held a more static, Aristotelian notion of God. Whereas love is a *permanent* quality and *characterizes* God, wrath does *not last eternally* and does not reach beyond time. The other important feature of wrath is that it can be remedied, or be prompted by love.

The opposite of love is not wrath, but *indifference.* We can readily compare the responsibilities of parents and grandparents. If a parent genuinely cares about his or her children, he or she is likely to experience anger if their child is bent on self-destruction or quite deliberate disobedience or damage to others. A modicum of consistent discipline is part of caring parental love. Grandparents may have a more relaxed, indulgent love. . . . After all, the children are not their immediate responsibility. They may experience anger at outrageous behavior, but they are far more likely to "spoil" the child with extra gifts or treats, in normal circumstances. The parents' care does not signal less love than that of the grandparents. Indeed, parental "spoiling" may arise from a relative subordination of selfless love to more selfish competition for the child's approval. Anders Nygren observes, "As long as God is God, He cannot behold with indifference that His creation is destroyed."[53]

The Hebrew Old Testament contains a bewildering variety of words which may be translated as "wrath" or "anger." The main five are *'aph* (Exod. 22:24; 32:10-12; Job 16:9; 19:11; Pss. 2:5, 12; 95:11; well over 200 occurrences; one writer suggests many more); *chēmâ,* sometimes also fury (Deut. 29:23, 28; 2 Kings 22:13, 17; Job 21:20; Pss. 59:13; 79:6; Ezek. 13:15; over 35 occurrences); *chārôn,* fierce wrath (Exod. 15:7; Pss. 69:24; 88:16; Ezek. 7:12, 14;

---

52. Moltmann, *Sun of Righteousness,* 145.

53. Anders Nygren, *Commentary on Romans* (London: S.C.M., 1952), 98.

more than six uses); ʿebrâ, wrath (Pss. 78:49; 85:3; Prov. 14:35; Isa. 9:19; 14:6; Ezek. 21:31; 38:19; Zeph. 1:15, 18; about 40 occurrences); qetseph (Num. 16:46; Josh. 22:20; 2 Chron. 24:18; 29:8; Pss. 38:1; 102:10; Isa. 60:10; Jer. 10:10; 21:5; 50:13; about 25 occurrences). In addition to these five forms, zāʿaph means to be enraged; zāʿam means to be indignant or angry; and kaʿas means anger or vexation (1 Kings 15:30; 21:22; 2 Kings 23:26). Eight or more Hebrew words are used. Most uses, but not all, are used of the wrath or anger of God, including the references which we have cited.

The Greek New Testament, by contrast, tends to use only two words, orgē and thymos. According to Moulton and Geden, there are only about 35 occurrences of orgē (eleven in Romans) and eighteen of thymos, although some do not denote the anger of God.[54] The Septuagint, however, translated nineteen different Hebrew words as orgē from the Old Testament, and Hatch and Redpath list between 300 and 350 occurrences of the Greek orgē.[55] They also list about 300 occurrences of thymos, to translate twenty-six Hebrew words, although, again, not all of these apply to God.[56]

The Hebrew chēmâ characteristically refers to the wrath of God, and is often associated with fire or burning, from which the word is derived. A typical example would be: "My wrath will go forth like fire and burn, with no one to quench it" (Jer. 21:12; cf. Isa. 42:25: "So he poured upon him the heat of his anger, and the fury of war; it set him on fire all around. . . . It burned him, but he did not take it to heart"). The word clearly implies emotion in God. Schunck observes, "chēmâ probably . . . lent expression to the hot inward excitement accompanying anger."[57] Hence it is often "kindled" (2 Kings 22:13, 17). But chēmâ is not permanent; it can be "turned away" (Prov. 15:1; 21:14), and one can refrain from it (Ps. 37:8) or give it up. It is used 85 times in the Old Testament for the wrath of God, sometimes against disobedient Israel but often against idolatrous foreign nations. Although it often brings punishment (Ps. 6:2) or even destruction (Deut. 9:19; Ezek. 13:13), it may also have a remedial purpose. God may also turn away his anger through the interventions of humans (Num. 25:11; Ps. 106:23). God's wrath may also be against oppressors, and therefore lead to the vindication and rescue of the weak and oppressed.

54. W. F. Moulton and A. S. Geden, A Concordance of the Greek Testament (Edinburgh: T&T Clark, 1899), 703 and 463-64.

55. Edwin Hatch and Henry A. Redpath, A Concordance to the Septuagint (2 vols.; Athens: Beneficial Book Publishers, 1977), 1008-10.

56. Hatch and Redpath, Concordance to the Septuagint, 660-62.

57. K.-D. Schunck, "Chēmâ," TDOT, vol. 4, 463; cf. 462-65.

The most frequent cause of divine wrath in the Old Testament is idolatry, of which the worship of the golden calf constitutes a well-known example (Exod. 32:22-24). But the oppression of the poor and social injustice provide another example. "Despising the word of the Holy One" (Isa. 5:24) is another provocation; so is breaking the Sabbath (Exod. 20:8-11). But the sin of a hardened or self-centered character counts for more than a series of external acts. Pannenberg rightly speaks of an "autonomy of the will that puts the self in the center, and uses everything else as a means to the self as an end."[58] "Self-willing . . . alienates from God by putting the self in the place that is God's alone."[59] Sin is not merely an individual act, but a condition of the human heart. That is why to the Hebrew terms "rebellion" or "apostasy" (Hebrew, *pāsha'*, verb, and *pesha'*) and "missing the mark" (*chāta'*, verb, and *chattā't*) is added the even more serious term "wickedness of heart," "guilt," or "distortion" (Hebrew, *'āwôn*). Augustine clearly recognized this, and Athanasius sees sin as a state of corruption (Greek, *phthora*), by which he means not so much corruption as such, but being in a "natural" state *without knowledge of God*. Sin is above all "not knowing God" or not contemplating him.[60] Karl Rahner adopts a similar view.

In the New Testament the term *wrath* (Greek, *orgē*) applies almost exclusively to God, especially in Romans and Revelation. Whereas in the Old Testament this often concerns present history, the New Testament concerns both present and future. Rom. 2:5 and Rev. 6:17 both refer to the Day of Wrath. The reference in Romans, however, recalls C. H. Dodd's famous (his critics would say "infamous") comment on Romans that Paul "retains the concept of 'the wrath of God' . . . not to describe the attitude of God . . . but to describe an inevitable process of cause and effect in a moral universe."[61] In other words, it is not externally imposed, but represents the internal or natural outworking of actions and behavior which are said to arouse God's wrath. Any haste to reject this interpretation as "impersonal" should be delayed, for sometimes the consequences of what provokes God to wrath do have self-destructive consequences, and do not necessarily depend on direct divine intervention. Nevertheless Dodd's view has met with a storm of controversy. Stephen Travis has tried to combine a limited recognition of its in-

---

58. Wolfhart Pannenberg, *Systematic Theology* (3 vols.; Grand Rapids: Eerdmans, 1991-98), vol. 2, 243.

59. Pannenberg, *Systematic Theology*, vol. 2, 261.

60. Athanasius, *Incarnation of the Word*, sect. 11 (also *NPNF*, ser. 2, vol. 4, 42).

61. Charles H. Dodd, *The Epistle of Paul to the Romans* (London: Hodder & Stoughton, 1932), 23.

sight with a careful emphasis on God's personal action. He admits that "in a divinely controlled universe, if people's sins lead to negative consequences, that can only be because God has willed it so. . . . Dodd . . . was wrong to distance the operation of wrath from God's personal involvement in human affairs." However, he suggests, Dodd is right to underline the notion of "*internal*" consequences as a frequent expression of it.[62] But he is mistaken in risking a depersonalized, quasi-mechanical approach.

We constantly experience "internal" effects in daily life. If a child refuses to practice the piano, he or she will never become a good pianist. If someone refuses to work at school, normally he or she will never enter university, and perhaps end with a humdrum job. It is surprising how many times people miss this approach in biblical passages. When Isaiah exclaims, "His reward is with him" (Isa. 40:10; 62:11), he is not portraying God bringing some such reward as a bag of gold; he is saying that to enjoy God's presence *is* his reward. Simply looking at language, Ludwig Wittgenstein remarks in the *Tractatus*, "An internal property of a fact can also be called a feature of that fact. . . . A property is internal if it is unthinkable that its object should not possess it."[63] Similarly, it is built into the concept of God's wrath and of human sin that undesirable consequences follow from both. Later, in the *Philosophical Investigations*, Wittgenstein prefers to speak of "the grammar of the proposition."[64] Stephen Travis, among others, correctly points out that not every instance of "wrath" in the New Testament can be readily explained in this way.[65] For example, in his missionary preaching in Thessalonica, to which he alludes in 1 Thess. 1:9-10, Paul says that Jesus Christ "rescues us from the wrath that is coming." We are delivered from condemnation at the Last Judgment. A similar reference occurs in 1 Thess. 5:9. 1 Thess. 2:16 may possibly be a reference to historical outworking of judgment, although 1 Thessalonians would seem to be much earlier than the fall of Jerusalem. We cannot somehow explain away all references to future wrath.

Yet while Rom. 1:18-32 reflects standard Jewish synagogue sermon ma-

---

62. Stephen H. Travis, *Christ and the Judgement of God: The Limits of Divine Retribution in New Testament Thought* (Milton Keynes and Colorado Springs: Paternoster and Hendrickson, 2008), 55.

63. Ludwig Wittgenstein, *Tractatus Logico-Philosophicus* (Ger. and Eng.; London: Routledge & Kegan Paul and New York: Humanities Press, 1961), 4-1221 and 4-123 (on p. 53).

64. Ludwig Wittgenstein, *Philosophical Investigations* (Oxford: Blackwell, 2nd ed. 1958), sect. 353; cf. sects. 371 and 373.

65. Travis, *Christ and the Judgement of God*, 56.

terial in its attack on idolatry and immorality, this passage does focus on the inherent consequences of these alienating sins. Sin breeds yet more sin, and alienates God. Clearly Paul is commenting on the unbelieving Gentile world. Charles E. B. Cranfield criticizes Dodd's interpretation on the grounds that if God genuinely loves the world, he will not be unmoved by oppressors, injustice, and moral evil.[66] God's wrath perhaps includes the futilities and disasters that result from impiety and injustice, but it is also "revealed" in the gospel, in view of the parallelism between v. 17, "God's righteousness is revealed," and v. 18. Cranfield writes, "The two revelations . . . are . . . two aspects of the same process."[67] Present disasters are significant, but they do not exhaust the full meaning of "wrath." The phrase "from heaven" does seem to link this theme with apocalyptic discourse found in Judaism, in the teaching of Jesus, elsewhere in Paul, and in Revelation. Many take this to be a criticism of the passage, but Klaus Koch, Ernst Käsemann, Christiaan Beker, Alexandra Brown, and others reflect the indispensability of apocalyptic.

The Greek *paredōken*, "[God] gave them up" (Rom. 1:24, 26, 28), represents a term taken from Psalm 106:41, where God endorses the choice of people to abandon God. Barth observes, "The confusion . . . becomes its own punishment. . . . The enterprise of setting up the 'No-God' is avenged by its success. . . . Our conduct becomes governed precisely by what we desire."[68] Rom. 2:1-11 also speaks of God's wrath in the context of human hypocrisy, guilt, and the Last Judgment. Rom. 4:15 associates wrath with the Law: "The Law brings wrath." This effectively marks off the relation of grace and faith. Stählin comments, "Everything depends on whether a man rejects Christ, or . . . lets himself be appropriated to, what Christ is and brings."[69] In Rom. 9:23, what looks very harsh, namely, "objects [lit. 'vessels'; Greek, *skeuē*] of wrath," is part of Paul's argument about God's mercy and patience. Cranfield writes of "God's patient enduring of vessels of wrath."[70] Travis similarly writes, "God's sovereign purpose is a positive one, in which 'vessels of wrath' may become 'vessels of mercy' (cf. Eph. 2:3-10)."[71]

To be sure, we cannot go all the way with Origen to suggest that "the

---

66. C. E. B. Cranfield, *The Epistle to the Romans,* ICC (2 vols.; Edinburgh: T&T Clark, 1975), vol. 1, 108-10.

67. Cranfield, *Romans,* vol. 1, 110.

68. Karl Barth, *The Epistle to the Romans* (London: Oxford University Press, 1933), 51.

69. Gustav Stählin, *"orgē,"* TDNT, vol. 5, 446; cf. 419-47.

70. Cranfield, *Romans,* vol. 2, 497.

71. Travis, *Christ and the Judgement of God,* 65.

wrath of God" is *always* educative, remedial, or reformative. This may account for many, but not all, references to his wrath. Moreover, those who imagine that the coming and work of Christ mean a sudden cessation of wrath are out of tune with a gradually "realized" eschatology. Whiteley offers a helpful analogy, in a different context, to the Christian's liberation from sin, which I have cited elsewhere because it is so helpful. The Christian's deliverance from sin, he suggests, is like being transferred from the icy cold into a warm room.[72] The heat is the *decisive* force: it cannot be reversed. In this sense the Christian is not to fear the wrath to come. He or she is free from it. But as someone stands in front of a roaring fire or a hot radiator, the person still suffers from pockets of cold in his or her toes or other joints. They know that they will eventually *become* thoroughly warm. "Sin will no more have dominion over you" (Rom. 6:14). But in the present both heat and cold still exercise an influence. Christian sin may incur disappointment and wrath, as well as confidence and love.

It is more difficult to come to clear conclusions about unbelievers. As a *general* conclusion, one aspect of the Last Judgment is that for some it will inevitably bring confrontation with the wrath of God. But this should not be exaggerated. In the awesome passage in Revelation about "the winepress," G. B. Caird urged, "Even here the object of the reaping is the storing of the crop, not the bonfire."[73] "Wrath" in the book of Revelation mainly falls upon those who have killed the martyrs and oppressed the Church, though "Babylon," for whom trade seems to be the only goal in life, also stands in judgment. John sees "Babylon" as "drunk with the blood of the saints [i.e., God's people] and on the blood of the witnesses to Jesus" (17:6). The references to wrath in Rev. 15:1 and 7 seem to look back to God's liberation of his people from Egypt. 16:1, about "bowls of wrath," also looks back to the plagues of Egypt in the Exodus, and probably to historical experiences. Yet in Rev. 19:15 "the winepress of the fury of the wrath of God the Almighty" does seem to refer to the Last Judgment, which we examine in the next chapter.

None of this means, however, that as Wright warns us about hell, we can make anticipatory judgments about this or that person, or group of people. Paul explicitly warns his readers, "Do not pronounce judgment be-

---

72. D. E. H. Whiteley, *The Theology of St. Paul* (Oxford: Blackwell, 1964, 2nd ed. 1971), 126-27; Anthony C. Thiselton, *The Living Paul* (London: S.P.C.K. and Downers Grove: IVP Academic, 2009), 12.

73. G. B. Caird, *The Revelation of St. John the Divine* (London: Black, 1966), 190.

fore the time, before the Lord comes, who will bring to light the things now hidden" (1 Cor. 4:5). These things are not only beyond our knowledge, but beyond our time. We do know that believers are justified, even if they fail many times (Rom. 8:31-39). We do know that the wrath of God is more often remedial and saving than we may imagine (cf. 1 Cor. 5:5). Above all, we do know that it is not a permanent quality of God, like righteousness and love. There is much that we can leave only in the merciful and loving hands of God.

Perhaps the final point to stress is that the popular idea that the Old Testament portrays a God of wrath and the New Testament a God of love is utterly mistaken. Psalm 103:8-11 declares, "The LORD is merciful and gracious, slow to anger and abounding in steadfast love. He will not deal with us according to our sins, nor repay us according to our iniquities. For as the heavens are high above the earth, so great is his steadfast love toward those that fear him." This reminds us of Rom. 8:31-39: "If God is for us, who is against us? . . . It is God who justifies; who is to condemn? . . . Who will separate us from the love of Christ?" Paul's list of conquered obstacles includes death (v. 38).

CHAPTER 10

The Last Judgment and
Justification by Grace through Faith

10.1. Judgment Anticipated with Joy? Vindication and Truth

It is natural and to be expected that we should contemplate the Last Judgment with some degree of trepidation, and perhaps even terror. Paul states very clearly: "For all of us must appear before the judgment seat of Christ, so that each may receive recompense for what has been done in the body, whether good or evil" (2 Cor. 5:10). Paul does not seem to exempt Christians.

Yet much of the Old Testament anticipation of the Last Judgment seems to arouse the very opposite emotions. The Psalmist writes, "He [God] will judge the peoples with equity. Let the heavens be glad, and let the earth rejoice. . . . Then shall all the trees of the forest sing for joy before the LORD; for he is coming, for he is coming to judge the earth. He will judge the world with righteousness . . . and truth" (Ps. 96:10-13). It might be suggested that this is the joy of creation and nature after human exploitation of the earth. But Psalm 67 speaks of the joy of nations: "Let the nations be glad and sing for joy, for you [God] judge the peoples with equity, and guide the nations upon earth" (Ps. 67:4). These words are said or sung regularly in Anglican liturgy, both in the 1662 Book of Common Prayer and in Common Worship.

Three reasons for joy in the face of judgment can be detected. First, the disclosure of God's righteousness and truth puts an end to all deception, seduction, and illusion. We shall come to see whether self-proclaimed achievers and so-called celebrities are what they claim to be, and just what "worldly success" really amounts to. Second, God will publicly and definitively vindicate the oppressed. Psalm 98 declares, "He [God] has revealed his vindication in the sight of the nations. . . . Make a joyful noise to the

LORD, all the earth; break forth into joyous song. . . . For he is coming to judge the earth. He will judge the world with righteousness, and the peoples with equity" (Ps. 98:2, 4, 9). Third, God publicly reveals himself as universal King of all creation, one of whose roles is to defend the wronged, and to put things right. The Church could believe only in faith (2 Cor. 5:7; Heb. 11:1, 2, 13). Now hidden faith is vindicated in plain sight. Moreover, the theme of "putting things right" constitutes the key connecting thread between justification by grace and the Last Judgment.

Whatever may be our view of Liberation Theology, José Porfirio Miranda is quite right to make this a central theme of his *Marx and the Bible*. He quotes Otto Michel as affirming that in Paul the "justice of God is at the same time judicial sentence and eschatological salvation."[1] The Hebrew for judgment *(mishpāt)* regularly finds expression in the LXX as the Greek *krima* or *krisis*, but the verb "to judge" (Hebrew, *shāphat*) is often related to the Greek *dikaiosynē*, "righteousness," as José Porfirio Miranda claims.[2] Peter Stuhlmacher and Karl Kertelge make the same connection. Ernst Käsemann rightly relates both aspects to "God's sovereignty over the world, revealing itself eschatologically in Jesus."[3] Hence for Miranda this "putting right" concerns not only an individual relationship with God, but more especially the social situation of societies of humans.

In the Last Judgment the whole world is accountable and responsible to God. His will be the definitive verdict on all human claims and endeavors. Stephen Travis comments, "The emphasis on restorative justice is not on 'paying back' the offender, but on positively 'putting right' what has gone wrong between the offender and the victim."[4] But while agreeing that restorative justice needs more recognition and emphasis, he disagrees with Klaus Koch that justice is *never* retributive in the biblical writings. Koch, he claims, overstates his case. Retribution exists in both Testaments.[5] In Rom. 12:19 Paul enjoins Christians not to repay evil for evil, for "Vengeance is mine. I will repay, says the Lord." Similarly, 2 Thess. 1:6, 8 uses Old Testament concepts of

1. José Porfirio Miranda, *Marx and the Bible* (London: S.C.M., 1977), 173; Otto Michel, *Der Brief an die Römer*, Meyer Commentary (Göttingen: Vandenhoeck & Ruprecht, 4th ed. 1966), 254.

2. Miranda, *Marx and the Bible*, 111-12.

3. Ernst Käsemann, "'The Righteousness of God' in Paul," in *New Testament Questions of Today* (London: S.C.M., 1969), 180; cf. 168-82.

4. Stephen H. Travis, *Christ and the Judgement of God* (Milton Keynes: Paternoster and Colorado Springs: Hendrickson, 2008), 8.

5. Travis, *Judgement*, 17-19, 64-66, and 74-84.

punishment (Greek, *ekdikēsis*) and "repay" (Greek, *antapodidōmi*) in a retributive sense. More controversially he appeals to Käsemann's notion of *lex
talionis* in 1 Cor. 3:17 and elsewhere. Yet Travis points out that the remedial
and restorative use of judgment is more frequent than these references, and
often refers to the inbuilt consequences of sin (discussed above).

It is important not to confuse biblical understandings of justice and
judgment with those formulated by Aristotle, and mediated to the Church
especially through Thomas Aquinas. In Aristotle equivalence and equality
played a major part. But Eichrodt comments that in the Old Testament "it
is not a question of impartiality with which a formal standard of justice is
applied. . . . [In a righteous judgment] every relationship was as it should
be" (Lev. 19:15; Deut. 16:18; 25:1; 2 Sam. 15:1-6; Ps. 72:1-2).[6] God shows his
righteousness by vindicating and delivering his people. To this effect God
raises up "Judges" to do this work in ancient Israel. The book of Judges
portrays the task of the Judges in a consistent way, depicting a cyclical pattern of four or five acts. Their common aim is to bring salvation, liberation, and prosperity to Israel (Hebrew, *hōshia'* and *shālôm*). The following
cycle of events occurs a number of times: (1) Israel sins against the Lord;
(2) God sells Israel into the hands of Philistines; (3) Israel cries to the Lord
in their distress; (4) God raises up a "Savior" or "Judge" to redeem Israel
into a state of well-being and security; (5) Israel again dwells in safety and
security, until Israel recommences the same cycle of events again.

The book of Judges begins with the death of Joshua. The first cycle of
events occurs in Judg. 2:13-23, where Israel "abandoned the LORD" (2:13) and
"he gave them over to plunderers, . . . and he sold them into the power of
their enemies" (2:14). Israel was "in great distress" (2:15), and "Then the
LORD raised up judges, who delivered them out of the power of those who
plundered them" (2:16). The narrator adds: "But whenever the judge died,
they would relapse" and behave wickedly (2:19). The second cycle begins in
chapter 3, with the "raising up" of Othniel. The Israelites "did what was evil
in the sight of the LORD" (3:7); the Lord "sold them" into the hands of their
enemy (3:8); Israel "cried out to the LORD"; and "the LORD raised up a deliverer, . . . Othniel, . . . and he judged Israel. . . . So the land had rest" (3:9-11).

The third full cycle concerns Ehud (3:12-31). After Israel "cried out to
the LORD" (3:15), Ehud delivered the Israelites. But after his death a fourth
cycle concerns Deborah (4:1–5:31). A fifth full cycle includes the episode of
Sisera and Barak, which culminates in Jael's murder of Sisera with a tent peg

6. Walter Eichrodt, *Theology of the Old Testament*, vol. 1 (London: S.C.M., 1961), 240-41.

(4:21). Deborah's victory is celebrated in poetry in chapter 5, and chapter 6 introduces the sixth cycle of this pattern of events, in which the judge and savior was Gideon (6:1–8:35). The seventh cycle concerns Abimelech (9:1-57); then Tola (briefly, 10:1-2); Jair (10:3-18); Jephthah is the focus of a tenth cycle (11:1–12:7); and after three more judges we reach the story of Samson (13:24–16:31). The final chapters of Judges constitute appendices that emphasize that there was anarchy when "there was no king in Israel" (18:1).

Although these twelve or thirteen judges are human figures, God empowers them with his Holy Spirit to act on his behalf. Indeed, it is important to note that all or most of these all-too-human figures were flawed or limited in some conspicuous way, showing that the deliverance may be seen as God's, who truly is "judge." Clearly they were all mortal and fallible. They were effective only when "the LORD was with the judge" (Judg. 2:18), "the LORD raised up a deliverer" (3:9), or "the Spirit of the LORD came upon him" (3:10). Famously Ehud was "a left-handed man," a sign of weakness or abnormality in the ancient world (3:15). Deborah and her assistant Jael were women, who were not normally warriors or leaders (4:4, 17). Gideon was commanded drastically to reduce the size of his army to only three hundred. "The LORD said to Gideon, 'The troops with you are too many. . . . [It would] take the credit away from me'" (7:2); moreover, he was full of doubt (6:36-40). Abimelech was flawed by ambition (9:1-57). Jephthah was impulsive, and his mistaken vow led to the sacrifice of his daughter (11:34-40). Samson was a philanderer who wasted his time on practical jokes (14:1–16:22). Yet in all these examples, the Spirit of the Lord used imperfect instruments to "judge" or to deliver and vindicate a repentant Israel. It was God who, through them, acted as "Judge."

There are few better comments on all this than that of a writer at the turn of the nineteenth and twentieth centuries. A. B. Davidson wrote correctly in 1904, "The function of a judge was wider than with us; he was both judge and advocate, not judging as judges do now, on evidence set before him by others. . . . 'Turn to me and be saved! . . . For I am God, and there is none else — a righteous God and a Saviour' (Isa. 45:21, 22). The antithesis which in dogmatics we are familiar with is a righteous or just God and *yet* a Saviour. The Old Testament puts it differently — a righteous God and *therefore* a Saviour. It is His own righteousness that causes Him to bring in righteousness" (his italics).[7]

---

7. A. B. Davidson, *The Theology of the Old Testament* (Edinburgh: T&T Clark, 1904), 133 and 143-44.

Gerhard von Rad underlines these points when he observes, "There is absolutely no concept in the Old Testament with so central a significance for all the relationships of human life as that of *ts-d-q-h*" (Hebrew, "righteousness").[8] It *includes* a person's relation with God, but *also* his or her relationship to one's fellows. This is not simply an *ethical* norm; it shows how a human's personal *relationship* with God affects everything. Hence the Old Testament may regularly use *sh-ph-ṭ*, "to execute judgment" or "to execute" and also *dyn*, "to judge" or "to discern." There is a conscious wordplay in Abraham's plea for Sodom and Gomorrah when he cried, "Shall not the Judge [Hebrew, *shōphet*] of all the earth do what is just [Hebrew, *mishpāt*]?" (Gen. 18:25). Abraham prays that God will not sweep away the innocent with the guilty, but will judge in accordance with his own righteous nature. The maintenance of covenant justice constitutes part of God's role as sovereign governor of the world. Again, this forms part of his kingly role. Hence the Hebrew *sh-ph-ṭ* may also mean "to rule, to govern."[9]

In the New Testament the teaching of Jesus provides an angle on this which is even clearer than many other parts of Scripture. In the "parables of reversal," Jesus regularly grants that there is often ambiguity in the present situation, which still awaits definitive clarification. Weeds and wheat, for example, may become so entwined together that to try to root out one now may risk the survival of the other (Matt. 13:24-30). J. Jeremias rightly classifies the Parable of the Tares among the Wheat and the Seine-net (Matt. 13:47-48) as parables of the consummation.[10] He comments, "Conditions are reversed; what is hidden becomes manifest (Matt. 10:26 and parallels), poor become rich (Luke 6:20), the last are first (Mark 10:31), the small become great (Matt. 18:4), the hungry are filled (Luke 6:21), the weary find rest (Matt. 11:28), those who weep laugh (Luke 6:21), the mourners are comforted (Matt. 5:4), the sick are healed, the blind receive their sight, lame walk, lepers are cleansed, deaf hear (Matt. 11:5), . . . the oppressed [are] relieved (Luke 4:18), the lonely are exalted (Matt. 23:12; Luke 14:11; 18:14), . . . the dead live (Matt. 11:5)."[11]

8. Gerhard von Rad, *Old Testament Theology*, vol. 1 (Edinburgh: Oliver & Boyd, 1962), 70.

9. Richard Schultz, "*sh-ph-ṭ*," *NIDOTTE*, vol. 4, 213-20, esp. 215; Francis Brown, with S. R. Driver and C. A. Briggs, "*shāphaṭ*," "judge," "govern," in *The New Hebrew and English Lexicon* (Lafayette: Indiana Associated Publishers and Authors, 1980), 1047-48.

10. Joachim Jeremias, *The Parables of Jesus* (London: S.C.M., 1963), 224-27.

11. Jeremias, *Parables of Jesus*, 221-22.

It is crucial for the Church *not* to assume that this consummation comes in full before the Last Judgment. Certainly processes which find future fulfillment have been set in train in the present. But to interpret all these goals as undergoing fulfillment in the present is radically to mistake God's timing. The harvest has yet to be gathered; the new temple has yet to be fully built; the scattered people of God have yet to be gathered together into one. Ambiguity persists in the present. Saints still sin; the Church is not yet pure and free from stain. Donatists and more extreme Puritans represent only two examples of the trend to demand a "pure" Church in the present. The present order of life has still to be reversed.[12] The Beatitudes provide an example of the difference between proleptic fulfillment in Jesus and complete fulfillment in the final judgment.

The work of John L. Austin, John Searle, and their successors helps to explain how the "illocutionary" performative act of God's verdictive speech-act in judgment will constitute a transformative verdict which involves action as well as speech, or a speech-act. God's definitive verdict in Christ will not only bring clarity to all ambiguity and hiddenness; it will also fully establish what God's decree enacts. In God's distinctive, definitive judgment we find combined the two functions which Austin calls "verdictives" and "exercitives."[13] The verdictive is an exercise of judgment, as when a jury returns the verdict "guilty" or "not guilty"; the exercitive, in Austin's terms, is the exercising of a power in a judicial sentence, as when a judge might say, "I condemn you to life imprisonment." As Austin's immediate successor, Donald Evans, expresses it, "In a Verdictive utterance I say what *is* so; in an Exercitive utterance I authoritatively say what is to *be* so because I say so. One cannot draw a sharp line between the two, however" (his italics).[14]

Because God makes a verdictive pronouncement with authority, whatever verdict God utters *is* definitively and universally the case. His verdict is final. An exercitive will draw out implications of this verdict in a more-than-verbal way. It will express a sentence, a consignment, or a liberation and a deliverance. It will set the prisoner free. The response of God's people will be to accept and endorse the definitive verdict, whether or not it may have been predicted or will come as a surprise: "Great and amazing

12. Norman Perrin, *The Kingdom of God in the Teaching of Jesus* (London: S.C.M., 1963), 83.

13. John L. Austin, *How to Do Things with Words* (Oxford: Oxford University Press, 1962), 88-91, 152-53, 154-56, 162.

14. Donald D. Evans, *The Logic of Self-Involvement* (London: S.C.M., 1963), 36.

are your deeds, Lord God the Almighty" (NRSV) or "Just and true are your ways" (AV/KJV; Rev. 15:3). We shall explain further the significance of "performatives" below.

Yet Paul is no less insistent than Jesus that God's verdict should not be mis-timed. He declares, "Do not pronounce judgment before the time, before the Lord comes, who will bring to light the things now hidden in darkness, and will disclose the purposes of the heart. Then each one will receive commendation from God" (1 Cor. 4:5). He applied this at once to "success" in the ministry. We simply cannot tell "before the time" whether in God's eyes our ministry is a stunning success or a futile effort. "I do not even judge myself. I am not aware of anything against myself, but I am not thereby acquitted. It is the Lord who judges me" (4:3-4). This applies to Paul and to Apollos, and perhaps to others (4:6-7). By jumping the gun in terms of timing, the Corinthians commit a radical error. They observe the struggles and persecution of the apostles and their own supposed "reigning as kings" or satiated state with supposed "riches," and mistake the situation. They have become, in their own eyes, armchair spectators of a gladiatorial combat in which the apostles still simply struggle, as if they were the scrapings from everyone's shoes, or mere dirt (1 Cor. 4:8-13).

The point is that any attempt to evaluate life in mid-process before the Last Judgment is doomed to futility. God has his own "righteous judgment," and merely human standards of accountability are misleading and false. Christians await not only vindication and justification, but also a definitive transformative verdict. Only at the end will they see, as it were, with God's eyes. Only such a picture can prove itself to be "true." Christians may indeed look forward to the Last Judgment as a stripping away of disguises, a true verdict on life and struggle, as well as vindication and an act of covenant righteousness. "We shall all appear before the judgment seat of Christ" (2 Cor. 5:10) need not be intimidating; it may well be a moment when illusion is swept aside, and we experience freedom and deliverance from error and fear.

A third theological witness in the New Testament is just as emphatic as Jesus and Paul. The Epistle to the Hebrews is not Pauline, but represents the work of a highly articulate theologian. The argument relates to priesthood, sacrifice, and mediation, but within a framework of eschatology. C. K. Barrett rightly argues that eschatology is the "determining element" in Hebrews.[15] The work of the Aaronic priests remained incomplete, and

---

15. C. K. Barrett, "The Eschatology of the Epistle to the Hebrews," in *The Background of*

even Joshua could not lead Israel into complete "rest" (Heb. 4:4-9; 7:23). Barrett likens the pilgrim existence featured in Hebrews to a journey which remains incomplete until we enter the "new Jerusalem." The present "Jerusalem" is merely a copy of the true Jerusalem to come. In this present life Christians have "no abiding city; they seek the city which is to come" (Heb. 13:14). Ernst Käsemann and Robert Jewett similarly underline this perspective.[16] In terms of its Alexandrian affinities of expression, this city is not a contingent entity but "the city which has foundations," anchored in the realm of futurity. Heavenly realities belong to realms of truth or genuineness (Greek, *alēthina*, in contrast to *hypodeigmata*).

1 Peter and John also share this perspective, contrary to some popular assumptions about John. In Selwyn's words, in 1 Peter Christians "live in grace, but not yet in glory."[17] On John, Raymond Brown comments, "The establishment or realization of the *basileia* (kingdom) is yet to come, and the Church is oriented toward that future *basileia*. . . . There is a future vision of glory," even if there are also elements of "realized" eschatology.[18] Jesus declares, "I should lose nothing, but raise it up on the last day" (John 6:39-40). Promise, hope, and pilgrimage are an integral part of the main voices of the New Testament. The Last Judgment is not a source of fear to be repressed or swept under the carpet as a mere relic of Jewish apocalyptic, but an event to which Christians may look forward with joyful anticipation, although never with complacency or presumption.

An arbitrary sample of modern theologians suggests that the transformation of ambiguity into clarity and of hiddenness into vindication and openness has a place in many streams of thought. Paul Tillich, for example, spends more than a hundred pages of his *Systematic Theology* on the ambiguities of life. Human fallenness suggests a tendency toward disintegration, lack of stability, and the need for a "centre."[19] Even various ethical norms, he argues, encounter ambiguity, including those of moral law. Kant

---

the *New Testament and Its Eschatology: In Honour of C. H. Dodd,* ed. W. D. Davies and D. Daube (Cambridge: Cambridge University Press, 1956), 366; cf. 363-93.

16. Ernst Käsemann, *The Wandering People of God: An Investigation of the Letter to the Hebrews* (Minneapolis: Augsburg, 1984), esp. 26-37; Robert Jewett, *Letter to Pilgrims: A Commentary on the Epistle to the Hebrews* (Cleveland: Pilgrim Press, 1981).

17. E. G. Selwyn, "Eschatology in 1 Peter," in *Background of the New Testament,* ed. Davies and Daube, 396; cf. 394-401.

18. Raymond Brown, *The Gospel according to John,* AB (London: Chapman and New York: Doubleday, 1971), cxvii and cxviii.

19. Paul Tillich, *Systematic Theology,* vol. 3 (London: Nisbet, 1964), 34-113.

spoke of an "unconditional command," but is this always applicable in interpersonal situations? He asks, "How is moral self-interrogation possible within the ambiguous mixture of essential and existential elements which characterize life? . . . The content of the moral law is historically conditioned."[20] Law, Tillich insists, expresses a person's estrangement from himself, even if this is seen as a command to love. Even growth and self-creativity do not escape ambiguity.

Tillich looks in part to the divine Spirit's transformation of the new being and our life situation. But only in Christ does this appear without distortion.[21] Yet within this world order, there is always the danger of "projections of all the ambiguous materials of temporal life . . . into transcendent realms."[22] We need "the ultimate judgment" to defeat the illusory claim of the negative to be positive.[23] Only with the advent of a new heaven and a new earth will God's final judgment reveal what is genuinely the case, without the pretensions of the penultimate to be seen as ultimate, even in "religion" and in "culture." The Last Judgment, even if interpreted symbolically for Tillich, represents, like the divine life, "the eternal conquest of the negative."[24]

Thus even a theologian who, we might imagine, would perhaps see eschatology as the domestication of anthropocentric doctrine surprisingly insists on eschatology as a disambiguating feature of religion, culture, law, and ethics. We cannot truly see "with God's eyes" until every relic of illusory misunderstanding has become obsolete in the light of God's Final Judgment. The absence of a temple in the "heavenly Jerusalem" signifies the end of "religion" and the public verdict of God.[25] We must now look more closely at the relation between the Last Judgment and performative language, and the relation between the Last Judgment and justification by grace through faith.

10.2. The Last Judgment, "Verdictives," and Justification by Grace

C. F. D. Moule approaches the relation between judgment and justification through a theology of the sacraments. Baptism, he argues, clearly represents the death of the Christian (Rom. 6:2-11) as well as the Christian's be-

20. Tillich, *Systematic Theology,* vol. 3, 49.
21. Tillich, *Systematic Theology,* vol. 3, 153-59.
22. Tillich, *Systematic Theology,* vol. 3, 423.
23. Tillich, *Systematic Theology,* vol. 3, 424-27.
24. Tillich, *Systematic Theology,* vol. 3, 431.
25. Tillich, *Systematic Theology,* vol. 3, 430.

ing raised to life. Moreover, death in biblical thinking represents the ultimate verdict on sin. Hence, "If Baptism is voluntary death, then it is also a pleading guilty, an acceptance of the sentence," which will be made publicly at the Last Judgment.[26] Alan Richardson follows Moule's verdict. He writes, "Baptism involves judgement. God's judgement upon sin was executed in the baptism of death which Christ underwent. To be baptized is to accept God's verdict of guilty, and so to be brought past the great assize and the final judgement of the last day into the life of the Age to Come."[27]

Moule proceeds to examine the relation between Holy Communion and the Last Judgment. The case for baptism may appear stronger because it is "once-for-all." But Holy Communion is also a preaching of the gospel of the cross and the resurrection. Moule writes, "The only explicit reference in the New Testament to preparation for the Lord's Supper is in terms of *judgement* [his italics] . . . 'Examine yourselves [Greek, *dokimazetō de anthrōpos heauton*] and only then eat of the bread and drink of the cup' (1 Cor. 11:28)."[28] He continues, "In 1 Cor. 11:28-32 *dokimazein* (sift, test), *krima* (judgement), *diakrinein* (discern, discriminate), *krinein* (to judge) and *katakrinein* (thoroughly judge, condemn) are used in quick succession in a very striking way."[29] The climax comes in 11:31-32: "But if we judged ourselves, we should not be judged. But when we are judged by the Lord, we are disciplined, so that we may not be condemned along with the world." Heb. 10:29 has another closely relevant comment about judgment. Heb. 6:6 speaks of "crucifying again the Son of God."

On the other hand, rightful participation in the Lord's Supper means accepting God's verdict on sin in advance of the Last Judgment, and receiving the verdict that falls on those who die and are raised with Christ. Christ bears any condemnation on our behalf, and we are "put right with God" in advance of the Last Judgment. In traditional Reformation language, the Christian, if he or she faces judgment at all, faces it "clothed in the righteousness of Christ." "Who will bring any charge against God's elect? Who is to condemn?" (Rom. 8:33-34).

---

26. C. F. D. Moule, "The Judgement Theme in the Sacraments," in *Background of the New Testament*, ed. Davies and Daube, 465; cf. 464-81.

27. Alan Richardson, *An Introduction to the Theology of the New Testament* (London: S.C.M., 1958), 341.

28. Moule, "The Judgement Theme in the Sacraments," in *Background of the New Testament*, ed. Davies and Daube, 469-70.

29. Moule, "The Judgement Theme in the Sacraments," in *Background of the New Testament*, ed. Davies and Daube, 470.

When Paul exclaims, "There is therefore now no condemnation for those who are in Christ Jesus" (Rom. 8:1), this is not because Christians will escape the Last Judgment, but because at the Last Judgment they will receive God's definitive verdict "things have been put right," or "justified," in Christ. This emerges not only in polemical passages about the Law in Galatians and perhaps in Romans, but elsewhere in Paul. Paul writes to the Corinthians that they will be "blameless on the day of our Lord Jesus Christ" (1 Cor. 1:8; Greek, *anenklētous*, free from any charge, unimpeachable, irreproachable). They receive a verdictive pronouncement, but it includes the themes of "not guilty" and "right with God." Such a verdict is public, definitive, and irreversible. What has been appropriated by faith in hiddenness is revealed publicly to be the case. Hence justification through faith and Final Judgment are indissolubly linked: faith is transformed into sight.

Johannes Weiss is crystal clear, and rightly so, that justification by grace is a "pre-dating of what is really an eschatological act of salvation. . . . *Justification is an occurrence which will take place only on the day of the divine judgement* (Rom. 2:12, 13, 16)."[30] Weiss's formulation helps to explain such passages as Gal. 5:5, "We eagerly wait for the hope of righteousness." This angle of approach also opens up the nature and scope of illocutionary, performative, verdictive speech-acts. For Weiss insists, "This . . . does not indicate a *description* of the real *facts* of the case. It does not say what a man *is* in himself, but it states that he is *considered, in the eyes of God and according to his judgment, right 'with God'*" (my italics).[31] God declares the ungodly just (Rom. 4:5): "we are justified freely" (Rom. 3:24; Greek, *dōrean*, "as a gift").

We acknowledge that Weiss approaches justification in overly narrow legalistic terms. Whether justification is not a *description* of Christian existence may be open to question. But it invites a careful discussion of J. L. Austin's long discussion to the effect that illocutionary performatives are *not* examples of description, but precisely the opposite, and yet he reluctantly concludes that "perhaps there is no great distinction between statements and performative utterances."[32]

Since we have not yet fully explained the distinctive logic of verdictive

---

30. Johannes Weiss, *Earliest Christianity*, vol. 2 (New York: Harper Torchbooks, 1959), 502 (my italics); cf. 497-504.

31. Weiss, *Earliest Christianity*, vol. 2, 499.

32. Austin, *How to Do Things with Words*, 52; cf. 45-52.

illocutionary performatives, we must do so now, even at the risk of repeating what we have written in greater detail elsewhere.[33] Austin comments, "An 'illocutionary' act [is the] performance of an act *in* saying something, as opposed to performance of an act *of* saying something" (his italics).[34] Typical examples include saying "I do" in a wedding service as an effective act of marriage, declaring "I baptize you" in a baptism service, or stating "I promise to come" in a solemn declaration. Austin is at pains to emphasize that we do not speak of a *"false"* promise, or "christening," or marriage, if the words are uttered by a bigamist, a masquerader, or an insincere hypocrite; but an "infelicitous" or ineffective speech-act when these fail, because they are *not descriptions or true-or-false statements.*

John Searle equally distances performatives from statements. In his famous shopping-list analogy, borrowed from Elizabeth Anscombe, Searle argues that when a man acts on a shopping list, he is in effect changing conditions in the world to match the instructions of the shopping list. But this is quite different from, even opposite to, "the direction of fit between words and the world" in assertions.[35] To *describe* or to *report* is to make the words of assertions fit the nature of the world. "Propositional content" gets words to match the world; illocutionary force gets the world to match the words: "Assertions are in the former category, promises and requests are in the latter."[36]

Yet both Austin and Searle recognize that "for a certain performative utterance to be happy, certain statements have *to be true*" (Austin's italics).[37] I have applied this to New Testament Christology: Jesus cannot effectively say "Your sins are forgiven" unless he has authority to forgive sins. Donald Evans, however, rightly distinguishes between such "institutional" facts and brute causal power.[38] God's promises, for example, are linked with the covenant as well as with his faithfulness.

We may now return to Weiss's ambiguous language about "facts." What counts as a "fact" often depends on the circumstances or frame of

---

33. Anthony C. Thiselton, *Thiselton on Hermeneutics: The Collected Works and New Essays of Anthony Thiselton*, Ashgate Contemporary Thinkers on Religion (Aldershot: Ashgate and Grand Rapids: Eerdmans 2006), Part II: Hermeneutics and Speech-Act Theory, 51-150.

34. Austin, *How to Do Things with Words*, 99.

35. John R. Searle, *Expression and Meaning: Studies in the Theory of Speech Acts* (Cambridge: Cambridge University Press, 1979), 3.

36. Searle, *Expression and Meaning*, 3; cf. 1-29.

37. Austin, *How to Do Things with Words*, 45.

38. Evans, *The Logic of Self-Involvement*, 69-79.

reference within which we use the term. Without question, justification by grace primarily expresses a verdict; it is verdictive, among which Austin cites as typical: acquit, convict, reckon, assess, characterize, and so on.[39] He writes, "Verdictives consist in the delivering of a finding . . . upon evidence. . . . A verdictive is a judicial act."[40] An umpire who calls the batsman "out," however, thereby makes the batsman out "in virtue of an official position."[41] Verdictives are often linked with "exercitives," which decree a course of action that matches the verdict.

Since Paul, Luther, and the Reformers state clearly that God's verdict of justification by grace will acquit, or put in the right, those who are sinners, many critics notoriously call this a legal fiction or pretense. How can both be "true"? My consistent approach has been not only to broaden the scope of "justification" but also to invoke Donald Evans's category of *onlooks*.[42] We considered this approach in Chapter 5, where we wished to urge the far-reaching effects of making a distinction between participatory perspectives and observer ones. An "onlook" is not simply true-or-false, but may be true or false *within a given system* or context. Evans writes, "'Looking on *x* as *y*' involves placing *x* within a structure, organization, or scheme. This often involves the assumption of a status, function, or role."[43] This applies to verdicts. I have argued that in the New Testament God "looks on" Christians as sinners *within the realm of law and history:* God *"looks on" Christians as "put right with God" within the framework of eschatology and Christology.*

I have pressed this argument before because I am convinced of its importance, though it has suffered neglect.[44] It seems to me to be vital in both discrediting the idea of a "legal fiction" or contradiction, and vindicating the Last Judgment as the proper context or frame of reference of justification by grace. The role of "faith," as Paul and Luther stress, is the *appropriation* of this hidden verdict now in the present, though it has yet to be ratified and made public and definitive. Faith, as it were, allows the Christian to enjoy his or her eschatological deliverance *before* the Last Judgment. Hence Paul may bring the experience into the present: "since

---

39. Austin, *How to Do Things with Words,* 152.
40. Austin, *How to Do Things with Words,* 152.
41. Austin, *How to Do Things with Words,* 153.
42. Evans, *The Logic of Self-Involvement,* 124-44.
43. Evans, *The Logic of Self-Involvement,* 127.
44. Anthony C. Thiselton, *The Two Horizons* (Grand Rapids: Eerdmans and Exeter: Paternoster, 1980), 407-28.

we are justified by faith" (Rom. 5:1). Faith is certainly *not* a secondary *cause* of justification alongside grace. D. E. H. Whiteley rightly comments, "Faith is not the reason why God justified some and not others, but the 'response' of those who are justified."[45] Faith is not a Protestant substitute for good works.

Yet if God is the one who makes a definitive pronouncement at the last day, will not what he pronounces become a matter of fact and assertion? Will performative verdictives remain distinctive over against statements? Clearly in the *present* time, God's verdict is not yet statement. But at the last day, will the realm of law and history any longer be relevant to a Christian's status? More than ever, the verdict "sinner" slips from view as history and law, and is overcome in God's final definitive act of vindication. He has said it; it stands accomplished.

10.3. Universal Judgment: Will It Involve Retribution? Will All Be Judged?

We have more than once repeated Paul's words "For *all of us* [Greek, *tous pantas hēmas*] must appear before the judgment seat of Christ, so that each may receive recompense for what has been done in the body, whether good or evil" (2 Cor. 5:10). Paul has been expounding the hidden nature of Christian ministry. Our inner nature is being renewed even if people see our outer nature wasting away (2 Cor. 4:16). We look not at what can be seen, but at what cannot be seen (4:18). At present "we walk by faith, not by sight" (2 Cor. 5:7). But if it is our aim "to please him [God]" (5:9), one day this hidden action will be made public and vindicated. Everything will be exposed for what it really is. Paul's use of "the body" is like Luke's concern about "riches." Both what a person does in his "body" and how he uses his pocket are indicators in advance of what a person's aspirations are really worth. Paul does not exempt Christians. Writing explicitly to Christians at Corinth, he asserts: "All of us must appear before the judgment seat of Christ," although his main thought here is that of the vindication of what Christians did by faith.

In other places Paul speaks of God's "righteous judgments" as that which will be revealed in relation to those who are not Christians (Rom. 2:5-11). In other contexts God's "righteous judgment" is, as we have seen,

---

45. D. E. H. Whiteley, *The Theology of St. Paul* (Oxford: Blackwell, 1964 and 1970), 165.

part of his governance of the world (Rom. 3:4-8). Occasionally the judgment of God is portrayed as not restorative but retributive: "It is just of God to repay with affliction those who afflict you" (2 Thess. 1:6, on the assumption of Paul's authorship). On the other hand, from a different viewpoint this can be seen as an act of vindication on behalf of the oppressed or martyrs who remained faithful when everything seemed to point away from God's concern. Yet this is not worked out in terms of matching rewards for goodness and corresponding penalty points for evil deeds. Stephen Travis rightly urges, "There is no suggestion here of reward or punishment in accordance with the quality of good or evil deeds done."[46] Kent L. Yinger expresses the same thought differently. He writes, "Within the larger pattern of soteriology . . . it is not a deed for deed inspection, but rather one's entire pattern of life is in view, one's 'way.'"[47] He continues, "Questions as to the *quantity* of transgressions or righteous deeds are pointless. There is . . . no tension or paradox between salvation by grace and judgement according to deeds. . . . Thus the whole world, both Jew and Gentile, stands under the wrath of God (Romans 1–3), and vengeance awaits the enemies of the Gospel (2 Thess. 1:1-10), whereas 'God has destined us (Christians) not to wrath, but for obtaining salvation' (1 Thess. 5:9, also 1:10)."[48]

Yinger perhaps represents a particular phase of Pauline scholarship, for he accepts without reserve E. P. Sanders's case for the "New Look on Paul" of covenantal nomism. No doubt Sanders has broadened some issues about grace and law, but we need not follow Yinger's virtually uncritical account of Sanders. Nevertheless Yinger rightly argues that "righteousness is conferred solely by means of faith in Christ. . . . Eschatological recompense according to deeds *confirms* [his italics], on the basis of deeds, one's justification," because deeds show publicly who has appropriated God's gift of righteousness through Christ.[49]

Again, Stephen Travis expresses the same thought differently. He writes, "The real clue to the apparent problem of the relation between justification by faith and judgement according to works is to be found in the discovery of the true meaning of justification. Justification involves not only a verdict of acquittal, but a relationship with God in which people ex-

---

46. Travis, *Christ and the Judgement of God*, 94.

47. Kent L. Yinger, *Paul, Judaism, and Judgement according to Deeds*, SNTSMS 105 (Cambridge: Cambridge University Press, 1999), 284.

48. Yinger, *Paul, Judaism, and Judgement*, 287.

49. Yinger, *Paul, Judaism, and Judgement*, 290.

perience God's power at work."[50] Käsemann, Stuhlmacher, and Kertelge have long made this point. If Christians experience judgment in this life, it can only be restorative or remedial (1 Cor. 5:1-5). If the Last Judgment reveals the truth of affairs as they are, this judgment can only take the form of seeing Christians in Christ. Incidentally, this also addresses a curiosity. It is strange that Christians should worry about being exposed to other people's views, as if this were to matter more than how God sees them. But the truth is that if God will see all Christians "clothed in the righteousness of Christ" (Rom. 5:17; 6:2-11; Gal. 2:16, 20-21; 3:27), this is how other Christians will see us.

Some passages may seem at first sight to suggest "grades" of rewards or penalty, as when Paul speaks of builders who build with different types of materials (1 Cor. 3:10-15). But the text makes it clear, as James Dunn insists, that there are not six types of work (gold, silver, precious stones, wood, hay, straw), but simply combustible and noncombustible material (gold, silver, marble). This will survive the fire. Dunn comments, "Those who have Christ as the foundation of their lives will be saved . . . (even if in some cases) saved only by a whisker."[51] God is faithful in completing what he has begun. The Last Judgment will reveal that those in Christ are in a right relation with God.

On the subject of graded "rewards" and penalties, we must refer back to what we asserted about "internal" consequences when we discussed the wrath of God in the last chapter. Clearly there will be no "external" distribution of these Christians. Any external "reward" would pale into insignificance compared with the privilege of being admitted to the glory and presence of God in Christ. If "heaven" means perfect bliss, there is hardly room for personal comparisons of achievement. But this may not preclude the "reward" of knowing that God's grace and gifts have been effective in unimagined ways. When Isaiah declares, "His reward is with him, and his recompense before him" (Isa. 40:10; 62:11), the meaning is that the very presence of God is his reward. Yet whether each believer will have the special satisfaction of knowing that his work had borne fruit and remains a significant factor, or will be eclipsed by the sheer glory of God and privilege of justification, is difficult to say with certainty. Certainly Paul suggests that deeds done "in the body" will feature somehow; but whether in

---

50. Travis, *Christ and the Judgement of God*, 95.

51. James D. G. Dunn, *The Theology of Paul the Apostle* (Edinburgh: T&T Clark, 1998), 491.

individual terms or as contributory to the new creation as a whole is not clear. On the other hand, being in Christ cannot imply any sense of regret without questioning the all-sufficiency of the work of Christ.

We are left with the complex problem of whether any aspect of judgment may be retributive in the case of hardened unbelievers. That everyone without question will be reconciled with accepting the sovereign verdict of God cannot be doubted. But whether judgment remains *wholly* restorative largely depends on the issues which were discussed under "hell" and "wrath." Probably the most thorough study of restorative justice at the Last Judgment is Christopher Marshall's helpful study, *Beyond Retribution*.[52] Marshall thoroughly examines the use of "righteousness" (Greek, *dikaiosynē*, with its cognate verbs and adjectives ["to justify, setting free"]) in Romans and elsewhere in the New Testament. Romans alone contains about sixty-three instances of the word.[53] He comments, "Paul shows that the gospel is all about justice . . . *God's* justice" (his italics; Rom. 1:17; 3:21, 22, 25).[54] It is especially about justice for the oppressed, and "God's rectifying power to accomplish justice."[55]

We too readily forget, however, *what it means to be "oppressed."* Liberation Theology has made it fashionable to speak of "the poor" and "the disempowered." But this approach is too narrow. Hegel, Heidegger, Gadamer, Pannenberg, and others have shown that humans may be imprisoned by *their historical finitude or "thrownness."* In other words, society and their situation in history have foreclosed certain options. A thoroughly "rationalist" or evidentially "scientific" society *may make Christian belief more difficult, and this becomes therefore a force of oppression.* Sometimes churchpeople may become a little complacent about their privilege of not being among unbelievers. But if God's vindication of the oppressed includes *those weighed down with constraints imposed upon them,* by their race, gender, or society, who is to say how far God's act of vindication can reach? To be born outside of the heritage of the Christian Church or a Christian family is thereby to be exposed to the dominating and oppressive structures of "principalities and powers," whether in the form of aggressive secularism or religious paganism. While we are not seeking to second-guess the testing of many unbelievers, it is wise to see them as victims of

52. Christopher D. Marshall, *Beyond Retribution: A New Testament Vision for Justice, Crime, and Punishment* (Grand Rapids: Eerdmans, 2001).

53. Marshall, *Beyond Retribution*, 38.

54. Marshall, *Beyond Retribution*, 41.

55. Marshall, *Beyond Retribution*, 41.

oppression, for whom in certain cases "judgment" may come as deliverance. This is not to compromise the fate of those who deliberately and consciously reject Christ, preferring their own "independence" and self-achieved righteousness.

Where Marshall is perhaps at his strongest is in showing once again that "Paul's interpreters have unwittingly brought to the text an essentially Western concept of retributive justice, which is largely based on metaphysical law, rather than a Hebraic concept of covenant justice based on relationship. The Hebrew idea of righteousness is *comprehensively relational*" (his italics).[56] He adds, "It is debatable whether retribution, strictly understood, is as foundational to biblical conceptions of law and justice as is sometimes claimed."[57] The most explicit advocate of the Aristotelian or "Western" view is probably Thomas Aquinas. Thomas discusses justice in his *Summa Theologiae*, 2:2 (Q. 57-122). He states, "Justice implies equality. . . . God is satisfied if we accomplish what we can. . . . Justice tends to make man repay God as much as he can."[58]

Related to this is what exactly constitutes "sin." Just as many in Western society would glibly repeat Aquinas's formulations, so many consider "sin" a matter of balancing right and wrong deeds. But, as Pannenberg insists, sin goes much deeper than individual acts. Pannenberg writes, "The decay of the doctrine of original sin led to the anchoring of the concept of sin in acts of sin, and finally the concept was reduced to the individual act. . . . The problem is that our inability to master the fact of evil manifests itself in its destructive effects. . . . The turning away from God has made the problem all the more severe. . . ."[59] Sin involves not only evil acts, but also "fixation on the self . . . we are caught fast in the self."[60]

In this sense, humankind is more like oppressed victims than those who freely choose to do good or evil acts. Sin is not a matter of ethics or morals, as F. R. Tennant might imply, which view Paul Ricoeur firmly rejects. But does Marshall overstate his case? Travis broadly approves of Marshall's approach, but hesitates to accept a generalizing answer in all cases.[61] We have tried to signpost some firm landmarks, but cannot claim that ev-

---

56. Marshall, *Beyond Retribution*, 43 and 47.

57. Marshall, *Beyond Retribution*, 120.

58. Aquinas, *Summa Theologiae*, 2:2, Q. 57, art. 1.

59. Wolfhart Pannenberg, *Systematic Theology*, vol. 2 (Grand Rapids: Eerdmans and Edinburgh: T&T Clark, 1994), 236.

60. Pannenberg, *Systematic Theology*, vol. 2, 251; cf. 255.

61. Travis, *Christ and the Judgement of God*, 4-12, 74-86.

erything is neatly tied up without loose ends, much as many may wish for this. The question of "ways of judgment" may be too complex a question to admit of easy answers, and in this life much still remains hidden.[62] But Oliver O'Donovan opens up a raft of further issues which relate to the judgment theme.

62. See Oliver O'Donovan, *The Ways of Judgment* (Grand Rapids: Eerdmans, 2005).

CHAPTER 11

The Beatific Vision of God: From Glory to Glory — The Final State of the Redeemed

11.1. Two Meanings of Glory: God's Presence and His Glory as God's Self

We shall consider four distinct meanings or aspects of God's glory, spread over the first two sections. Of these four the first is most vital for an understanding of "the Last Things."

First, of the varied meanings of "glory," one controlling theme is that of *glory as God's presence.* A popular maxim asserts, "It is not in heaven that we find God, but *in God* that we find heaven." "Heaven" is precisely *not* a construct of the imagination. Plato postulated a timeless realm of pure Forms or essences, of which the present world of earth was seen to be an inferior, timebound, and spacebound copy. He reached this idea by speculating about perfection and the nature of "the soul" as being of a different order of reality from that of the body. But Christian "heaven" does not consist of a realm of perfect "essences" projected by human imagination. The "glory" which awaits every Christian is precisely and primarily *the presence of God.* Very much secondarily, it then involves not a human projection, but God's new creation.

It is simply impossible to imagine or to predict what being "face to face" with God (1 Cor. 13:12) in the *fullest* sense will mean. Admittedly this revelation will not come as a complete surprise, since the New Testament writers see Jesus Christ as "the reflection of God's glory and the exact imprint of God's very being" (Greek, *apaugasma tēs doxēs kai charactēr tēs hypostaseōs autou,*" Heb. 1:3). Stephen "gazed into heaven and saw the glory of God, and Jesus standing at the right hand of God" (Acts 7:55; i.e., standing as God's honored executive authority). Because there are theological contrasts between Stephen's speech and the general thrust of Luke-Acts, Marcel Simon and others argue convincingly for the authenticity and early date of Stephen's speech.[1] Yet even though Christ is the definitive revelation of God, we cannot claim that to know Christ in this life is thereby to know the *inexhaustible* depths of God. Any language about "glory for me" does not denote some "external" personal reward, but the inestimable privilege of full access to the wonder and beauty of God, namely, to God's glory.

Jude speaks of God as the One who will "make you stand without blemish in the presence of his glory with rejoicing" (Jude 24). Revelation tells of the Christian martyrs in heaven, who in full knowledge of God cry, "Just and true are your ways"; heaven was opened, and "the temple was filled with smoke from the glory of God and from his power" (Rev. 15:3, 8). Heaven is permeated with "the glory of God and radiance like a very rare jewel" (Rev. 21:11). The "city" has no need of sun or moon, "for the glory of God is its light, and its lamp is the Lamb" (Rev. 21:23). The Christians in Colossae "will be revealed with him in glory" (Col. 3:4). Those who are fully involved or share Christ's sufferings will "shout for joy when his glory is revealed" (1 Pet. 4:13). In 2 Thessalonians "the presence of the Lord" occurs in parallel with "the glory of his might" (2 Thess. 1:9), and "when he comes to be glorified by his saints" (1:10). In examining passages in Revelation, however, we will do well to heed Robert Gundry's recent comment, "Symbolic language fills the book of Revelation as it fills other apocalyptic literature. We may therefore presume that the description of the New Jerusalem in Rev. 21:1–22:5 deals in symbolisms . . . unheard-of dimensions, having gates that each consist of a single pearl. . . ."[2] It concerns people, not geography.

Glory not only indicates God's presence, but it also denotes a *visible manifestation* of God's presence. Much of the New Testament language draws on the Old Testament, where "the glory of the LORD" or "the glory of Yahweh" occurs no fewer than thirty-six times. Often seeing God becomes a source of strength. Isaiah writes, "They shall see the glory of the LORD. . . . Say to those who are of a fearful heart, 'Be strong, do not fear!'"

1. Marcel Simon, *St. Stephen and the Hellenists in the Primitive Church* (London: Longmans, Green, 1958), and Larry W. Hurtado, *One God, One Lord* (London and New York: Continuum and T&T Clark, 2nd ed. 1998), 118 and 121-22.

2. Robert H. Gundry, "The New Jerusalem," in *The Old Is Better: New Testament Essays* (Tübingen: Mohr Siebeck, 2005), 399; cf. 399-411. Cf. also George B. Caird, *The Language and Imagery of the Bible* (London: Duckworth, 1980), 160-67.

(Isa. 35:2, 4). Many examples suggest the *visible appearance or manifesta-tion* of God's glory in such phenomena as a cloud, a mountaintop, or the tabernacle, but other passages speak of God's glory as "filling," "rising," or "going up," and "coming" or "departing."

Ezekiel is typical here. Much of the symbolism of the book of Revela-tion is drawn directly from Ezekiel. "Like the bow in a cloud, . . . this was the appearance of the likeness of the glory of the LORD" (Ezek. 1:28). But God's glory also *moves*. "The glory of the LORD rose up from the cherub, . . . and the court was full of the brightness of the glory of the LORD" (Ezek. 10:4). "Then the glory of the LORD went out [or 'departed,' AV/KJB] from the threshold of the house and stopped above the cherubim" (Ezek. 10:18). "The glory of the LORD entered the temple" (Ezek. 43:4). Finally, "the glory of the LORD filled the temple of the LORD, and I fell upon my face" (Ezek. 44:4).

This clearly has parallels in Isaiah and elsewhere. In addition to Isa. 35:2-4, Isa. 40:5 declares, "The glory of the LORD shall be revealed, and all people shall see it together," and Isa. 66:18 adds, "They shall come and shall see my glory." Even with reference to Mosaic times, the writer says, "In the morning you shall *see* the glory of the LORD" (Exod. 16:7). "The glory of the LORD appeared in a cloud" (Exod. 16:10). "The cloud covered the tent of meeting, and the glory of the LORD filled the tabernacle" (Exod. 40:34). "The LORD our God has shown us his glory" (Deut. 5:24). In the Psalms, "the LORD will *appear* in his glory" (Ps. 102:16). Clearly in these verses "glory" refers to the presence of God in a form which can be *seen*, and be-cause it is a *manifestation of the living God*, it may move from place to place, or "fill" his temple. In the context of "the Last Things," it is equally clear that, if we choose to speak of "heaven" at all, its first characteristic, more important than any other, is that *God is present* in a directly accessi-ble way. "Glory" certainly conveys *more* than this, but this remains the starting point.

We may now pass to our *second* meaning or aspect of "glory." In terms of etymology and semantics, there is universal argument that the main Hebrew word for "glory," *kābôdh*, conveyed in origin "what weighed heavily" or was "weighty."[3] If "weight" was once the central idea, we can

---

3. See, e.g., Gerhard von Rad, "*kābôdh* in the Old Testament," *TDNT*, vol. 2, 238, and 238 n. 20; Francis Brown, with S. R. Driver and C. A. Briggs (eds.), *The New Hebrew and English Lexicon* (Lafayette, IN: Associated Publishers and Authors, 1980), 457-59; W. A. Van Gemeren (ed.), *NIDOTTE*, vol. 2, 577-83.

compare the Latin *gravis,* meaning "heavy," and the English loanword *gravitas,* meaning the possession of "dignity" or "weighty presence." Sometimes in England the Crown Nominations Commission (which appoints Diocesan Bishops) has discussed whether an able candidate possesses, in addition to other qualities, the *gravitas* needed for a leader, especially for a national role. It fundamentally conveys "what makes a person impressive." It is also here that we see the *divergence and uniqueness, in comparison with secular usage,* when this word is applied to God. For while, in Homer, Achilles may "glory" in his warrior-like qualities, or Odysseus may glory in his cleverness or guile, what makes God "impressive" is not only his majesty but also his *humility* in being willing to engage with, and forgive, humanity, and most of all his *self-emptying in the incarnation and the cross.*

This nuance ultimately derives from the Greek *doxa* as well as the Hebrew *kābôdh,* but it does not have the classical Greek sense of "opinion." In the Septuagint *doxa* translates the Hebrew *kābôdh* nearly 200 times, and the word occurs 280 times in the canonical books of the Old Testament, and even about 445 times if we include deuterocanonical books. Yet if *doxa* meant only "the visible manifestation of God," how might Israel or the Church "give glory" to God, or "glorify" (Greek, *doxazō*) him (Matt. 5:16; Luke 2:20; 5:26)? The meaning can shade into the Greek "reputation" or "favorable status." This meaning is less frequent in the Hebrew Old Testament than in the LXX and New Testament. It is easy to see how God's people can ascribe to him "power," "honor," "splendor," or the "reputation" that goes with his revealed acts as God of Israel and the Church.

Nevertheless this applies more closely to heavenly *worship* than to the *state* of enjoying God's presence. John the Divine or Seer writes, "The living creatures give glory and honor and thanks to the one seated on the throne, . . . singing, 'You are worthy, our Lord and God, to receive glory and honor and power . . .'" (Rev. 4:9, 11). In the Old Testament God may be praised as eternal sovereign, and for his splendor and radiance. There remain traces of this in the New Testament: "Knowledge of the glory of God shines in our hearts" (2 Cor. 4:6). Nevertheless Paul continues that this is "the glory of God in the face of *Jesus Christ*" (v. 6). The context is, "we proclaim Jesus Christ as Lord" (4:5). What makes God so eminently, incomparably impressive is not only his sovereign majesty and power but his focusing all his engagement with the world in Christ and the cross. Certainly the New Testament draws on visible manifestations of God in such symbols (almost sacraments, in the broadest sense) as the cloud and fire. However, Karl Barth rightly declares, "God's glory is God Himself in the truth and capacity and act in which He makes Himself known as God. . . . At its core, it is freedom to love. . . . In his glory God is the One who seeks and finds fellowship, creating and maintaining and controlling it. . . . It is a matter of God's *love*" (Barth's italics).[4]

Truly to see and to enjoy the glory of God, Barth resumes, is to "recognise the beauty of God in Jesus Christ. . . . The beauty of Jesus Christ is not just any beauty. It is the beauty of God. Or more concretely, it is the beauty of what God is and does in Him."[5] He writes further, "God's glory is the truth and power and act of His self-declaration and therefore of His love. . . . The beginning, centre and goal of these works of the divine glory is God's Son, Jesus Christ."[6] Now we know this glory, he concludes, in a hidden but also authentic way, by faith. Then shall we see him as he is openly, "face to face" (1 Cor. 13:12). The paradoxical reversal of "worldly" glory finds exposition in John, Paul, and Martin Luther. John records, "The hour has come for the Son of Man to be glorified" (John 12:23), as Jesus proceeds to *the cross*. When he faces an ignominious death, he prays, "Father, glorify your name" (John 12:28). The contrast shows that this was all about "the death he was to die" (12:33). Paul shows that Christ crucified is "foolishness" by the standards of the world, but "the power of God and the wisdom of God" (1 Cor. 1:18-25). Martin Luther rejects a *theologia gloriae*. He writes, "The visible and hinder parts of God . . . mean the humanity of God, his weakness . . ." (1 Cor. 1:25). "The theologian of glory says bad is good and good is bad. The theologian of the cross calls them by their proper name. For as long as a man does not know Christ, he does not know God, hidden in sufferings."[7]

God's glory, Luther shows us, is not a triumphalist glory of sheer power as such, but a glory of God's humility, centered on the *cross*. The God whom we shall encounter when we meet *face to face* in the post-resurrection life is God *in Christ*, or, as one writer calls it, "The *Christlikeness* of God." If Christians have as their goal to be like Christ, what a face-to-face meeting that will be! A *Christlike* God will meet and embrace us, yet offering *inexhaustible depths* of further discovery. Paul writes, "How unsearchable are his judgments, and how inscrutable his ways! For who

---

4. Karl Barth, *Church Dogmatics*, II/1, *The Doctrine of God* (Edinburgh: T&T Clark, 1957), sect. 31, part 3, 641.

5. Barth, *Church Dogmatics*, II/1, sect. 31, part 3, 665.

6. Barth, *Church Dogmatics*, II/1, sect. 31, part 3, 666 and 667.

7. Martin Luther, "The Heidelberg Disputation," in *Luther: Early Theological Works*, ed. James Atkinson (London: S.C.M., 1962), 290 and 291.

has known the mind of the Lord?" (Rom. 11:33-34). This aspect also forms part of Karl Barth's stress on the *beauty* of God. This aspect of beauty is also expounded by the Roman Catholic theologian Hans Urs von Balthasar.[8] Balthasar's approach may be broader, and emphasizes *aesthetics*. But Barth's comment on God's glory as "God Himself," and God's beauty as part of that glory, carries us on to a third major theme of "glory."

11.2. Two Further Meanings of Glory: Loving God for His Sake, and Seeing Him Face-to-Face

The third aspect of glory to be considered is suggested by Jürgen Moltmann. He declares, *"To 'glorify' God means to love God for his own sake, and to enjoy God as he is in himself."*[9] He notes that this idea derives from Augustine. Augustine argued that sinners "make use" of God in order to enjoy the world, but believers "make use" of the world in order *to "enjoy" God.* He wrote, "Men, who in their eagerness to enjoy the creature instead of the Creator had grown into the likeness of this world, are therefore most appropriately named 'the world.'"[10] The praise of God, Moltmann insists, "has no purpose, no utility . . . in common with the child's self-forgetting delight in its game."[11] It is the sheer joy of celebration.

Many devotional writers have urged that worshippers should be more ready to "waste time," in this sense, in pure adoration. But, as our chapter on instant holiness by the Holy Spirit in the resurrection has shown, Christians will see, after the resurrection, the relative worthlessness of the created order in comparison with God himself. This is not to belittle the beauty of creation; it is to take up the faultless logic of Augustine and of Athanasius that, in spite of the beauty of what God creates (his "creatures"), their beauty cannot compete with that of the God who created them. We shall be face-to-face with the One whose infinite beauty and resourcefulness created the beautiful things from which we were reluctant to part as we faced death.

To cite Moltmann again, after the resurrection, *"self-love* must become

---

8. Hans Urs von Balthasar, *The Glory of the Lord* (7 vols.; Edinburgh: T&T Clark, 1982-91), e.g., vol. 6 (1991), 31-86, and vol. 7.

9. Jürgen Moltmann, *The Coming of God: Christian Eschatology* (London: S.C.M., 1996), 323 (my italics).

10. Augustine, *On Christian Doctrine*, bk. 1, ch. 12 (*NPNF*, ser. 1, vol. 2, 525); also ch. 5.

11. Moltmann, *The Coming of God*, 323.

the creative love for the other, that is to say, *selfless love*" (his italics).[12] Everything will be in God. But does this mean that friends, historic figures, and beautiful objects cease to play any part in our thoughts? We can only speculate. But if believers are "face-to-face" with God, this must in some sense include access to, and knowledge of, *the mind of God*. Hence we can be certain that part of the purpose of resurrection, rather than the pagan notion of "immortality" (as in Plato and some Eastern religions), is God's preservation of recognizable and communicable individuality. One of the best treatments on which we draw, as we noted, was that of Ernst Käsemann on the "body" as the visible expression of Christ's lordship, involving also human "ability to communicate" and "personal shape."[13] But this implies that God will cherish the recognizable forms of individuals. Through him, we shall enjoy God's affirmation of them in Christ. If, as is probable, we shall still value friendships and human love, this will all be seen, to use a phrase borrowed from Paul and the Reformers, as "clothed in the righteousness of Christ."

When all becomes enfolded in the mind and presence of God, there can be no competitive conflict between God's performing for his own sake and for the sake of his creatures. The biblical assertion, "My glory I give to no other" (Isa. 42:8), will not be applicable in an exclusive sense, for all creatures will recognize that the glory is God's. Nor will there be any jealousy or competitiveness about "rewards" or places in heaven: for we shall see one another as filtered through the all-encompassing mind of God.

We now reach our *fourth* theme or aspect of God's glory. Admittedly some of this meaning may remain a little speculative, and may stretch language. No one can describe the conditions of being *face-to-face with God* with certainty, except insofar as these rest on the promises of the faithful God, as revealed in Christ. But this does unfold all the main themes of "glory." If the main or first meaning of "glory" is the visible manifestation of the presence of God, the Old and New Testaments offer two further ways of conceiving of this "presence." First in Hebrew, *presence* uses the very same word as that which regularly translates also as "face," namely, *pānîm*. Sometimes a different Hebrew word, *'ayîn*, can also be translated both as *presence* and *eyes*.

David Ford has shown us much of the significance of *face*. He writes,

---

12. Moltmann, *The Coming of God*, 326.

13. Ernst Käsemann, "Primitive Christian Apocalyptic," in *New Testament Christians of Today* (New York: Harper & Row, 1967 and London: S.C.M., 1969), 135.

"It conjures up past events, stories, associations, a world of meaning. . . . Each face is uniquely individual, yet it is also a primary focus for relating to others. . . . The face as relating, welcoming, incorporating others, is fundamental to social life. . . . Faces can interanimate each other and at the same time each seems to become more fully and distinctively itself."[14] Ford speaks of "the inexhaustibility of the face of the beloved."[15] In Rev. 1:16 we read, "His face was like the sun shining with full force." What inexhaustible depths, what experiences of God "as he is in himself," what welcome, what meeting, there will be when we are face-to-face with God! Ford comments, "Seeing his face in worship is here the picture of unsurpassable joy and perfection."[16]

The second association is that of shining as light. Numerous passages, including the great priestly blessing, pray that God's face may "shine upon you" (Num. 6:25). During the Intertestamental period the rabbis and Judaism spoke of God's glory as the *Shekinah*, although this is not a biblical term. Moltmann comments, "The *Shekinah* is God himself and yet distinct from God himself," involving "God's self-distinction," as Georg Hegel and Franz Rosenzweig called it.[17] Hence it becomes possible to speak of God's suffering with Israel.[18] *Brightness* is associated with fire and beauty, but also inspires awe. In Exod. 24:16-17, we read: "The glory of the LORD settled on Mount Sinai. . . . Now the appearance of the glory of the LORD was like a devouring fire on top of the mountain." "Moses was not able to enter the tent of meeting because the cloud settled on it, and the glory of the LORD filled the tabernacle" (Exod. 40:35). The King of glory is the Lord of hosts (Ps. 24:10). "The God of glory thunders. . . . The voice of the LORD flashes forth flames of fire" (Ps. 29:3, 7). "For I will be a wall of fire all around it [Jerusalem], says the LORD, and I will be the glory within it" (Zech. 2:5). Finally, one of the most famous verses is: "Arise, shine, for your light has come, and the glory of the LORD has risen upon you" (Isa. 60:1). It is not surprising that New Testament writers use "clouds" in connection with glory. But the point in the majority of references is to stress the *transcendence* of God's glory. Humans should approach it only with trepidation

---

14. David F. Ford, *Self and Salvation: Being Transformed* (Cambridge: Cambridge University Press, 1999), 18-19.

15. Ford, *Self and Salvation*, 21.

16. Ford, *Self and Salvation*, 175.

17. Jürgen Moltmann, *The Spirit of Life: A Universal Affirmation* (London: S.C.M., 1992), 48.

18. Moltmann, *The Spirit of Life*, 49; cf. 47-51.

and awe. Any attempt to approach the throne "with boldness" (Heb. 4:16) depends on the work of Christ as Mediator, or the One who stands between (Heb. 4:14–10:22).

This fourth aspect of meaning, however, should not obscure the fact that "heaven" primarily means God's presence, and the "glory of God" means the visible manifestation of that presence. It then carries meaning of the Christological and cruciform aspect because his self-emptying in humiliation and the cross "makes God impressive"; and his *glory* entails loving and honoring God for his own sake.

11.3. The Symbolism and Purpose of the Book of Revelation

We have observed that Ezekiel and other Old Testament books are necessary for understanding the symbolism of the book of Revelation. This statement, however, is not adequate. Although Revelation draws most of all on Ezekiel for its vision of God and the glory of God, especially as enthroned, Isaiah, Psalms, and Daniel contribute an influence, and postcanonical Jewish literature, including most of all *1 and 2 Enoch,* are decisive sources of imagery. They often hold the key to what otherwise obscure symbols in Revelation mean, and the first readers would be aware of them. Most symbolism has a specific background which controls its primary level of meaning. But the whole point of using symbol is to fire the imagination with multiple layers of meaning. Umberto Eco, following J. Lotman, calls these "open" texts, which deliberately have more than one level of application.[19] They stand in contrast to "closed" texts and meanings, where a sentence such as "Jesus was crucified under Pontius Pilate" has one meaning. Calvin insisted, against the use of allegory, that the Bible contained meanings that were genuine answers *(germanus et simplex).*[20] This can be applied to texts from which doctrine is derived, or which make historical claims, but hardly to language which is poetic or symbolic. Even language about the Suffering Servant in Isaiah 53 may have more than one level of application.

Before we look at the importance of the postbiblical apocalyptic Jewish writings, we may consider two relatively minor examples of how Reve-

19. Umberto Eco, *The Role of the Reader: Explorations in the Semiotics of Texts* (London: Hutchinson, 1981), 8-11.

20. John Calvin, *The Epistles of Paul to the Galatians, Ephesians, Philippians, and Colossians* (Edinburgh: Oliver & Boyd, 1965), 85.

lation uses symbols. "Seven" was a significant number for many creatures in the ancient world. The book of Revelation is written to seven churches (Rev. 1:4, 20); it speaks of seven stars and seven lampstands (Rev. 1:20), seven spirits and seven angels (Rev. 1:4; 4:5; 5:6); the Lamb with seven horns and eyes (Rev. 5:6); a beast with seven heads (Rev. 12:3); seven plagues (Rev. 15:1); seven kings and seven mountains (Rev. 17:9); seven seals (Rev. 5:1, 5; 6:1–8:1); seven trumpets (Rev. 8:2–11:15); and seven bowls (Rev. 15:7–16:17). Revelation in fact uses "seven" sixty times. It has ancestry in Genesis (67 times) and Leviticus (nearly 80 times). Its meaning is not agreed unanimously. David Aune expresses reservations, but George Caird, G. K. Beale, and the majority of commentators believe that "seven" usually denotes wholeness or completeness. The seventh day completed the work of creation and the week (Gen. 2:2). The "seven churches" may include specific or particular churches, as Rev. 1:11–3:22 implies, but here it also denotes the Christian Church as a whole. G. K. Beale rightly comments, "Sometimes *seven* is both literal and figurative. . . . Other times it is purely figurative for completeness . . . all churches in Asia Minor and probably, by extension, the church universal."[21] Caird states that the book "is really addressed to the church at large."[22] The symbol means "completeness or wholeness."[23]

In specific contexts "the beast with seven heads" almost certainly refers to the seven hills of Rome. Such a reference is so obvious that it counts against the old but otherwise attractive theory that Revelation used obscure symbols to escape the notice of Roman authorities who promoted the imperial cult. That explanation does not therefore account for every piece of symbolism. In most cases the symbolic significance of *seven* as completeness or wholeness holds good.

The four horsemen of Rev. 6:2-8, our second example, seem almost self-explanatory, with hints from the writer. The rider of the white horse is a conqueror, probably representing "the victorious course of the gospel."[24]

21. G. K. Beale, *The Book of Revelation: A Commentary on the Greek Text*, NIGTC (Grand Rapids: Eerdmans and Carlisle: Paternoster, 1999), 186.

22. G. B. Caird, *The Revelation of St. John the Divine* (London: Black, 1966), 15.

23. Caird, *The Revelation of St. John*, 14; cf. William Hendriksen, *More than Conquerors* (Grand Rapids: Baker and London: Tyndale, 1962 [1940]), 52 (who agrees); and David E. Aune, *Revelation 1–5*, WBC 52A (Dallas: Word, 1991), 29 (who dissents). He sees "seven" as cosmic authority, but others hold to the "wholeness" view, e.g., Hendriksen, *More than Conquerors*, 16.

24. Caird, *The Revelation of St. John*, 80. See also Beale, *The Book of Revelation*, 375.

This may look back to Ps. 43:3-5. The "bright red" horse (Greek, *hippos pyrros*) with a sword (Rev. 6:4) is an agent of violence. The black horse (Greek, *hippos melas*) represents hunger and food shortage, with scales in the rider's hand (Rev. 6:5-6). The "pale green" horse (Greek, *hippos chlōros*) explicitly bears the name Death.

These two examples of symbols, however minor, provide a clue to the purpose and interpretation of Revelation. The historical situation of the first readers in Asia Minor may constitute the immediate application. They suffer oppression from time to time and spasmodic persecution, especially when "the forces of evil" take the form of the Imperial Cult of Rome. This would apply especially if, as Irenaeus suggested, the book is to be dated during the last years of Domitian (c. 95-96). But the Church of the late first century does not exhaust the meaning and application. "Global" conflict may continue in later years and thus provide a message of assurance and final victory, and the absolute sovereignty of God, whenever the Church is struggling against pressures, and when it seems as if God is far away. Even the slaughtered Lamb (Rev. 5:6) retains his prominence, with "seven horns and seven eyes," denoting his complete knowledge and power, i.e., his omnipotence, omniscience, and perhaps omnipresence.

What is difficult to believe is that John's message somehow bypassed his first readers, and provided only a prediction of events which would occur in the distant future. This does not exclude *all* "futurist" interpretation, but suggests that early readers were not required to suspend involvement until some future period of the church. Where Revelation, however, explicitly embodies visions of the End-time, this clearly refers to the New Jerusalem and the postresurrection state.

The key theme of Revelation is *the sovereignty of God,* as it is in the first three Gospels' language about the kingdom, rule, or reign of God. The first three Gospels and Revelation agree that this sovereign rule took special form in Jesus, but that its climax or consummation was reserved for the Last Times. (The relation between the book of Revelation and the Fourth Gospel is considered by Joseph Estlin Carpenter in his book *The Johannine Writings.*[25]) Revelation thus encouraged Christians who were undergoing oppression that the forces of evil would never have the last word. God is, and will be, on the throne.

This brings us to Ezekiel and to such postcanonical books as *1 and*

---

25. J. Estlin Carpenter, *The Johannine Writings: A Study of the Apocalypse and the Fourth Gospel* (London: Constable, 1927).

2 *Enoch,* whose influences on the language and symbols of Revelation cannot be overestimated. Passages in Ezekiel and *1 and 2 Enoch* constitute
"throne visions" of God, of the same kind as we find in Rev. 4:2-11 and Rev.
15:2-4. *1 Enoch* likewise recounts, "I saw a lofty throne — its appearance was
like crystal and its wheels like the shining sun . . . and the Great Glory was
setting on it — as for his gown, which was shining more brightly than the
sun, it was whiter than any snow. None of the angels was able to come in
and see the face of . . . the Glorious One. . . . a great fire stood before him"
(*1 Enoch* 14:18-21).[26] The *Testament of Levi* has a closely parallel throne vision (*T. Levi* 3–5). The "Great Glory" is, as we have seen, the visible manifestation of God himself. 2 *Enoch* depicts an anthropomorphic vision of God,
but adds, "The face of the Lord is not to be talked about; it is so very mar-
vellous and supremely awesome. . . . Who can give account of his beautiful
appearance . . . indescribable, and his great glory?" (*2 Enoch* 22:1-4).

The *Apocalypse of Abraham* writes, "the heavens opened, and I saw . . .
a fire . . . and multitude of angels and a host of the invisible glory, and . . .
the living creatures" (*Apoc. Abr.* 19:4). 2 *Enoch* saw "the Lord. His face was
very strong and very glorious and terrible. . . . And I fell down flat. . . . And
the Lord . . . called to me, . . . 'Stand up.' . . . And the glorious ones did obei-
sance and said, 'Let him come up'" (*2 Enoch* 22:1-8). We may compare,
"When I saw him, I fell at his feet as though dead. But he [said], 'Do not be
afraid. . . . Now write . . .'" (Rev. 1:17, 19). "A door stood open. And the first
voice . . . said, 'Come up'" (Rev. 4:1). "Around the throne . . . are four living
creatures" (Rev. 4:6). Further: "I heard the voice of many angels surrounding the throne and the living creatures" (Rev. 5:11). "Great and amazing are
your deeds, Lord God, the Almighty" (Rev. 15:3). We may even compare the
symbolism of "He was sitting on the throne of his glory, and the books . . .
were open before him" (*1 Enoch* 47:3) with "The books were opened" (Rev.
20:12).

Among Old Testament sources, most scholars, including Christopher
Rowland, recognize the decisive influence of Ezekiel.[27] But Psalms, Isaiah,
Daniel, and other books shape the allusions of Revelation also. Daniel reflects Ezekiel 1: "The Ancient One took his throne, his clothing was white
as snow, and the hair of his head like pure wool; his throne was fiery

---

26. This translation comes from Carey C. Newman, *Paul's Glory — Christology: Tradition and Rhetoric,* NovTSup 69 (Leiden: Brill, 1992), 83.

27. Christopher Rowland, *The Open Heaven: A Study of Apocalyptic in Judaism and
Early Christianity* (New York: Crossroad, 1982).

flames, and the wheels were burning fire" (Dan. 7:9). We may compare Rev. 1:14: "his head and his hair were white as white wool, white as snow; his eyes were like a flame of fire." Dan. 7:13 traditionally refers to the Son of Man, although the NRSV translates "one like a human being," and the Septuagint "Son of Man" (Greek, *huios anthrōpou*); "Son of Man" also occurs in Rev. 1:13. It would be foolish and bizarre to imagine these symbols as literal components of a portrait. Carey Newman suggests that the ascription to the transcendent God of human-like parts of the body and even "garments" is to promote intertextual resonances between passages in Revelation and Ezekiel 1, Isaiah 6, Daniel 7, *1 and 2 Enoch*, 1Q405 (from Qumran), and a host of other passages in the Old Testament and postcanonical Jewish literature.[28] Far from compromising divine glory and transcendence, often the ambiguity of the imagery actually points to God's "otherness" or transcendence.

11.4. The Symbolic Language concerning the Last State of the Redeemed in Revelation

In the light of this careful examination of the purpose and main keys to the symbolism of Revelation, we may now turn to some genuinely futurist or eschatological visions. The description of the New Jerusalem in Rev. 21:1–22:5 is a paradigmatic case. Jerusalem itself is a symbol. Robert Gundry offers a helpful approach. He writes: "The New Jerusalem symbolizes the saints. . . . John is not describing the eternal dwelling place of the saints. He is describing *them* and them *alone*" (his italics).[29] D. Mathewson also shows how the climactic vision of Rev. 21:1–22:5 draws on a variety of Old Testament texts to produce resonances and allusions which enrich this vision.[30] If in any sense the New Jerusalem is a dwelling place, Gundry argues, it is primarily *God's* dwelling place. It underlines that to be in heaven really means to be *with God*. Certainly the link with Rev. 20:11-15 is the community who were once dead but have passed through the judgment and the resurrection. Death has been abolished.

28. Newman, *Paul's Glory — Christology*, 83-104.

29. Gundry, "The New Jerusalem: People as Place, Not Place for People," in *The Old Is Better*, 400; cf. 399-411.

30. D. Mathewson, *A New Heaven and a New Earth: The Meaning and Function of the Old Testament in Revelation 21:1–22:5*, JSNTS 238 (London and New York: Sheffield Academic Press, 2003).

One symbol is expressed in the words "as a bride adorned for her husband" (Rev. 21:2). But we know from Rev. 19:7-8 that the "bride" who "made herself ready" (19:7) stands "for the saints," arrayed in righteous acts. Further, when "the Spirit and the bride say, 'Come'" (Rev. 22:17), this is a plea to Christ to come to vindicate the saints who suffer and are oppressed. The imagery moves from "New Jerusalem" to "bride," and if it is relevant to compare Ephesians, Eph. 5:25 also implies that the Church is the bride of Christ. The "adornment" of the bride (Greek, *hōs nymphēn kekosmēmenēn*) draws on several Old Testament passages (esp. Isa. 52:1; 61:10; cf. *Joseph and Aseneth* 4:1).[31] The marriage metaphor, complete with the usual trousseau, conveys the joy, celebration, and intimacy of the entire believing community face-to-face with God. The plural "peoples" in Rev. 21:3 may allude to the international composition of the one Church (Greek, *laoi*).

It is difficult to be certain whether "Jerusalem, coming down out of heaven from God," is simply an expression for "appeared," or perhaps more probably an assertion that nothing in the new creation is merely a development out of old capacities, but fresh creation by God, which nevertheless takes account of continuity with the old. More important is that the new Jerusalem is "holy," and that "coming down out of heaven" in v. 10 does not describe an event repeated for the second time, as if the city descended from heaven *twice*, as David Aune also insists.[32] It is typical of Revelation that events are often repeated, which points toward rejecting the whole book as a chronological sequence. It does often move forward, and for this reason some have suggested that it presents a series of spirals: some events are repeated as literary devices, but they look toward the climax of the Last Things.

A number of symbols follow in Rev. 21:4-14, which Gundry suggests characterize the "sheer happiness" of the city.[33] "He [God] will wipe every tear from their eyes; death will be no more; mourning and crying and pain will be no more" (21:4). "To the thirsty I will give water as a gift from the spring of the water of life" (21:6). A blessing comes to "those who conquer" (21:7). Destruction is symbolized as "the lake that burns with fire and sulphur" (21:8). The first symbol is almost literal speech. Gundry calls it "a

---

31. David E. Aune, *Revelation 17–22*, WBC 52C (Nashville: Nelson, 1998), 1121; Beale, *The Book of Revelation*, 1043-44.

32. Aune, *Revelation 17–22*, 1120.

33. Gundry, "The New Jerusalem," in *The Old Is Better*, 404.

happiness unadulterated by tears."[34] But this will mean any postmortal counterpart to tears and eliminates the counterpart of what, in this life, would give rise to tears. Hence clearly "mourning and crying" is abolished. "Thirst" must be seen against the background of a Near Eastern desert culture. Clearly Isa. 49:10 and 55:1 provide the interpretative background: "They shall not hunger or thirst, neither the scorching wind nor sun shall strike them down."[35] This is frequently used as a metaphor in Isaiah: "With joy you will draw water from the wells of salvation," where "wells of salvation" are not literal springs. "Water *of life*" (Rev. 21:6) or *flowing* water denotes water from a spring. It is a literal description of running water, as opposed to *stagnant* water in pools or jugs. Otherwise the significance of water as mediating life is well known in the ancient oriental and Greek worlds and is often metaphysical.[36] Throughout the Old Testament, Goppelt shows, metaphors and comparisons point to God as a source of living water (Jer. 2:13 is a classic: "they have forsaken me, the fountain of living water, and dug out cisterns, . . . cracked cisterns"). In the New Testament Jesus is "living water" (John 4:10, 14; cf. John 7:37). As in Isa. 55:1, the water in Rev. 21:6 is a free gift, "without price." Goppelt suggests, "Passages in Revelation take water figuratively, like Isa. 55:1."[37] *Flowing* water suggests satisfaction to longing which can be constantly renewed. After all, God is "the living God."

"Those who conquer" (Rev. 21:7; Greek, singular *ho nikōn*) has an almost technical meaning in Revelation. The martyrs typically "conquer" when they remain faithful to death under persecution. Beale comments, "This conquering of sin (Rev. 2:26-28; 3:5; 21:7) entails being conquered by the world . . . when believers refuse to compromise with the world."[38] The purpose of this verse, Beale comments, is *to encourage Christians to persevere* through hardship. He continues, "The figurative point of all these multiple pictures of the End-time blessings is interpreted at the conclusion of v. 7 to be God's presence with his people."[39]

John the Seer uses many more symbols, which superficially appear to describe a heavenly location. The holy city is perched on a great, high

---

34. Gundry, "The New Jerusalem," in *The Old Is Better*, 404.

35. Beale, *The Book of Revelation*, 1056.

36. Leonhard Goppelt, "*hydōr*" ("water"), *TDNT*, vol. 8, 316; cf. 314-33.

37. Goppelt, "*hydōr*," *TDNT*, vol. 8, 325.

38. Beale, *The Book of Revelation*, 269 and 1057.

39. Beale, *The Book of Revelation*, 1058; cf. Caird, *The Revelation of St. John*, 267; and Aune, *Revelation 17–22*, 1128-30.

mountain (Rev. 21:10). The glory of God is "like a very rare jewel, like jasper, clear as crystal" (21:11). It "has a great, high wall with twelve gates" (21:12). It has "twelve foundations" (21:14). All these, however, are symbols of security. The mountain is "so huge and high that no invading army could possibly gain a foothold on it."[40] The city wall, it is explained a few verses later (Rev. 21:15-21a), is so solid, thick, and high, that no army could breach it. Its "fifteen hundred miles," or 12,000 stadia, are not literal measurements, but indicate that in height, length, and width the walls cannot be breached. In addition to all this, an angel stands guard at each gate. It is not primarily the place, however, Gundry insists, that is secure, but God's own people. In their lifetime they have suffered deadly assaults from forces of evil, even from demonic forces, but this never happens again. They need no longer experience any anxiety. Because God is there, the cubic shape matches the holy of holies in the tabernacle and the temple (1 Kings 6:20).

It would be foolish to try to specify the individual meaning of each of the precious stones. The Church has often been poor and without much property, especially the first readers of the book. Gundry rightly observes, "John promises the saints the incalculable wealth of precious stones and precious metal. Again, we should resist the temptation to spiritualize."[41] But there are overtones to the symbols, as we should expect. God is often seen to dwell at the top of a "high" mountain. This chapter may also allude to the vision of God's glory in Ezekiel 43. This constitutes a secondary level of meaning.[42] The dimensions are measured (Ezek. 43:13-17); gates are mentioned (43:1); and the vision centers on the throne and glory of God. 2 *Enoch* 65:10 speaks of "a great indestructible wall" and the new "paradise." The *twelve* foundations are explicitly called "the twelve names of the twelve apostles" (21:14). It is difficult not to recall common Christian teaching in Eph. 2:20, "built upon the foundation of the apostles and prophets." Perhaps "twenty-four" in Rev. 4:4 refers to this "twice twelve" of the two covenants. The rock, or mountain, points to the security and stability, which complements the ever-new flowing river or flowing waters.

40. Gundry, "The New Jerusalem," in *The Old Is Better*, 404.

41. Gundry, "The New Jerusalem," in *The Old Is Better*, 405.

42. Beale, *The Book of Revelation*, 1066. Another "secondary" level of meaning may concern the jewels of the high priest's breastplate or the jewels worn by the king of Tyre in Ezek. 28:13. But although the jewels are similar, John relates them in a different sequence, and this link remains speculative. Cf. Caird, *Revelation of St. John*, 274-78.

Revelation 21:15-17, as we have noted, recalls Ezekiel 43, but it may re-flect the theme of Ezekiel 40–48. "Meaning" again has to do with security. But it is more important to note the repetition of what has been narrated before. W. Hendriksen has been influential among many who might other-wise have taken a sequential "futurist" view. He points out how John's vi-sions are *often repetitive and in parallel*. For example, he writes, "A careful study of chapter 20 will reveal that this chapter describes a period which is synchronous with that of chapter 12."[43] Chapters 12–14, he argues, cover the entire dispensation. He claims, "A careful reading of the book of Reve-lation has made it clear that the book consists of seven sections . . . parallel to one another. . . . The period is viewed now from one aspect, now from another."[44] The number of periods may be questioned, and the book em-bodies progression as well as cyclical themes. But, as the "meaning" pas-sage shows, it is *not* a sequential chronological narrative. The "Interlude" of Rev. 7:1-17 is a further decisive example.[45]

Revelation 21:22-27 tells us that there is "no temple in the city" (Rev. 21:22). The New Jerusalem is not "religious" in the usual sense of the term, meaning "religious aspiration." God himself is the temple (21:22). Simi-larly, because God is there, "the city has no need of the sun or moon to shine on it, for the glory of the Lord is its light" (Rev. 21:23). This is parallel with the hint given in John 2:21, "He [Jesus] was speaking of the temple of his body" (cf. Mark 14:58). But the most important reason for the obsoles-cence of the temple in the new creation is, as Caird suggests, that a "holy place" was needed for the glory of the Lord when the environment of the earth was "common," "secular," or "tainted."[46] But, this section tells us, "nothing unclean . . . nor anyone who practices abomination" will enter or remain in the city (21:27). Hence the whole people of God are holy, and God does not need to be "separate" (Hebrew, *qādôsh*, also "holy") any-more. There is a hint of inclusiveness in the verse "The nations will walk by its light, and the kings of the earth will bring their glory into it" (Rev. 21:24), and the gates will be open (21:25). This may, however, reflect Isa. 60:3, 5, 11, as Beale claims.[47] Richard Bauckham agrees that in vv. 24-26

---

43. Hendriksen, *More than Conquerors,* 19.

44. Hendriksen, *More than Conquerors,* 19.

45. Robert H. Mounce, *The Book of Revelation* (Grand Rapids: Eerdmans and London: Marshall, Morgan & Scott, 1977), 164; Judith Kovacs and Christopher Rowland, *Revelation through the Centuries* (Oxford: Blackwell, 2004), 98-99.

46. Caird, *The Revelation of St. John,* 278-79.

47. Beale, *The Book of Revelation,* 1004-1102.

"the nations" are those who were converted to Christian faith just before Christ's final Return, by the witness of the martyrs.[48]

This may appear to clash with Rev. 21:11-12 on the security of the "city" with its gates guarded by angels. But, as Ian Ramsey showed fifty years ago, symbols which may *seem* paradoxical readily complement one another. Ramsey, followed much later by Paul Ricoeur, showed that in a symbol two or more "universes of discourse" overlap or interact with each other to create "disclosure situations" where propositional language runs out.[49] The "whole" then yields its meaning, involving the reader's active reflection. Paul Ricoeur similarly comments that metaphor and symbol "bring two separate domains into cognitive and emotional relation by using language directly appropriate for one as a lens for seeing the other"; while Paul Tillich speaks of the capacity of symbols to open depths of the self and the depths of what is symbolized.[50] I have attempted to explain and expound the work of these authors in a short section elsewhere, and to show the importance of symbol for biblical interpretation.[51]

In the vision of the New Jerusalem the final set of symbols comes in Rev. 22:1-5. Again there is a referral back to the "water of life," or living water, bright or pure as crystal, flowing from God and the lamb (v. 1). The "tree of life" (22:2) looks back to Gen. 2:9-10, hinting at an *Urzeit-Endzeit* pattern, or suggesting a restoration at the End of the original Paradise of Eden. The number "twelve" features again in Rev. 22:2, where it is clearly not numerical. The leaves of the tree "are for the healing of the nations" (v. 2). Most of the first readers would see an allusion to a reversal of the curse of eating from the tree of knowledge of good and evil (Gen. 2:17 and 3:17). Caird observes, "John has now exhausted all the riches of Old Testament imagery to describe the splendour of the New Jerusalem."[52] The pas-

---

48. Richard Bauckham, *The Climax of Prophecy: Studies in the Book of Revelation* (Edinburgh: T&T Clark, 1993), 313.

49. Ian T. Ramsey, *Religious Language: An Empirical Placing of Theological Phrases* (London: S.C.M., 1957), 19-48; and Ian T. Ramsey, *Models for Divine Activity* (London: S.C.M., 1973).

50. Paul Ricoeur, "Metaphor and Symbol," in Ricoeur, *Interpretation Theory: Discourse and the Surplus of Meaning* (Fort Worth, TX: Texas Christian University Press, 1976), 67; cf. 45-69; and Paul Ricoeur, *The Conflict of Interpretations* (Evanston, IL: Northwestern University Press, 1974), 287-334; also Paul Tillich, *Dynamics of Faith* (London: Allen & Unwin, 1957), 42-47.

51. Anthony C. Thiselton, *New Horizons in Hermeneutics* (Grand Rapids: Zondervan and London: Harper-Collins, 1992), 575-82.

52. Caird, *The Revelation of St. John*, 280.

sage now focuses on the words, "They will see his face, and his name will be on the foreheads" (22:4). Not only are the redeemed *face-to-face with God* (discussed above), but they bear the mark of God's own ownership and protection in their persons. God is their light (v. 5). As the old hymn has it, "I am his, and he is mine."

CHAPTER 12

The Beatific Vision and Trinitarian Work of God: More on the Final State of the Redeemed

The very fact that symbolic or poetic language has to use "indirect" speech to talk of God underlines what we have already concluded about the *glory* of God. God is an inexhaustible source of wonder. We shall not grow weary of exploring the depths of God himself. He is the living God, the God of promise, the ongoing God. He remains faithful and reliable, like a solid rock, which speaks of stability. But he will make possible surprising, new purposes and discoveries. Wolfhart Pannenberg argues several times that God's faithfulness does not exclude his fulfilling his promises in ways that may surprise us, or may seem unexpected. He comments, for example, in another context: "Its splendor . . . surpasses the whole range of the concrete forms it has taken . . . and points toward a future in which it is realized to the full. . . . They look for something hitherto unexampled which is still to come."[1] The unsurpassable and inestimable privilege of beholding, and participating in, each new wonder may be enjoyed not only with awe and reverence, but boldly and confidently in and with Christ (Heb. 4:16).

The New Testament uses many words for "joy." William Morrice examines eleven such words, in classical Greek, in the Septuagint, and in the New Testament.[2] He discusses *exultant joy* (Greek, *agallian, agalliasis*), used eleven times in the New Testament, as in Mary's "My spirit rejoices in God my Savior" (Luke 1:47), or in the case of the Philippian jailer, who "rejoiced with his whole household" (Acts 16:30-34). The Greek *euthymein,*

1. Wolfhart Pannenberg, *Basic Questions in Theology* (3 vols.; London: SCM, 1973), vol. 3, 61.

2. William G. Morrice, *Joy in the New Testament* (Exeter: Paternoster, 1984), 19-81. Cf. Rudolf Bultmann, *"agalliaomai," TDNT,* vol. 1, 19-21; and Hans Conzelmann, *"chairō, chara," TDNT,* vol. 9, 359-72.

used five times, conveys a mood of optimism (Jas. 5:13). The New Testament uses "gladness" (Greek, *euphrainein*) sixteen times, mainly in Luke-Acts, but not uniquely so (Gal. 4:27). Sheer pleasure (Greek, *hēdonē*) may be used of the pleasures of the world (Luke 8:14; Titus 3:3), but it may also be positive (2 Cor. 12:9. 15). *Hilaros*, "hilarity," may seem promising, but it occurs only twice. Morrice makes much of "boasting," or "glorying," especially Paul's thirty-five uses; but the usual contrast is between boasting in human achievements and glorying in God and glorying or boasting in the cross (1 Cor. 1:29-31; 3:21; Gal. 6:13-14). Blessedness is familiar from the Beatitudes (Greek, *makarios;* Matt. 5:3-12; Luke 6:20-23), and it occurs fifty-five times in the New Testament, mainly in the Gospels and Revelation. Morrice concludes with five more terms, of which "joy and delight" (Greek, *chairein* and *chara*) relate to the final state after suffering (Col. 1:11; 1:24; 1 Pet. 4:13; Rev. 19:7).

Morrice suggests that Luke constitutes "the Gospel of Joy," and he cites James Denney as saying that the New Testament is "the most buoyant, exhilarating, and joyful book in the world."[3] All the same, this touches only the outer edge of what joy would mean after the resurrection. Philosophers of religion constantly try to show the radical difference in logic or "grammatical" shape and content between words used in everyday life and the same words as applied to God. Even Wittgenstein observes how different "to hear" is. He remarks, "You can't hear God speak to someone else, you can hear him only if you are being addressed."[4] But such difference pales into insignificance compared with the difference between earthly joy and postresurrection joy. For example, the analogy of singing hymns of praise in this life for an eternal duration becomes quite misleading for at least two reasons. First, we have seen that "eternity" denotes neither endless *duration,* nor timelessness, nor even simultaneity, but time as this may be experienced in a *new dimension.* Second, even the most exalted experiences of singing God's praises on earth are marred by distractions and other attractions, concerns about time, repetitious imperfections, and, above all, remains of self-concern, self-love, or sin. These things will not detract from the sheer joy of praising God "for his own sake" and of beholding his beauty "face-to-face."

The glorification of God *after* the resurrection of the dead will involve at least three key factors. (1) First, *Christ's* own sufferings, death, and resur-

---

3. Morrice, *Joy in the New Testament,* 81; and James Denney, *Studies in Theology* (London: Hodder & Stoughton, 1895), 171.

4. Ludwig Wittgenstein, *Zettel* (Oxford: Blackwell, 1967), sect. 717.

rection will permeate everything. They will provide the lens through which everything else is seen, including even our fellow humans. (2) Secondly, the "spiritual body," or mode of existence after resurrection, as marked by the character and action of the Holy Spirit, will *embrace* our experience of God to a degree hitherto unimaginable. (3) Third, just as prayer on earth was *by* the Holy Spirit, *through* Jesus Christ the Son, *to* God the Father (Rom. 8:26-27), this *Trinitarian* process will move from faith to sight, and we shall participate in it with heightened awareness.

12.1. Joy, Wonder, and Christ's Crucifixion and Resurrection

The first of our three points, namely, *focus on the cross of Christ*, has profound consequences for everything else. These things concern not only giving glory to Christ, but a clearer understanding, in retrospect, of the depths and meaning of Christ's incarnation and sufferings, and the glory of his resurrection. We have already spoken of the continuing wounds of Christ as an aspect of his enduring identity after the resurrection (John 20:27-29). In this life joy often comes through or after the experience of pain, persecution, or suffering. Who is not to say that *for the redeemed "in Christ," his very suffering and the wounds of the cross will not transform and enhance the joy of victory into something more meaningful than it otherwise would be? Just as someone who once formerly experienced thirst and dehydration will appreciate living water more fully than one who has never experienced true thirst, so one who knows weeping, mourning, and pain will appreciate a future of "no more crying or tears" more fully than one who has known only happiness and prosperity in life.*

When my aunt died in profound Christian faith, her constant thought in her last hours was that even the angels will not be able to glorify Jesus Christ for personal forgiveness of sins, personal involvement in the cross, and new life, while she would share with all Christians in that distinctive witness and testimony. The theme of sharing in the death and resurrection of Christ will never become outdated. Further, every piece of suffering or oppression and death amid faithful trust in his sovereignty and love remains precious to God: "Precious in the sight of the Lord is the death of his faithful ones" (Ps. 116:15). Similarly, those who have suffered, with Christ, constraint and deprivation will all the more appreciate liberation from such deprivation: "My flesh faints for you, as in a dry and thirsty land where there is no water" (Ps. 63:1).

Although *life before death* is, as Moltmann insists, *more* than a preparation for the afterlife, it is hardly *less* than this. In this life we have learned how to experience joy, to express it, and to share it with others. Most poignantly of all, we have experienced joy *through or after trials and suffering.* If we know Wittgenstein's observations about "private" language and "public" criteria of meaning, previous experiences of interaction with others and of suffering will play a profound part in enhancing the currency of what it will mean *to rejoice, and to share this rejoicing with others.*[5] Without that background, it would become as individualistic as Wittgenstein's negative analogies. He asks, "Why can't my right hand give my left hand money?"; ". . . as if someone were to buy several copies of the morning paper, to assure himself that what it said was true"; or "saying: 'But I know how tall I am!' and laying his hand on top of his head to prove it."[6] Part of the wonder of God through Christ making creation as it is and as it has been is not restricted to this world. Why should joy after resurrection not be inestimably enhanced in the light of Christ's incarnation, suffering, and death? Can Jesus Christ not carry into eternity the memories and the marks of those constraints and torments from which he has become released forever in the resurrection and in eternity? Will the whole community who is "in Christ" *no longer "glory in the cross"*? Will not the very wounds of Christ enhance "the joy that was set him"? It is not only in the story of Thomas that we read of the wounds of Christ after his resurrection (John 20:27). In the book of Revelation the One who is worthy to open the seal is the *"Lamb standing as if he had been slaughtered"* (Rev. 5:6). The four living creatures and twenty-four elders sing: "You are worthy, . . . for *you were slaughtered,* and *by your blood* you ransomed for God saints from every tribe and language and people and nation" (5:9).

Again the elders and "myriads of myriads and thousands of thousands" sing, "Worthy is the Lamb that was slaughtered to receive power and wealth and wisdom and might and honor and glory and blessing" (Rev. 5:11-12). But this is not only the bare narrative of the Passion of Christ as we know it. We shall then, after the resurrection, see new understandings of the suffering and love that was involved. This will not be lost in the past, but *transformed and enhanced* in the resurrection to provide a surplus

---

5. Ludwig Wittgenstein, *Philosophical Investigations* (Ger. and Eng.; Oxford: Blackwell, 2nd ed. 1958), sects. 243-317; and a good exposition and critique in O. R. Jones (ed.), *The Private Language Argument* (London: Macmillan, 1966).

6. Wittgenstein, *Philosophical Investigations,* sects. 268, 265, and 279 respectively.

of unsurpassable joy. The cross and the resurrection will not simply be celebrated as a condition of Christian redemption, but as that which concerns the very basis of life and hope, as God created this, and most of all the love and glory of Christ, the slain Lamb with whom all the redeemed are intimately involved. What may be said of Jesus Christ may perhaps be said of the martyrs and even of all Christians who have suffered either from oppressors or from illness or natural calamity. It will not be "redemptive for others" in the unique sense used once-for-all of Christ's sacrifice, but it may be viewed in retrospect as something positive, even as a derivative "showing" of the afflictions of Christ (Rom. 6:1-11; Col. 1:24). John declares, "Blessed are the dead who . . . die in the Lord. . . . Their deeds follow them" (Rev. 14:13). "These are they who have come out of the great ordeal [great tribulation]; they have washed their robes and made them white in the blood of the Lamb" (Rev. 7:14).

12.2. The Continuing and Ever-Fresh Work of the Holy Spirit after the Resurrection: The Transformation and Enhancement of Sense Experience

The second feature with which we need to reckon is the *power of the Holy Spirit in the resurrection of Christ and the dead.* We have already argued that if, with O. R. Jones, we understand "holiness" as a *disposition* which is heavily dependent on a concrete situation, it is quite intelligible that the resurrection state can make possible instant sanctification by the Holy Spirit when we see God as he is, and appreciate the interconnectedness of all things. Nothing other than the will of God will any longer seem attractive or worthy of seeking; much else will appear deceitful and seductive. To suggest otherwise is to diminish in our minds the glory and beauty of God.

But so far we have considered only holiness. We know that on this earth and in this life we can grasp only traces of what it is *to wonder, to be satisfied, to be blessed, and to contemplate "glory."* The difference between the use of this language in the everyday world and its *application to God by faith* (in *this* life) is great enough. But the difference between these terms, even when used in life, and the "same" terms when applied to God by the most devout and learned *in faith,* is nothing compared with what they *will* be *when this is applied to God by sight in the fullest understanding of that to which they point,* and are fully trying to say. Paul has already laid out the ground for this in 1 Corinthians. He explains, "What human being knows what is truly human except the human spirit that is within? So also no one comprehends what is truly God's except the Spirit of God" (1 Cor. 2:11). Paul adds that even though in this life we may be "taught by the Spirit" (2:13), nevertheless this openness to the Holy Spirit is not perfect and not without fallibility. The Spirit is not *wholly* immanent, as the widely misused word "spirituality" too often suggests. The Holy Spirit is transcendent.

The Holy Spirit guards Israelite cattle from marauders (Isa. 63:14); he falls upon Samson, and he tears apart a lion barehanded as if it were a kid (Judg. 14:6); he takes possession of Gideon to perform unprecedented military leadership (Judg. 6:34); and Paul describes him as "the Spirit that is from [perhaps, better, 'issues from' or 'comes forth from'] God [Greek, *to pneuma to ek tou theou*]" (1 Cor. 2:12).[7] The Holy Spirit well deserves the title "The Beyond Who Is Within." We tend to have an inadequate idea of his transcendent power perhaps, first, because we have the wrong idea of "like a dove" at the Baptism of Jesus as representing gentleness (Mark 1:10; Matt. 3:16). In Mark the Spirit then "drives" Jesus into the wilderness to face messianic temptations, which action is hardly "gentle"; whereas in Gen. 1:2 the Spirit's brooding (like a dove) over the waters represents his creative and nurturing power. The second reason is that the Holy Spirit "does not speak on his own" (John 16:13, NRSV, but better translated "on his own initiative"), but witnesses to Christ. J. E. Fison speaks in this Johannine sense of "his self-effacement," and Moltmann similarly speaks of "his self-emptying."[8]

A further aspect of the Holy Spirit's work in the postresurrection situation is the *dynamic, moving, ever-new* experience which is "reduced" if we equate it with static satisfaction. By what logic should we assume that the very nature of the Holy Spirit to refresh us, and to lead us *beyond* familiar horizons, somehow ceases after the resurrection? The only argument of this kind that may be encountered is an appeal to the Greek notion of static "perfection," which derives its static nature from the Greek claim, rooted in Plato and Aristotle and echoed in Thomas Aquinas, that "the *perfect* forbids any improvement," as if to imply a "more" perfect. This suggests that progress implies that the earlier was less than perfect. On this basis, a perfect baby could never develop into a perfect boy or girl, or eventually into a perfect man or woman. But each stage will indeed be "perfect."

---

7. Anthony C. Thiselton, *The First Epistle to the Corinthians,* NIGTC (Grand Rapids: Eerdmans and Carlisle: Paternoster, 2001), 257-64, esp. 261.

8. J. E. Fison, *The Blessing of the Holy Spirit* (London and New York: Longmans, Green, 1950), 140; and Jürgen Moltmann, *The Spirit of Life: A Universal Affirmation* (London: S.C.M., 1992), 12.

The stage beyond the perfect is *not* "*more* perfect" but *equally* perfect or flawless *for the next stage*. Which pulls us in its direction? We can either opt for a Greek and Thomist view of timeless perfection and "essence" or for the biblical view of the living God, who is always on the move, and the Spirit of God, who likewise is never static but will "renew" whatever delights the glory of God inspires. We see the seductive influence of the Greek view in the Greek Septuagint's translating the Hebrew *imperfect* tense "I will be" (Exod. 3:14) by the static present tense, "I AM."

We may next consider how the postresurrection mode of being and the new creation may provide counterparts to the sensory experience of earthly life, which *far surpass it*. Matter is not annihilated but transformed, as Moltmann and many argue. The scientist and theologian David Wilkinson includes in his work a chapter on "the Future of Matter."[9] He points out that there are both continuity and discontinuity in the transformation of matter, and that in any case questions about the nature of matter, like time, are exceedingly complex. The Bible and the early Church, he stresses, saw matter as the medium of the divine. The whole of creation will share in the glory of the children of God. He quotes with approval John Polkinghorne, who is also a distinguished scientist and theologian. Polkinghorne writes, "The matter-energy of the world to come will certainly have to be radically different . . . [from] the matter-energy of this present creation. . . . If the world to come is to be free from death and suffering, its matter-energy will have to be given a different character."[10] Paul's comment, which culminates in ". . . all things in subjection under him, so that God may be all in all" (1 Cor. 15:28), is important to Polkinghorne, Wilkinson, and Moltmann. On the resurrection, Wilkinson repeats: "The resurrection encourages a picture of transformation. . . . Scientific and theological insights into the embodiment of and the psychosomatic unity of the human person mean that matter is important in the new creation. . . . Matter will be transformed."[11] This, in turn, coheres with T. F. Torrance's emphasis on the bodily resurrection of Christ and its consequences. He writes, "The irruption of the new creation . . . brings with it

9. David Wilkinson, *Christian Eschatology and the Physical Universe* (London: Continuum and T&T Clark, 1994), 137-58.

10. John C. Polkinghorne, "Eschatology," in *The End of the World and the Ends of God: Science and Theology on Eschatology,* ed. J. C. Polkinghorne and M. Welker (Harrisburg, PA: Trinity Press International, 2000), 39; cf. 29-41; and Wilkinson, *Christian Eschatology and the Physical Universe,* 153.

11. Wilkinson, *Christian Eschatology and the Physical Universe,* 156-57.

the capacity to create in us new conceptions and new categories of thought with which to apprehend and to speak appropriately . . . about it."[12]

We may pause for about two pages to speculate on what this might suggest. Sensory experience depends on the media of the eye, the ear, the tongue, smell, and tactile communication. The five senses are the basic source of sense experience. In spite of human perception of the beauty of the world, the enjoyment of music and sounds, the experience of exquisite tastes and cuisine, the marvelous fragrance of flowers and perfume, and the enjoyment of texture or the intimacy and comfort of a tactile communication with friends or a husband or wife, all of these five senses are limited in what they can convey. Yet at death we are reluctant to part with them. Will these not be transformed and surpassed, rather than annihilated?

The ancients Euclid, Aristotle, and Galen disagreed about the mechanics of visual perception. Near the beginning of the modern era of research, the end of the nineteenth century, Hermann von Helmholz, a neo-Kantian colleague of Heinrich Hertz, claimed that optical reception was of poorer or less efficient quality than it might ideally have been. Much is left to the brain to "fill in" gaps in our vision. Theories of the *Gestalt* approach in the 1930s and 1940s have been largely abandoned. It is generally agreed that the lens of the eye focuses an image onto the retina to convey neuronal signals by photoreceptive cells of the retina to the human brain.[13] The eye functions broadly like a simple camera. The brain, however, plays a major part in interpreting the raw visual data, which are transmitted through the nerves. In theory, sight could be greatly enhanced if "sight" were to be transformed into its postresurrection counterpart.

When we consider seeing beautiful colors, this becomes more striking. Even the philosopher John Locke argued that colors are not "there" but constitute a secondary quality, depending on how we perceive them. We now know that violet and blue are generated by shorter waves of 400-475 nanometers at the high-frequency end of the visual spectrum, while dark red and orange are generated by larger waves of 600-700 nanometers at the low-frequency end of the color spectrum. What colors might we "see" beyond these upper and lower limits if the postresurrection counterpart to our medium of visual perception were to be available?

Another phenomenon which provokes thought is that of synesthesia

12. T. F. Torrance, *Space, Time, and Resurrection* (Edinburgh: T&T Clark, 1976 and 1998), 177.

13. W. D. Wright, *The Rays Are Not Coloured* (Bristol: Hilger, 1967).

or inter-sensorial transfer. Synesthesia in the use of metaphor is well known from earliest times. Homer speaks of being "lily-voiced" (Homer, *Iliad* 3.152), where sight is applied to sound. The music (hearing) of the spheres (sight) occurs in Dante and in Chaucer. But synesthesia can perhaps be a physiological or neurological phenomenon, and not only a semantic one. Two senses may be linked and interchanged. Some, even if a few, view numerals as suggesting colors, or blur the distinction between the senses in other ways.[14] Does this imply a transcending of the senses which potentially suggests that sense experience itself can be transcended? At minimum, it allows us to imagine such transcendence as a possibility.

No doubt much of this remains speculative and hypothetical. Many will dismiss some of it. But suppose we consider briefly the capacities of the human ear. We may set aside the physiology of the outer, middle, and inner ear, and its dependence on the brain likewise. Whatever that may mean, it is common knowledge that, in terms of pitch, the lowest that a human can hear is 20-30 cycles per second in frequency of sound vibrations, and the highest is 20,000 cycles per second, dropping off for most of the elderly to a significantly lower frequency with an inability to hear the highest notes or highest overtones. But God has created dogs who can hear up to 60,000 cycles per second. If God can provide this for dogs, can his Holy Spirit not provide a counterpart for the postresurrection condition? This may not mean only the capacity to hear higher or lower notes, but may profoundly affect the overtones and the texture of what for the present we must still call music or song.

Taste provides a third suggestive example. We are told that even the most subtle culinary delights are generated by only five elements, together with a sense of smell: saltiness, sourness, bitterness, and sweetness, with perhaps "unami" or a savory protein, found sometimes in fermented or aged foods, and added to the traditional Western four by the Japanese and Indians. Apparently thousands of tastes are mediated through the "taste buds" (or gustatory calyculi) restricted to the upper surface of the tongue. Is it impossible for God to conceive of an enhanced generation of taste? As for smell and touch, we can only try to imagine how these might be enhanced and transformed. These three examples must suffice.

We do not have to imagine such things, however. When Paul expounded the meaning of resurrection, his appeal was not to human imagi-

---

14. See Stephen Ullmann, *The Principles of Semantics* (Oxford: Blackwell, 2nd ed. 1957 and 1963), 266-89.

nation, but to the sovereign power of the Creator God to create, to transform, and to shape a new creation. It was up to *God alone* whether he could or would design appropriate "bodies" for new environments, the counterpart of stars for the heavens, birds for the sky, fish in the sea, or animals for the land (1 Cor. 15:35-41).

12.3. The Purposes of God the Father: Divine Dialogue; God as All in All

The third feature about the shaping of the resurrection mode of existence by the Holy Spirit concerns the final purposes of God, who is the source and goal of all things (Rom. 11:36). Part of God's Trinitarian action concerns prayer, worship, and adoration after the resurrection, based on what we know of the Spirit's work in prayer in this life. In this life we constantly find that we do not know how we should pray. This is a common experience, often reported to pastors, whether by Christians or by others. Paul explicitly recognizes and acknowledges this. He explains: "The Spirit helps us in our weakness; for we do not know how to pray as we ought, but that very Spirit intercedes with sighs too deep for words. . . . The Spirit intercedes for the saints according to the will of God" (Rom. 8:26-27). But Paul has also just explained that we derive our common sonship of God from the status of Christ as God's Son. *The Holy Spirit* directs our prayers as God's children primarily to *God the Father as our Father,* mediated *through Christ as our Redeemer and Mediator* (Rom. 8:15-17). In the Church of England Doctrine Commission Report of 1987, to which I was a contributor, we wrote of "the experience of being 'prayed in,'" and of being "graciously *caught up in a divine conversation,*" in which prayer is strictly *by the Holy Spirit to God the Father through Jesus Christ the Son.*[15]

"Sighs too deep for words" (Rom. 8:26) may well describe aspects of this experience of prayer during the ambiguities and struggles of this life. But the "divine conversation" will hardly stumble or stutter in communication after the resurrection. If we are still privileged to be participants in the Divine Conversation, communication will come readily, since nothing will have remained hidden or ambiguous, and our status as "unimpeachable and blameless on the Day of our Lord Jesus Christ" will surely curb any un-

---

15. The Doctrine Commission of the Church of England, *We Believe in God* (London: Church House Publishing, 1987), 108.

due reticence. Again, we shall "boldly" approach God's throne (Heb. 4:16). What further purposes might God have? We do not know, since God has revealed only those purposes which concern this present world. But will the living God have run out of good purposes? It is difficult to imagine. This would not exclude the symbolism of "rest" for an interval. But for most of us, "everlasting rest" may not sound inviting. All, we may be thankful, lies locked up in the mind of God, who loves us and seeks our welfare.

Further, to be "with" the Lord, as he has promised (1 Thess. 4:17), does not imply merely a passively dumb proximity of location, for "location," as well as duration, has disappeared from view. To be "with" someone implies activity, communication, or at least empathy and oneness of spirit. Thus Paul speaks of being manifested with him in glory (Col. 3:4), and John declares, "When he [God] is revealed, we will be like him, for we will see him as he is" (1 John 3:2). The vision of Rev. 7:14-17 expresses the main point, necessarily combining prose with poetry: "These are they who have come out of the great ordeal: they have washed their robes and made them white in the blood of the Lamb.

> "For this reason they are before
>   the throne of God,
> and worship him day and night
>   within his temple;
> and the one who is seated on
>   the throne will shelter them.
> They will hunger no more, and
>   thirst no more;
> the sun will not strike them,
> nor any scorching heat.
> For the Lamb at the center of the
>   throne will be their shepherd,
> and he will guide them to
>   springs of the water of life:
> and God will wipe away every
>   tear from their eyes."
>
> (Rev. 7:14-17)

Yet the center of the stage in the visions in Revelation is not the people of God, however blessed and happy. It is God himself who is and will be the source of all this. The "great multitude" cries,

"Hallelujah!
For the Lord our God
 the Almighty reigns.
Let us rejoice and exult
 and give him the glory."

(Rev. 19:6-7)

Bibliography

Allo, E.-B., *Saint Paul: Première Épitre aux Corinthiens* (Paris: Gabalda, 2nd ed. 1956).

Ambrosiaster, *Commentarius in Epistolas Paulinas,* ed. Henricus J. Vogels (Vienna: Hoelder-Pichler-Tempsky, 1969).

Aquinas, Thomas, *Commentary on 1 Thessalonians* (New York: Magi, 1969).

————, *Summa Theologiae,* Blackfriars ed., 60 vols. (London: Eyre & Spottiswoode, 1963 and *New Advent* online).

Athanasius, *On the Incarnation,* in *Christology of the Later Fathers,* ed. E. R. Hardy (London: S.C.M. and Philadelphia: Westminster Press, 1954); also in *NPNF* (Grand Rapids: Eerdmans, 1991), ser. 2, vol. 4, 31-67.

Attridge, H. W., *The Epistle to the Hebrews* (Philadelphia: Fortress, 1989).

————, "Let Us Strive to Enter That Rest," *HTR* 73 (1980): 279-88.

Augustine, *City of God,* in *NPNF,* ser. 1, vol. 2.

————, *Confessions,* ed. Henry Chadwick (Oxford: Oxford University Press, 1991).

————, *On Christian Doctrine* in *NPNF,* ser. 1, vol. 2.

————, *On Rebuke and Grace* in *NPNF,* ser. 1, vol. 5.

————, *On the Psalms,* in *NPNF,* ser. 1, vol. 8.

Aune, David E., *Revelation 1–5, 6–16, and 17–22,* WBC (3 vols.; Nashville: Nelson, 1998).

Austin, John L., *How to Do Things with Words* (Oxford: Oxford University Press, 1962).

Ayer, Alfred J., *Language, Truth and Logic* (London: Gollancz, 1946).

Baird, William, *History of New Testament Research,* vol. 2 (Minneapolis: Fortress, 2003).

Barr, James, "Has the Bible Any Authority?" in James Barr, *Explorations in Theology* 7 (London: S.C.M., 1980).

————, *The Semantics of Biblical Language* (Oxford: Oxford University Press, 1961).

Barrett, C. K., "The Eschatology of the Epistle to the Hebrews," in *The Background of the New Testament and Its Eschatology: Studies in Honour of C. H. Dodd,* ed. W. D. Davies and D. Daube (Cambridge: Cambridge University Press, 1956), 363-93.

Barth, Karl, *Church Dogmatics* (14 vols.; Edinburgh: T&T Clark, 1957-75).

————, *The Epistle to the Romans* (London: Oxford University Press, 1933).

————, *The Word of God and the Word of Man* (London: Hodder & Stoughton, 1928).

Basil of Caesarea, *Letters,* in *NPNF,* ser. 2, vol. 8.

Bauckham, Richard, *The Climax of Prophecy: Studies in the Book of Revelation* (Edinburgh: T&T Clark, 1993).

———, *The Fate of the Dead: Studies in the Jewish and Christian Apocalypses,* NovTSup 93 (Atlanta: Society of Biblical Literature, 1998).

Beale, G. K., *The Book of Revelation: A Commentary on the Greek Text,* NIGTC (Grand Rapids: Eerdmans and Carlisle: Paternoster, 1999).

Beasley-Murray, G. R., *Jesus and the Last Days* (Peabody, MA: Hendrickson, 1995).

Beker, J. Christiaan, *Paul the Apostle: The Triumph of God in Life and Thought* (Edinburgh: T&T Clark, 1980).

———, *Paul's Apocalyptic Gospel: The Coming Triumph of God* (Philadelphia: Fortress, 1982).

Bengel, Johann, *Gnomon Novi Testamenti* (Stuttgart: Steinkopf, 1866).

Berdyaev, Nicholas, *The Beginning and the End* (London: Bles, 1952).

———, *The Destiny of Man* (London: Bles, 1937).

Berkhof, L., *Systematic Theology* (Grand Rapids: Eerdmans and London: The Banner of Truth, 1959).

Best, Ernest, *The First and Second Epistles to the Thessalonians* (London: Black, 1972).

Black, Max, *Perplexities: Rational Choice, Metaphor, Poetic Ambiguity* (Ithaca: Cornell University Press, 1990).

Botha, J. Eugene, *Jesus and the Samaritan Woman: A Speech-Act Reading of John 4:1-42* (Leiden: Brill, 1991).

Botterweck, G. J., and Helmer Ringgren (eds.), *Theological Dictionary of the Old Testament (TDOT)* (Grand Rapids: Eerdmans, 1980).

Bowald, Mark A., *Rendering the Word in Theological Hermeneutics: Mapping Divine and Human Agency* (Aldershot and Burlington, VT: Ashgate, 2007).

Briggs, Richard S., *Words in Action: Speech Act Theory and Biblical Interpretation* (Edinburgh and New York: T&T Clark, 2001).

Brown, Alexandra R., *The Cross and Human Transformation: Paul's Apocalyptic Word in 1 Corinthians* (Minneapolis: Fortress, 1995).

———, "Paul and the Parousia," in *The Return of Jesus in Early Christianity,* ed. John T. Carroll with Alexandra Brown and J. S. Siker (Peabody, MA: Hendrickson, 2000), 47-76.

Brown, Francis, with S. R. Driver and C. A. Briggs (eds.), *The New Hebrew and English Lexicon* (Lafayette, IN: Associated Publishers and Authors, 1980).

Brown, Raymond, *The Gospel according to John,* AB (2 vols.; London: Chapman and New York: Doubleday, 1966 and 1971).

Bultmann, Rudolf, "*agalliaomai,*" in *TDNT,* ed. G. Kittel and G. Friedrich, vol. 1, 19-21.

———, *Theology of the New Testament,* vol. 1 (London: S.C.M., 1952).

Burkitt, F. C. (ed.), *The Book of Rules of Tyconius,* Texts and Studies 3 (Cambridge: Cambridge University Press, 1894).

Caird, George B., *The Language and Imagery of the Bible* (London: Duckworth, 1980).

———, *The Revelation of St. John the Divine* (London: Black, 1966).

Calvin, John, *Commentary on 1 and 2 Thessalonians* (Wheaton, IL: Crossway/Good News, 1999).

————, *The Epistles of Paul to the Galatians, Ephesians, Philippians, and Colossians* (Edinburgh: Oliver & Boyd, 1965).

————, *Institutes of the Christian Religion*, ed. H. Beveridge (2 vols.; London: James Clarke, 1957).

Carpenter, J. Estlin, *The Johannine Writings: A Study of the Apocalypse and the Fourth Gospel* (London: Constable, 1927).

Carroll, John T. (with Alexandra Brown et al.), *The Return of Jesus* (Peabody, MA: Hendrickson, 2000).

Chadwick, Henry, *Boethius* (Oxford: Clarendon, 1981).

Charles, R. H., *A Critical and Exegetical Commentary on the Revelation of St. John*, ICC (2 vols.; Edinburgh: T&T Clark, 1920).

————, *A Critical History of the Doctrine of a Future Life in Israel, in Judaism, and in Christianity;* also entitled *Eschatology* (London: Black, 2nd ed. 1913).

Chauvet, L.-M., *Symbol and Sacrament* (Minneapolis: Collegeville, 1955).

Christiansen, Ellen J., *The Covenant in Judaism and Paul: A Study of Ritual Boundaries as Identity Markers* (Leiden: Brill, 1997).

Chrysostom, John, "Homilies on 1 and 2 Thessalonians," in *NPNF,* ser. 1, vol. 13.

Clement, *The Stromata,* in *ANF,* vol. 2.

Clifford, W. K., "The Ethics of Belief," in W. K. Clifford, *Lectures and Essays* (1879), reprinted in W. K. Clifford, *The Ethics of Belief and Other Essays* (New York: Prometheus, 1999).

Collins, R. F., *First Corinthians* (Collegeville, MN: Glazier/Liturgical Press, 1999).

Conzelmann, Hans, "*chairō, chara,*" in *TDNT,* vol. 9, 359-72.

Cranfield, Charles E. B., *The Epistle to the Romans,* ICC (2 vols.; Edinburgh: T&T Clark, 1975).

————, *The Gospel according to Mark,* Cambridge Greek Testament (Cambridge: Cambridge University Press, 1963).

Cullmann, Oscar, *Christ and Time: The Primitive Conception of Time and History* (London: S.C.M., 1951).

————, *Immortality of the Soul or Resurrection of the Dead? The Witness of the New Testament* (London: Epworth, 1958).

————, and F. J. Leenhardt, *Essays on the Lord's Supper* (London: Lutterworth, 1958).

Dahl, M. E., *The Resurrection of the Body* (London: S.C.M., 1962).

Daley, Brian E., *The Hope of the Early Church: A Handbook of Patristic Eschatology* (Cambridge: Cambridge University Press, 1991).

Danker, Frederick W., *A Greek-English Lexicon of the New Testament and Other Early Christian Literature,* based on W. Bauer's Lexicon (BDAG) (Chicago: University of Chicago Press, 3rd ed. 2000).

Davidson, A. B., *The Theology of the Old Testament* (Edinburgh: T&T Clark, 1904).

De Boer, M. C., *The Defeat of Death: Apocalyptic Eschatology in 1 Corinthians 15 and Romans 5* (Sheffield: J.S.O.T., 1988).

Denney, James, *Studies in Theology* (London: Hodder & Stoughton, 1895).

Dillenberger, John (ed.), "The Sacrament of Penance," in *Martin Luther: Selections from His Writings* (New York: Doubleday, 1961).

The Doctrine Commission of the Church of England, *The Mystery of Salvation* (London: Church House Publishing, 1995).

————, *We Believe in God* (London: Church House Publishing, 1987).

Dodd, Charles H., *The Epistle of Paul to the Romans,* Moffatt Commentary (London: Hodder & Stoughton, 1932).

————, "The Mind of Paul: I" (1933) and "The Mind of Paul: II" (1934), in *New Testament Studies* (Manchester: Manchester University Press, 1953), 67-127.

Donfried, Karl, "The Epistolary and Rhetorical Context of 1 Thessalonians 2:1-12," in *The Thessalonians Debate: Methodological Discord as Methodological Synthesis,* ed. K. P. Donfried and J. Beutler (Grand Rapids: Eerdmans, 2000).

————, "The Imperial Cults and Political Conflict in 1 Thessalonians," in *Paul and Empire: Religion and Power in Roman Imperial Society,* ed. Richard Horsley (Harrisburg, PA: Trinity Press International, 1997), 215-23.

Duffy, Mervyn, *How Language, Ritual and Sacraments Work according to John Austin, Jürgen Habermas, and Louis-Marie Chauvet* (Rome: Pontifical Gregorian University, 2005).

Dunn, James D. G., *The Theology of Paul the Apostle* (Edinburgh: T&T Clark, 1998).

Eco, Umberto, *The Role of the Reader: Explorations in the Semiotics of Texts* (London: Hutchinson, 1981).

Eichrodt, Walther, *Theology of the Old Testament* (2 vols.; London: S.C.M., 1961 and 1967).

Eriksson, Anders, *Traditions as Rhetorical Proof: Pauline Argumentations in 1 Corinthians,* ConBNT 29 (Stockholm: Almqvist & Wiksell, 1998).

Evangelical Alliance Commission, *The Nature of Hell* (London: Acute, 2000).

Evans, Craig A., *Mark 8:27–16:20,* WBC 34B (Nashville: Nelson, 2001).

Evans, Donald D., *The Logic of Self-Involvement: A Philosophical Study of Everyday Language with Special Reference to the Christian Use of Language about God as Creator* (London: S.C.M., 1963).

Fison, J. E., *The Blessing of the Holy Spirit* (London and New York: Longmans, Green, 1950).

Fitzmyer, Joseph A., *First Corinthians,* The Anchor Yale Bible 32 (New Haven and London: Yale University Press, 2008).

Flannery, Austin P. (ed.), *Documents of Vatican II* (Grand Rapids: Eerdmans, 1975).

Ford, David F., *Self and Salvation: Being Transformed* (Cambridge: Cambridge University Press, 1999).

France, R. T., *The Gospel of Mark: A Commentary on the Greek Text,* NIGTC (Grand Rapids and Cambridge: Eerdmans and Carlisle: Paternoster, 2002).

————, *Matthew* (Leicester: Inter-Varsity Press and Grand Rapids: Eerdmans, 1985).

Fried, Charles, *Contract as Promise: A Theory of Contractual Obligation* (Cambridge, MA: Harvard University Press, 1981).

Funk, Robert W., *Parables and Presence* (Philadelphia: Fortress, 1982).

Gadamer, Hans-Georg, *Truth and Method* (London: Sheed & Ward, 2nd rev. ed. 1989).

Gillespie, Thomas W., *The First Theologians: A Study in Early Christian Prophecy* (Grand Rapids: Eerdmans, 1994).

Goldingay, John, *Models of the Bible* (Grand Rapids: Eerdmans and Carlisle: Paternoster, 1994).

Goppelt, Leonhard, *"hydōr"* (water), in *TDNT*, vol. 8, 314-33.

Green, Joel B., *The Gospel of Luke*, NICNT (Grand Rapids and Cambridge: Eerdmans, 1997).

Gundry, Robert H., "The New Jerusalem," in *The Old Is Better: New Testament Essays in Support of Traditional Interpretation*, WUNT 178 (Tübingen: Mohr Siebeck, 2005), 399-411.

Habermas, Jürgen, *Knowledge and Human Interests* (London: Heinemann, 2nd ed. 1978).

———, *The Theory of Communicative Action* (2 vols.; Cambridge: Polity Press and Beacon Press, 1987).

Hachlili, Rachel, *Jewish Funerary Customs: Practices and Rites in the Second Temple Period*, JSJSup (Leiden: Brill, 2005).

Hamilton, N. Q., *The Holy Spirit and Eschatology in Paul*, SJT Occasional Paper 6 (Edinburgh: Oliver & Boyd, 1957).

Hatch, Edwin, and Henry A. Redpath, *A Concordance to the Septuagint* (2 vols.; Athens: Beneficial Book Publishers, 1977).

Hays, Richard B., *First Corinthians* (Louisville: John Knox, 1997).

Heinbeck, R. S., *Theology and Meaning* (London: Allen & Unwin, 1969).

Helm, Paul, *Eternal God: A Study of God without Time* (Oxford: Clarendon, 1988).

Hendriksen, William, *More than Conquerors: An Interpretation of the Book of Revelation* (Grand Rapids: Baker and London: Tyndale Press, 1962 [1940]).

Hengel, Martin, *The Cross of the Son of God* (London: S.C.M., 1986).

Henry, Matthew, *Concise Commentary on the Whole Bible* (C.D., Gospel Forum, n.d.).

Hick, John H., *Philosophy of Religion* (Englewood Cliffs, NJ: Prentice Hall, 4th ed. 1990).

Hill, David, *New Testament Prophecy* (London: Marshall, Morgan & Scott, 1979).

Hofius, Otfried, *Katapausis: Die Vorstellung vom endzeitlichen Ruheort in Hebräerbrief* (Tübingen: Mohr, 1970).

———, "The Lord's Supper and the Lord's Supper Tradition," in *One Loaf, One Cup: Ecumenical Studies on 1 Corinthians 11 and Other Texts*, ed. Ben F. Meyer (Macon, GA: Mercer University Press, 1993).

Hogg, A. G., *Redemption from This World* (Edinburgh: T&T Clark, 1924).

Holleman, J., *Resurrection and Parousia: A Traditio-Historical Study of Paul's Eschatology in 1 Corinthians 15*, NovTSup 84 (Leiden: Brill, 1996).

Hooker, Morna D., *The Gospel according to Saint Mark* (London: Black and Peabody, MA: Hendrickson, 1991).

Hughes, J. A., "Revelation 20:4-6 and the Question of the Millennium," *WTJ* 35 (1973): 281-302.

Hughes, Kevin L., *Constructing Antichrist* (Washington: Catholic University of America Press, 2005).

Hurtado, Larry W., *One God, One Lord* (London and New York: Continuum and T&T Clark, 2nd ed. 1998).

Irenaeus, *Against Heresies*, in *ANF*, vol. 1 (Grand Rapids: Eerdmans, 1993), 309-567.

Janik, A., and S. Toulmin, *Wittgenstein's Vienna* (London: Wiedenfeld and Nicolson, 1973).

Jeremias, Joachim, *The Eucharistic Words of Jesus* (London: S.C.M., 1966).

———, "Flesh and Blood Cannot Inherit the Kingdom of God (1 Cor. 15:50)," *NTS* 2 (1955): 151-59.

———, "*hadēs*," in *TDNT*, vol. 1, 146-49.

———, *The Parables of Jesus* (London: S.C.M., 2nd ed. 1963).

Jerome, *Commentary on Matthew*, ed. Thomas P. Scheck, FC 117 (Washington: Catholic University of America Press, 2008).

———, "Preface to Daniel," in P. Schaff and H. Wach, *Nicene and Post-Nicene Fathers (NPNF)*, ser. 2, vol. 6 (Edinburgh: T&T Clark and Grand Rapids: Eerdmans, 1989).

Jewett, Robert, *Letter to Pilgrims: A Commentary on the Epistle to the Hebrews* (Cleveland: Pilgrim Press, 1981).

———, *Paul's Anthropological Terms* (Leiden: Brill, 1971).

Johnson, Luke T., *The Gospel of Luke*, Sacra Pagina 3 (Collegeville, MN: Glazier/Liturgical Press, 1991).

Jones, O. R., *The Concept of Holiness* (London: Allen & Unwin, 1961).

Jones, O. R. (ed.), *The Private Language Argument* (London: Macmillan, 1966).

Jüngel, Eberhard, *God as the Mystery of the World* (Grand Rapids: Eerdmans and Edinburgh: T&T Clark, 1983).

Käsemann, Ernst, *New Testament Questions of Today* (London: S.C.M., 1969).

———, "On the Subject of Primitive Christian Apocalyptic," in his *New Testament Questions of Today* (New York: Harper & Row, 1967 and London: S.C.M., 1969), 108-37.

———, *The Wandering People of God: An Investigation of the Letter to the Hebrews* (Minneapolis: Augsburg, 1984).

Kierkegaard, Søren, *Fear and Trembling*, ed. Walter Lowrie (New York: Doubleday, 1941 and 1954).

Kline, M. G., "The First Resurrection," *WTJ* 37 (1975): 360-75.

Koch, Klaus, *The Rediscovery of Apocalyptic: A Polemical Work on a Neglected Area of Biblical Studies and Its Damaging Effects on Theology and Philosophy* (London: S.C.M., 1972).

Kovacs, Judith, and Christopher Rowland, *Revelation through the Centuries* (Oxford: Blackwell, 2004).

Kübler-Ross, Elisabeth, *On Death and Dying* (New York: Simon & Schuster, 1969 and London: Tavistock Publications, 1970).

Kuschel, Karl-Joseph, *Born before All Time: The Dispute over Christ's Origin* (London: S.C.M., 1992).

Lactantius, *Divine Institutes*, in *ANF*, vol. 7, ed. A. Roberts and J. Donaldson (Grand Rapids: Eerdmans, 1989), 2-223.

Lane, William L., *The Epistle to the Hebrews* (Waco: Word, 1991).

———, *The Gospel according to Mark* (Grand Rapids: Eerdmans and London: Marshall, Morgan & Scott, 1974).

Lewis, C. S., *The Problem of Pain* (London: Bles, 1940).

Lindsey, Hal, *The Late Great Planet Earth* (Grand Rapids: Zondervan, 1970).

Lincoln, Andrew T., *Paradise Now and Not Yet*, SNTSMS 43 (Cambridge: Cambridge University Press, 1981).

Locke, John, *Works* (London: Rivington, 12th ed. 1824).

Louw, Johannes P., and Eugene A. Nida (eds.), *Greek-English Lexicon of the New Testament Based on Semantic Domains* (2 vols.; New York: United Bible Societies, 2nd ed. 1989).

Lowe, John, "An Examination of Attempts to Detect Developments in St. Paul's Theology," *JTS* 42 (1941): 129-42.

Luther, Martin, "The Heidelberg Disputation," in *Luther: Early Theological Works*, ed. James Atkinson (London: S.C.M., 1962), 276-307.

———, "Letter to Michael Stiefel and Table Talk Recorded by Anthony Leuterbach" (1533), in *Luther: Letters of Spiritual Counsel*, ed. T. G. Tappert, LCC 18 (London: S.C.M., 1955).

———, *Luther: Early Theological Works: The Epistle to the Hebrews*, ed. James Atkinson, LCC 16 (London: S.C.M., 1962).

———, *LW*, vol. 28: *Commentary on 1 Corinthians 7 and 15 and 1 Timothy*, ed. Hilton Oswald (St. Louis: Concordia, 1973) or *Luthers Aufgabe* (WA 36).

———, "Sermons in Castle Pleissenburg, 1539," in *LW*, vol. 51 (Philadelphia: Muhlenberg, 1959).

Lyons, John, *Introduction to Theoretical Linguistics* (Cambridge: Cambridge University Press, 1968).

———, *Semantics* (2 vols.; Cambridge: Cambridge University Press, 1977).

Malherbe, Abraham J., *The Letters to the Thessalonians*, AB 32B (New Haven and London: Yale University Press, 2000 and 2004).

Marcel, Pierre C., *The Biblical Doctrine of Infant Baptism* (London: James Clarke, 1953).

Marshall, Christopher D., *Beyond Retribution: A New Testament Vision for Justice, Crime, and Punishment* (Grand Rapids: Eerdmans, 2001).

Marshall, I. Howard, *1 and 2 Thessalonians: A Commentary* (Vancouver: Regent College Publishing, 1983).

Martin, James P., *The Last Judgement in Protestant Theology from Orthodoxy to Ritschl* (Edinburgh: Oliver & Boyd, 1963).

Martyn, J. Louis, "Apocalyptic Antinomianism in Paul's Letter to the Galatians," *NTS* 31 (1985): 410-24.

———, "Epistemology at the Turn of the Ages," in *Christian History and Interpretation: Studies Presented to John Knox*, ed. W. R. Farmer et al. (Cambridge: Cambridge University Press, 1967).

Mathewson, D., *A New Heaven and a New Earth: The Meaning and Function of the Old Testament in Revelation 21:1–22:5*, JSNTSup 238 (London and New York: Sheffield Academic Press, 2003).

McCool, Gerald A. (ed.), *A Rahner Reader* (London: Darton, Longman & Todd, 1975).

McGinn, Bernard, *Antichrist: Two Thousand Years of the Human Fascination with Evil* (San Francisco: Harper, 1994).

McGrath, Alistair, *The Making of Modern German Christology* (Oxford: Blackwell, 1986).

Melanchthon, Philipp, *Loci Communes Rerum Theologicarum,* in *Melanchthon and Bucer,* ed. Wilhelm Pauck, LCC 19 (London: S.C.M., 1969).

Moberly, R. W. L., *The Bible, Theology and Faith* (Cambridge: Cambridge University Press, 2000).

———, Hebrew, "*b-ṭ-ḥ,*" in *NIDOTTE,* vol. 1, 644.

———, *Prophecy and Discernment* (Cambridge: Cambridge University Press, 2006).

Moffatt, James, *The First Epistle of Paul to the Corinthians,* Moffatt Commentary (London: Hodder & Stoughton, 1938).

Moltmann, Jürgen, *The Coming of God: Christian Eschatology* (London: S.C.M., 1996).

———, "God's Kenosis in the Creation and Consummation of the World," in *The Work of Love: Creation as Kenosis,* ed. John Polkinghorne (Grand Rapids: Eerdmans and London: S.P.C.K., 2001), 137-51.

———, *In the End — In the Beginning* (London: S.C.M., 2004).

———, *Is There Life after Death?* (Milwaukee: Marquette University Press, 1998).

———, *The Spirit of Life: A Universal Affirmation* (London: S.C.M., 1992).

———, *Sun of Righteousness, Arise! God's Future for Humanity and the Earth* (London: S.C.M., 2010).

———, *Theology of Hope: On the Ground and the Implications of a Christian Eschatology* (London: S.C.M., 1967).

———, *The Trinity and the Kingdom of God: The Doctrine of God* (London: S.C.M., 1981).

Moo, Jonathan, "Continuity, Discontinuity, and Hope," *Tyndale Bulletin* 61 (2010): 21-44.

Moore, Arthur L., *1 and 2 Thessalonians,* New Century Bible (London: Nelson, 1969).

———, *The Parousia in the New Testament,* NovTSup 13 (Leiden: Brill, 1966).

Morrice, William G., *Joy in the New Testament* (Exeter: Paternoster, 1984).

Morris, Leon, *The First and Second Epistles to the Thessalonians* (Grand Rapids: Eerdmans, 1959).

Moule, C. F. D., "The Judgement Theme in the Sacraments," in *Background of the New Testament: Studies in Honour of C. H. Dodd,* ed. W. D. Davies and D. Daube (Cambridge: Cambridge University Press, 1956), 464-81.

Moulton, J. H., and George Milligan, *The Vocabulary of the Greek Testament* (London: Hodder & Stoughton, repr. 1952).

Moulton, W. F., and A. S. Geden, *A Concordance of the Greek Testament* (Edinburgh: T&T Clark, 1899).

Mounce, Robert H., *The Book of Revelation* (Grand Rapids: Eerdmans and London: Marshall, Morgan & Scott, 1977).

Müller, Ulrich B., *Prophetie und Predigt im Neuen Testament* (Gütersloh: Mohn, 1975).

Munck, Johannes, "Paulus Tanquam Abortivus, 1 Cor. 15:8," in *New Testament Essays: Studies in Memory of T. W. Manson,* ed. A. J. B. Higgins (Manchester: Manchester University Press, 1959), 180-95.

Naudé, Jackie A., "*q-d-sh,*" in *NIDOTTE,* vol. 3, 878-83.

Neufeld, Dieter, *Re-conceiving Texts as Speech Acts: An Analysis of 1 John* (Leiden: Brill, 1994).

Newman, Carey C., *Paul's Glory — Christology: Tradition and Rhetoric*, NovTSup 69 (Leiden: Brill, 1992).

Niebuhr, Reinhold, *The Nature and Destiny of Man*, vol. 2: *Human Destiny* (London: Nisbet, 1943).

Nygren, Anders, *Commentary on Romans* (London: S.C.M., 1952).

O'Donovan, Oliver, *The Ways of Judgement* (Grand Rapids: Eerdmans, 2005).

Olyan, Saul M., *Biblical Mourning: Ritual and Social Dimensions* (Oxford: Oxford University Press, 2004).

Origen, *Against Celsus*, ANF, vol. 4 (Grand Rapids: Eerdmans, 1989), 395-669.

———, *De Principiis*; repr. in *ANF*, vol. 4, 239-384.

Page, S. H. T., "Revelation 20 and Pauline Eschatology," *JETS* 23 (1980): 31-45.

Pannenberg, Wolfhart. "Eschatology and the Experience of Meaning," in *Basic Questions in Theology* (3 vols.; London: S.C.M., 1970-73), vol. 3, 192-210.

———, "The Revelation of God in Jesus of Nazareth," in *New Frontiers in Theology*, vol. III: *Theology as History*, ed. James M. Robinson and John B. Cobb (New York: Harper & Row, 1967).

———, *Systematic Theology* (3 vols.; Grand Rapids: Eerdmans and Edinburgh: T&T Clark, 1991-98).

———, *Theology and the Philosophy of Science* (Philadelphia: Westminster, 1976).

———, *What Is Man? Anthropology in Theological Perspective* (Philadelphia: Fortress, 1970).

Parker, Colin M., *Bereavement* (Harmondsworth: Penguin, 3rd ed. 1998; Hove: Routledge, 4th ed. 2010).

Peacocke, Arthur, "The Cost of New Life," in *The Work of Love*, ed. John Polkinghorne (Grand Rapids: Eerdmans and London: S.P.C.K., 2001), 21-41.

Perrin, Norman, *The Kingdom of God in the Teaching of Jesus* (London: S.C.M., 1963).

Polkinghorne, John, "Eschatology," in *The End of the World and the Ends of God: Science and Theology on Eschatology*, ed. J. C. Polkinghorne and M. Welker (Harrisburg, PA: Trinity Press International, 2000), 29-41.

Polkinghorne, John (ed.), *The Work of Love: Creation as Kenosis* (Grand Rapids: Eerdmans and London: S.P.C.K., 2001).

Pope Benedict XII, *Benedictus Deus (On the Beatific Vision of God)*, in *Papal Encyclicals Online*, January 2008.

Porter, Stanley E., and Jacqueline C. R. de Roo (eds.), *The Concept of the Old Covenant in the Second Temple Period*, JSJSup (Leiden: Brill, 2003).

Powys, David, *"Hell": A Hard Look at a Hard Question* (Milton Keynes and Waynesboro, GA: Paternoster, 1997), with a Foreword by Graham Stanton.

Prat, Ferdinand, *The Theology of St. Paul* (2 vols.; London: Burns, Oates & Washbourne, 1945).

Price, H. H., *Belief* (London: Allen & Unwin and New York: Humanities Press, 1969).

Pritchard, H. A. A., "The Obligation to Keep a Promise," in *Moral Obligation: Essays and Lectures* (Oxford: Clarendon, 1949).

Rabanus, Maurus, *Opera Omnia*, in *Patrologia Latina*, ed. J.-P. Migne, vol. 112, part 6.

Rad, Gerhard von, *Old Testament Theology*, vol. 1 (Edinburgh: Oliver & Boyd, 1962).

Rahner, Karl, "Purgatory," in his *Theological Investigations* 19 (London: Darton, Longman & Todd, 1984).

Räisänen, Heikki, *Challenges to Biblical Interpretation: Collected Essays* (Leiden, Boston, Cologne: Brill, 2001).

Ramsey, Ian T., *Models for Divine Activity* (London: S.C.M., 1973).

————, *Religious Language: An Empirical Placing of Theological Phrases* (London: S.C.M., 1957).

Rendtorff, Rolf, *The Covenant Formula: An Exegetical and Theological Investigation* (Edinburgh: T&T Clark, 1998).

Reventlow, Henning Graf, *The Authority of the Bible and the Rise of the Modern World* (London: S.C.M., 1984).

Richard, Earl J., *First and Second Thessalonians,* Sacra Pagina 11 (Collegeville, MN: Glazier/Liturgical Press, 1995 and 2007).

Richardson, Alan, *An Introduction to the Theology of the New Testament* (London: S.C.M., 1958).

Richardson, Neil, *Paul's Language about God,* JSNTSup 99 (Sheffield: Sheffield Academic Press, 1994), 114-19.

Ricoeur, Paul, *The Conflict of Interpretations* (Evanston: Northwestern University Press, 1974).

————, "Metaphor and Symbol," in Paul Ricoeur, *Interpretation Theory: Discourse and the Surplus of Meaning* (Fort Worth, TX: Texas Christian University Press, 1976), 45-69.

————, *Time and Narrative* (3 vols.; Chicago: University of Chicago Press, 1984-88).

Rigaux, Béda, *Saint Paul: Les Épitres aux Thessaloniciens* (Paris: Gabalda, 1956).

Ringgren, Helmer, *The Prophetical Conception of Holiness* (Uppsala: Lundequistka, 1948).

Robinson, J. A. T., *The Body: A Study of Pauline Theology* (London: S.C.M., 1952 and Philadelphia: Westminster, 1977).

————, *In the End, God . . . : A Study of the Christian Doctrine of the Last Things* (London: James Clarke, 1950), 10.

Rolston, Holmes, "Kenosis and Nature," in *The Work of Love: Creation as Kenosis,* ed. John Polkinghorne (Grand Rapids: Eerdmans and London: S.P.C.K., 2001), 43-65.

Roth, Cecil (ed.), *The Haggadah* (London: Soncino Press, new ed. Heb. and Eng. 1934).

Rowell, Geoffrey, *Hell and the Victorians* (Oxford: Clarendon, 1974).

Rowland, Christopher, *The Open Heaven: A Study of Apocalyptic in Judaism and Early Christianity* (New York: Crossroad, 1982).

Rowland, Christopher, and Judith Kovacs, *Revelation* (Oxford: Blackwell-Wiley, 2004).

Rupp, E. Gordon, and Benjamin Drewery (eds.), *Martin Luther: Documents of Modern History* (London: Arnold, 1970).

Ryle, Gilbert, *The Concept of Mind* (London: Hutchinson, 1949).

————, *Dilemmas* (Cambridge: Cambridge University Press, 1966).

Schleiermacher, Friedrich, *The Christian Faith* (Edinburgh: T&T Clark, 1989 [Ger., 1st ed. 1821; 2nd ed. 1830]).

Schnackenburg, Rudolf, *Baptism in the Thought of St. Paul* (Oxford: Blackwell, 1964).

Scholem, Gershom, *Major Trends in Jewish Mysticism* (New York: Schocken, 1954 and 1995).

Schultz, Richard, "sh-ph-ṭ," in *NIDOTTE*, vol. 4, 213-20.

Schweizer, Eduard, "pneuma, pneumatikos," in *TDNT*, vol. 6, 415-55.

Searle, John R., *Expression and Meaning: Studies in the Theory of Speech Acts* (Cambridge: Cambridge University Press, 1979).

Selwyn, E. G., "Eschatology in 1 Peter," in *New Testament Background: Studies in Honour of C. H. Dodd*, ed. W. D. Davies and David Daube (Cambridge: Cambridge University Press, 1956), 394-401.

Simon, Marcel, *St. Stephen and the Hellenists in the Primitive Church* (London: Longmans, Green, 1958).

Simon, Ulrich, *The End Is Not Yet: A Study in Christian Eschatology* (London: Nisbet, 1964).

Smith, C. Ryder, *The Bible Doctrine of Salvation* (London: Epworth Press, 2nd ed. 1946).

Soskice, Janet Martin, *Metaphor and Religious Language* (Oxford: Clarendon, 1985).

Stählin, Gustav, "orgē," in *TDNT*, vol. 5, 419-47.

————, "thrēneō," in *TDNT*, vol. 3, 148-55.

Stephens, Joanna, Unpublished dissertation (Nottingham: St John's College, 2008).

Strawson, P. F., *Individuals: An Essay in Descriptive Metaphysics* (London: Methuen, 1959), 190-204.

————, *Introduction to Logical Theory* (London: Methuen, 1963).

Stuhlmacher, Peter, *Gerechtigkeit Gottes bei Paulus*, FRLANT 87 (Göttingen: Vandenhoeck & Ruprecht, 1965).

Stump, Eleonore, and Norman Kretzmann, "Eternity," in *Philosophy of Religion: The Big Questions*, ed. Eleonore Stump and Michael J. Murray (Oxford and Malden, MA: Blackwell, 1999).

Swinburne, Richard, *The Coherence of Theism* (Oxford: Clarendon, 1977).

Sykes, S. W., and J. P. Clayton (eds.), *Christ, Faith and History: Cambridge Studies in Christology* (Cambridge: Cambridge University Press, 1972).

Tertullian, *On Prescription against Heretics*, in *ANF*, vol. 3, 243-68.

Thayer, Joseph H. (ed.), *Greek-English Lexicon of the New Testament* (Edinburgh: T&T Clark, 4th ed. 1901, repr. 1953).

Theodore of Mopsuestia, *Commentarii in Epistolas B. Pauli*, vol. 2, ed. H. B. Swete (Cambridge: Cambridge University Press, 1880).

Thiselton, Anthony C., *A Concise Encyclopaedia of the Philosophy of Religion* (Oxford: Oneworld, 2002).

————, *1 Corinthians: A Shorter Exegetical and Pastoral Commentary* (Grand Rapids: Eerdmans, 2006).

————, *1 and 2 Thessalonians through the Centuries* (Oxford: Blackwell-Wiley, 2011).

————, *The First Epistle to the Corinthians: A Commentary on the Greek Text*, NIGTC (Grand Rapids: Eerdmans and Carlisle: Paternoster, 2000).

————, "Hebrews," in *Eerdmans Commentary on the Bible*, ed. J. D. G. Dunn and J. W. Rogerson (Grand Rapids: Eerdmans, 2003).

————, *The Hermeneutics of Doctrine* (Grand Rapids: Eerdmans, 2007).

————, *The Living Paul* (London: S.P.C.K. and Downers Grove, IL: Inter-Varsity Academic, 2009).

————, "The Logical Role of the Liar Paradox in Titus 1:12, 13: A Dissent from the Commentaries in the Light of Philosophical and Logical Analysis," *Biblical Interpretation* 2 (1994): 207-23; repr. in *Thiselton on Hermeneutics* (Grand Rapids: Eerdmans, 2006 and Aldershot: Ashgate, 2006).

————, *New Horizons in Hermeneutics* (London: Harper-Collins and Grand Rapids: Zondervan, 1992).

————, "Oath," in *New Interpreter's Dictionary of the Bible,* vol. 4 (Nashville: Abingdon, 2009), 309-12.

————, *Thiselton on Hermeneutics: The Collected Works and New Essays of Anthony Thiselton,* Ashgate Contemporary Thinkers on Religion (Aldershot: Ashgate and Grand Rapids: Eerdmans, 2006), Part II: Hermeneutics and Speech-Act Theory, 51-150.

————, *The Two Horizons* (Grand Rapids: Eerdmans and Exeter: Paternoster, 1980).

Tillich, Paul, *Dynamics of Faith* (London: Allen & Unwin, 1957).

————, *Systematic Theology,* vol. 3 (London: Nisbet, 1964).

Tollinton, R. B. (ed.), *Selections from the Commentaries and Homilies of Origen* (London: S.P.C.K., 1929).

Torrance, T. F., *Space, Time, and Resurrection* (Edinburgh: T&T Clark, 1976 and 1998).

Tracy, David, *The Analogical Imagination* (New York: Crossroad, 1981).

Travis, Stephen H., *Christ and the Judgement of God: The Limits of Divine Retribution in New Testament Thought* (Milton Keynes and Colorado Springs: Paternoster and Hendrickson, 2008).

Treier, Daniel, *Introducing Theological Interpretation of Scripture: Recovering a Christian Practice* (Grand Rapids: Baker Academic, 2008).

Tyndale, William, *A Pathway into the Holy Scripture,* in his *Doctrinal Treatises and Introduction to Portions of Scripture* (Cambridge: Cambridge University Press, Parker Society, 1848).

Ullmann, Stephen, *The Principles of Semantics* (Oxford: Blackwell, 2nd ed. 1957 and 1963).

————, *Semantics: An Introduction to the Science of Meaning* (Oxford: Blackwell, 1967).

Van Gemeren, Willem A. (ed.), *NIDOTTE* (5 vols.; Carlisle: Paternoster, 1997).

Vincent, Thomas, *Fire and Brimstone in Hell,* repr. *Gospel Truth Forum* C.D.

Von Balthasar, Hans Urs, *The Glory of the Lord* (7 vols.; Edinburgh: T&T Clark, 1982-91).

Walvoord, John F., *Armageddon: Oil and the Middle East* (Grand Rapids: Zondervan, 2nd ed. 1990).

————, *The Revelation of Jesus Christ* (Chicago: Moody, 1966).

Ward, Keith, "Cosmos and Kenosis," in *Work of Love,* ed. John Polkinghorne (Grand Rapids: Eerdmans and London: S.P.C.K., 2001), 152-66.

Watson, Francis, *Text and Truth: Redefining Biblical Theology* (Edinburgh: T&T Clark, 1997).

————, *Text, Church and World: Biblical Interpretation in Theological Perspective* (Edinburgh: T&T Clark, 1994).

Weiss, Johannes, *Earliest Christianity* (2 vols.; New York: Harper Torchbooks, 1959).

Wesley, John, *Notes on the New Testament* (Gospel Forum, C.D.).

Whiteley, D. E. H., *The Theology of St. Paul* (Oxford: Blackwell, 1964, 2nd ed. 1970).

Wilkinson, David, *Christian Eschatology and the Physical Universe* (London: Continuum and T&T Clark, 2010).

Wilson, S. G., *The Gentiles and the Gentile Mission in Luke-Acts*, SNTSMS 23 (Cambridge: Cambridge University Press, 1973).

Witherington, Ben, *1 and 2 Thessalonians: A Socio-Rhetorical Commentary* (Grand Rapids: Eerdmans, 2006).

———, *Jesus, Paul, and the End of the World* (Downers Grove, IL: InterVarsity Press, 1992).

Wittgenstein, Ludwig, *The Blue Book and Brown Books: Preliminary Studies for the "Philosophical Investigations"* (Oxford: Blackwell, 2nd ed. 1969).

———, *Philosophical Investigations* (Ger. and Eng.; Oxford: Blackwell, 2nd ed. 1958).

———, *Philosophical Remarks* (Oxford: Blackwell, 1975).

———, *Philosophische Bemerkungen* (Oxford: Blackwell, 1967).

———, *Tractatus Logico-Philosophicus* (Ger. and Eng.; London: Routledge & Kegan Paul and New York: Humanities Press, 1961).

———, *Zettel* (Oxford: Blackwell, 1967).

Wolterstorff, Nicholas, *John Locke and the Ethics of Belief* (Cambridge: Cambridge University Press, 1996).

———, *Lament for a Son* (Grand Rapids: Eerdmans, 1987).

Work, Telford, *Living and Active: Scripture in the Economy of Salvation* (Grand Rapids: Eerdmans, 2002).

Wright, N. T., *The Last Word: Scripture and the Authority of God* (London: Harper One and S.P.C.K., 2005).

———, *The Resurrection of the Son of God: Christian Origins and the Question of God*, vol. 3 (London: S.P.C.K., 2003).

———, *Surprised by Hope* (London: S.P.C.K., 2007).

Wright, W. D., *The Rays Are Not Coloured* (Bristol: Hilger, 1967).

Yinger, Kent L., *Paul, Judaism, and Judgement according to Deeds*, SNTSMS 105 (Cambridge: Cambridge University Press, 1999).

Ziesler, John, *The Meaning of Righteousness in Paul*, SNTSMS (Cambridge: Cambridge University Press, 1972).

Zimmerli, W., "Promise and Fulfilment," in *Essays in Old Testament Interpretation*, ed. Claus Westermann (London: S.C.M., 1963).

Zimmermann, Jens, *Recovering Theological Hermeneutics: An Incarnational-Trinitarian Theory of Interpretation* (Grand Rapids: Baker Academic, 2004).

Index of Names

Index of Subjects

Index of Scripture and Other Ancient Sources

243